Handbook of Forensic Toxicology for Medical Examiners

CRC SERIES IN
**PRACTICAL ASPECTS OF CRIMINAL
AND FORENSIC INVESTIGATIONS**

VERNON J. GEBERTH, BBA, MPS, FBINA *Series Editor*

Autoerotic Deaths: Practical Forensic and Investigative Perspectives
Anny Sauvageau and Vernon J. Geberth

Practical Crime Scene Processing and Investigation, Second Edition
Ross M. Gardner

The Counterterrorism Handbook: Tactics, Procedures, and Techniques, Fourth Edition
Frank Bolz, Jr., Kenneth J. Dudonis, and David P. Schulz

Practical Forensic Digital Imaging: Applications and Techniques
Patrick Jones

Practical Crime Scene Investigations for Hot Zones
Jacqueline T. Fish, Robert N. Stout, and Edward Wallace

Sex-Related Homicide and Death Investigation: Practical and Clinical Perspectives, Second Edition
Vernon J. Geberth

Handbook of Forensic Toxicology for Medical Examiners, Second Edition
D. Kimberley Molina and Veronica M. Hargrove

Practical Crime Scene Analysis and Reconstruction
Ross M. Gardner and Tom Bevel

Serial Violence: Analysis of Modus Operandi and Signature Characteristics of Killers
Robert D. Keppel and William J. Birnes

Bloodstain Pattern Analysis: With an Introduction to Crime Scene Reconstruction, Third Edition
Tom Bevel and Ross M. Gardner

Tire Tread and Tire Track Evidence: Recovery and Forensic Examination
William J. Bodziak

Officer-Involved Shootings and Use of Force: Practical Investigative Techniques, Second Edition
David E. Hatch and Randy Dickson

Practical Drug Enforcement, Third Edition
Michael D. Lyman

Principles of Bloodstain Pattern Analysis: Theory and Practice
Stuart James, Paul Kish, and T. Paulette Sutton

Global Drug Enforcement: Practical Investigative Techniques
Gregory D. Lee

Practical Investigation of Sex Crimes: A Strategic and Operational Approach
Thomas P. Carney

Principles of Kinesic Interview and Interrogation, Second Edition
Stan Walters

Practical Criminal Investigations in Correctional Facilities
William R. Bell

Practical Aspects of Interview and Interrogation, Second Edition
David E. Zulawski and Douglas E. Wicklander

Forensic Pathology, Second Edition
Dominick J. DiMaio and Vincent J. M. DiMaio

The Practical Methodology of Forensic Photography, Second Edition
David R. Redsicker

Quantitative-Qualitative Friction Ridge Analysis: An Introduction to Basic and Advanced Ridgeology
David R. Ashbaugh

Footwear Impression Evidence: Detection, Recovery, and Examination, Second Edition
William J. Bodziak

The Sexual Exploitation of Children: A Practical Guide to Assessment, Investigation, and Intervention, Second Edition
Seth L. Goldstein

Practical Aspects of Munchausen by Proxy and Munchausen Syndrome Investigation
Kathryn Artingstall

Practical Fire and Arson Investigation, Second Edition
David R. Redsicker and John J. O'Connor

Interpretation of Bloodstain Evidence at Crime Scenes, Second Edition
William G. Eckert and Stuart H. James

Investigating Computer Crime
Franklin Clark and Ken Diliberto

Practical Investigation Techniques
Kevin B. Kinnee

Friction Ridge Skin: Comparison and Identification of Fingerprints
James F. Cowger

Tire Imprint Evidence
Peter McDonald

Practical Gambling Investigation Techniques
Kevin B. Kinnee

Handbook of
FORENSIC
TOXICOLOGY for
MEDICAL EXAMINERS

Second Edition

D. Kimberley Molina, M.D.
Veronica M. Hargrove, Ph.D.

CRC Press
Taylor & Francis Group
Boca Raton London New York

CRC Press is an imprint of the
Taylor & Francis Group, an **informa** business

Cover image provided by, and used with permission from, Brian Hargrove.

CRC Press
Taylor & Francis Group
6000 Broken Sound Parkway NW, Suite 300
Boca Raton, FL 33487-2742

© 2019 by Taylor & Francis Group, LLC
CRC Press is an imprint of Taylor & Francis Group, an Informa business

No claim to original U.S. Government works

Printed on acid-free paper

International Standard Book Number-13: 978-0-8153-6581-5 (Hardback)
International Standard Book Number-13: 978-0-8153-6544-0 (Paperback)

Library of Congress Cataloging-in-Publication Data

Names: Molina, D. K., author. | Hargrove, Veronica, author.
Title: Handbook of forensic toxicology for medical examiners / D. Kimberley
Molina, M.D., Veronica M. Hargrove, Ph.D.
Description: Second edition. | Boca Raton, FL : CRC Press, Taylor & Francis
Group, [2019] | Includes bibliographical references and index.
Identifiers: LCCN 2018002264 | ISBN 9780815365815 (hardback : alk. paper) |
ISBN 9780815365440 (pbk. : alk. paper) | ISBN 9781351260602
Subjects: LCSH: Forensic toxicology--Handbooks, manuals, etc. | Medical
examiners (Law)--Handbooks, manuals, etc.
Classification: LCC RA1228 .M65 2019 | DDC 614/.13--dc23
LC record available at https://lccn.loc.gov/2018002264

Visit the Taylor & Francis Web site at
http://www.taylorandfrancis.com

and the CRC Press Web site at
http://www.crcpress.com

Editor's Note

This textbook is part of a series titled "Practical Aspects of Criminal and Forensic Investigations." This series was created by Vernon J. Geberth, a retired New York City Police Department lieutenant commander who is an author, educator, and consultant on homicide and forensic investigations.

This series has been designed to provide contemporary, comprehensive, and pragmatic information to the practitioner involved in criminal and forensic investigations by authors who are nationally recognized experts in their respective fields.

Contents

Series Editor

The Series Editor for *Practical Aspects of Criminal and Forensic Investigations* is Lieutenant Commander (retired) Vernon J. Geberth, New York City Police Department, who was the commanding officer of the Bronx Homicide Task Force, which handled more than 400 homicides a year. Commander Geberth has been president of P.H.I. Investigative Consultants, Inc., Marco Island, FL, since 1987. He has more than 47 years of law enforcement experience and has conducted homicide investigation seminars for more than 74,000 attendees from more than 8,000 law enforcement agencies.

Commander Geberth holds dual master's degrees in Clinical Psychology and Criminal Justice. He is a fellow in the American Academy of Forensic Sciences, Colorado Springs, CO, a graduate of the FBI National Academy, Quantico, VA, and the recipient of the Lifetime Achievement Award from the Vidocq Society.

He is an author, educator, and consultant on homicide and forensic investigations. He has published three best-selling books in this series, *Practical Homicide Investigation, Fifth Edition; Sex-Related Homicide and Death Investigation: Practical and Clinical Perspectives, Second Edition;* and *Practical Homicide Investigation: Checklist and Field Guide, Second Edition.*

He created, edited, and designed this series of more than 65 publications to provide contemporary, comprehensive, and pragmatic information to the practitioner involved in criminal and forensic investigations by authors who are nationally recognized experts in their respective fields.

He welcomes the opportunity to review new proposals for books covering any area of criminal and forensic investigation and may be reached through his email: vernongeberth@practicalhomicide.com.

List of Abbreviations

ABFT	American Board of Forensic Toxicology
aceta	acetaminophen
ACh	acetylcholinesterase
ASA	aspirin
BAC	blood alcohol (ethanol) content
bid	twice a day
CNS	central nervous system
CV	cardiovascular
d	day
g	gram
gtts	drops
h	hour
im	intramuscular
iv	intravenous
kg	kilogram
L	liter
mEq	milliequivalent
mg	milligram
min	minute
mL	milliliter
mo	month
NAME	National Association of Medical Examiners
ng	nanogram
NRI	norepinephrine reuptake inhibitor
NSAID	non-steroidal anti-inflammatory drug
OTC	over the counter
ppm	parts per million
po	by mouth (per os)
pr	per rectum
prn	as needed
q	every
qam	in the morning
qd	once a day
qHS	at bedtime
qid	four times a day

SC	subcutaneous
SNRI	serotonin and norepinephrine reuptake inhibitor
SSRI	selective serotonin reuptake inhibitor
supp	suppository
susp	suspension
TCA	tricyclic antidepressant
THC	delta-9-tetrahydrocannabinol
tid	three times a day
$\mathbf{V_d}$	volume of distribution
w/	with
wk	week
yr	year
λ	half-life
μg	microgram

How to Use This Book

1

For postmortem toxicology, the two most important concepts for any death investigator are:

1. Drug concentrations should never be interpreted in a vacuum.
2. There is no such thing as a "lethal drug concentration."

The purpose of this book is to assist forensic pathologists in the interpretation of common toxicology results. *This book is in no way meant as a substitute for a thorough death investigation and complete autopsy.*

Important points to consider are listed in the following:

- The concentrations given in this book are a compilation of the data from the literature.
  - The therapeutic/nontoxic concentrations given were determined either in serum during pharmacokinetic studies or were from whole blood samples taken from postmortem data from individuals dying of unrelated causes — who died with the drug present but without it contributing to death;
  - The toxic concentrations are serum concentrations obtained from individuals who suffered toxicities due to the drug listed but survived;
  - The lethal concentrations listed are for whole blood unless otherwise noted;
  - The lethal and toxic cases listed represent pure, single-drug intoxications unless otherwise noted.
- Consider the source.
  - Peripheral blood is preferable
    - Understand postmortem redistribution and the variables involved;
    - Some drugs are not as affected as others.
    - Not all peripheral blood is created equally — femoral is preferred.
  - Antemortem specimens may be serum and could affect interpretation.
  - Liver, urine, bile, and stomach contents do not necessarily indicate acute toxicity, only exposure.

- Consider the test.
  - Immunoassays may have cross reactivity giving false positive or false negative results.
  - Make certain to direct the testing for the drugs of interest.
    - Know which drugs are on the testing panels ordered and which drugs are found on which panels.
    - Some drugs may require specialized testing or sample collection.
- Consider the time.
  - Time elapsed since death may affect concentrations.
    - Some drugs may be metabolized after death or during the agonal period.
    - Postmortem redistribution may occur.
- Consider the circumstances.
  - When was the decedent last seen? What was the decedent doing? How was the deceased acting?
  - Are the terminal events consistent with a drug toxicity?
- Consider the decedent.
  - Are there other disease processes present?
  - How do the drugs and the diseases interact?
- Consider tolerance.
  - How long has the deceased been on the drug? At what dose? On what regimen?
    - Specifically consider in deaths with opiates/opioids, benzodiazepines, barbiturates, and ethanol.
  - Could withdrawal be possible?
    - Specifically consider with ethanol and benzodiazepines.
- Consider the presence of other drugs.
  - The presence of multiple drugs with similar effects can result in death or other adverse effects, such as serotonin syndrome.
- Consider intrinsic drug properties.
  - QT interval
    - Certain prescription and illicit drugs can prolong the QT interval.
    - Can be associated with sudden death, especially in the presence of underlying rhythm disturbances.
  - Metabolism
    - Approximately 30% of all drugs are affected by a drug metabolizing enzyme, the majority are part of the CYP450 system
    - Drug concentrations can vary by a factor of 600 between two individuals given the same dosage.
    - Genetic factors may play a role in how an individual absorbs, distributes, and metabolizes a drug.
      - A mutation in a drug metabolizing enzyme can lead to accumulation of a drug and toxicity.

Special Drug Groups 2

Acetylcholinesterase Inhibitors

While acetylcholinesterase inhibitors were historically used as pesticides and herbicides, in recent years they have been used to develop medications to treat Alzheimer's disease and myasthenia gravis. Commonly, their toxicity is measured by the percentage of acetylcholinesterase (ACh) activity with toxicity beginning 20% below the level of normal activity (or 80% activity level) and becoming pronounced by 50% activity level. Severe toxicity and death occur at 90% suppression (measured activity level = 10%). Postmortem testing should utilize the red blood cell (RBC), ACh as it better reflects neural ACh activity.

Table 2.1 is a non-comprehensive list of common drugs, nerve agents, and insecticide/pesticides that are acetylcholinesterase inhibitors.

Table 2.1   Acetylcholinesterase Inhibitors

Drugs—Alzheimer's disease	*Drugs—myasthenia gravis*	*Drugs—glaucoma*	*Poisons—nerve agents*
Donepezil (Aricept)	Ambenonium (Mytelase)	Demecarium (Humorsol)	Cyclosarin
Galantamine (Razadyne, Reminyl, Nivalin)	Edrophonium (Tensilon, Enlon, Reversol)	Echothiophate (Phospholine iodide)	Sarin
Huperzine A	Neostigmine (Prostigmin)		Soman
Ladostigil	Physostigmine (Antilirium)		Tabun
Metrifonate	Pyridostigmine (Mestinon, Regonol)		VX
Rivastigmine (Exelon)			VE
Tacrine (Cognex)			VG
			VM

Insecticides or pesticides

Acephate (Orthene)	Dichlorvos (DDVP, Vapona)	Formetanate (Carzol)	Oxydemeton-methyl (Meta systox-R)
Aldicarb (Temik)	Dicrotophos (Bidrin)	Fenthion (Baytex, Tiguvon, Entex)	Parathion (Niran, Phoskil)
Azinphos-methyl (Guthion)	Diisopropyl fluorophosphate (Dyflos)	Fonofos (Dyfonate)	Phorate (Thimet)
Bendiocarb (Ficam)	Dimethoate (Cygon, De-Fend)	Isofenphos (Oftanol, Amaze)	Phosalone (Zolonc)
Bufencarb	Dioxathion (Delnav)	Malathion (Cythion)	Phosmet (Imidan, Prolate)
Carbaryl (Sevin)	Disulfoton (Di-Syston)	Methamidophos (Monitor)	Phosphamidon (Dimecron)
Carbofuran (Furadan)	EPN	Methidathion (Supracide)	Pirimicarb (Pirimor)
Carbophenothion (Trithion)	Ethiofencarb	Methiocarb (Mesurol)	Propoxur (Baygon)
Chlorfenvinphos (Birlane)	Ethion	Methomyl (Lannate, Nudrin)	Temephos (Abate)
Chlorpyrifos (Dursban, Lorsban)	Ethoprop (Mocap)	Methyl parathion (Penncap-M)	TEPP
Coumaphos (Co-Ral)	Famphur	Mevinphos (Phosdrin)	Terbufos (Counter)
Crotoxyphos (Ciodrin, Ciovap)	Fenamiphos (Nemacur)	Monocrotophos	Tetrachlorvinphos (Rabon, Gardona)
Crufomate (Ruelene)	Fenitrothion (Sumithion)	Naled (Dibrom)	Trichlorfon (Dylox, Neguvon)
Demeton (Systox)	Fensulfothion (Dasanit)	Oxamyl (Vydate)	
Diazinon (Spectracide)			

Anesthetic Agents

General Anesthetics

General anesthetic agents are commonly used in the clinical setting to induce or maintain anesthesia. When used for this purpose, in a monitored clinical setting and in ventilated patients, the risk of death due to overdose is minimal. Some anesthetic agents are associated with other toxic effects, such as malignant hyperthermia, liver toxicities, and prolonged QT, but a discussion of these effects is beyond the scope of this book. However, when such agents are abused outside of the monitored clinical setting, **even therapeutic concentrations can be lethal**. Table 2.2 summarizes lethal concentrations of these medications, which have been reported in the literature.

Ketamine and propofol deserve special mention and are described in more detail below.

- Ketamine
  - In addition to being a widely used anesthetic agent, ketamine has become a drug of abuse known as Jet, Special K, Vitamin K, and Special K lube when combined with ethanol and gamma hydroxybutyric acid (GHB).
  - As ketamine is also used as a recreational drug, its presence alone may not indicate a lethal intoxication. The following nontoxic concentrations have been reported:

Blood (mg/L)	Liver (mg/kg)	Kidney (mg/kg)	Brain (mg/kg)	Cardiac Muscle (mg/kg)	Skeletal Muscle (mg/kg)
0.5–9	0.8	0.6	4	3.5	1.2

Table 2.2 Lethal Concentrations of General Anesthetic Agents

Anesthetic Agent	Blood (mg/L)	Vitreous (mg/L)	Liver (mg/kg)	Kidney (mg/kg)	Brain (mg/kg)	Lung (mg/kg)	Muscle (mg/kg)
Etomidate	0.4	0.3					
Halothane	3.4–720		1.7–880	12–14	104–1560	500	
Isoflurane	1.8–48		31–1000	27–53	29–307	9–34	9 (skeletal)
Ketamine	1.5–38		4.9–6.6	3.2–3.6	3.2–4.3		2.4 (cardiac)
Nitrous oxide	11–2030				47–2200	370–2420	
Propofol	0.03–5.5		1.4–27	1.8–5.5	2.9–17		222 (skeletal)
Sevoflurane	8–26	87	31–269	13–29			

- Propofol
  - With high volume of distribution and lipophilicity, it can be found several days following a surgical procedure at low tissue and blood concentrations and may not indicate an acute intoxication.
  - Can cause propofol infusion syndrome—characterized by metabolic acidosis, bradyarrhythmias, rhabdomyolysis, hypotension, and cardiac failure.
  - Therapeutic/nontoxic concentrations of propofol have been reported from 0.4 to 6.8 mg/L in blood.

Local Anesthetics

Local anesthetics usually result in toxicity and death by central nervous system excitation and seizure activity. They can also be cardiotoxic, resulting in arrhythmias and ventricular fibrillation.

Tables 2.3 and 2.4 summarize the pharmacokinetic properties and nonlethal and lethal concentrations of several local anesthetic agents.

Table 2.3 Pharmacokinetic Parameters and Toxic and Lethal Concentrations of Local Anesthetic Agents

Anesthetic Agent	κ (h)	Vd (L/kg)	Nontoxic Blood (mg/L)	Nontoxic Liver (mg/kg)	Toxic Blood (mg/L)	Lethal Blood (mg/L)	Lethal Liver (mg/kg)
Benzocaine	Unknown	Unknown	0.05–0.5		1.0–5.2[a]	3.5[a]	
Bupivacaine	1–3	0.4–1	0.2–3.5		0.3–20	3.8	
Lidocaine	0.7–5	1–4	0.3–5	0.01–4	8–12	12–44	10–96
Mepivacaine	1.5–2	0.5–4	0.1–5		4–9	16[b]–50	75
Prilocaine	0.5–2.5	0.7–4	0.9–5		0.3–2.8	13–15	14[a]–49
Procaine	7–8 min	0.3–1	4–43		18–96		
Ropivacaine	2–4	0.5–1	0.4–3		1.5–6	2	4.4

[a] Children.
[b] Mixed with lidocaine 4.9 mg/L.

Table 2.4 Additional Tissue Concentrations for Lidocaine and Mepivacaine

Anesthetic Agent	Nontoxic Concentrations				Lethal Concentrations			
	Kidney (mg/kg)	Brain (mg/kg)	Cardiac Muscle (mg/kg)	Skeletal Muscle (mg/kg)	Kidney (mg/kg)	Brain (mg/kg)	Cardiac Muscle (mg/kg)	Skeletal Muscle (mg/kg)
Lidocaine	0.01–15	0.01–5.9	0.8	0.9–2.9	12–204	6.6–135	9–13	20
Mepivacaine	51–59	51–83			51	51		

Lidocaine, benzocaine, and prilocaine deserve special mention and are described in additional detail below.

- Benzocaine and prilocaine toxicity can result in methemoglobinemia.
- Lidocaine is metabolized by CYP 1A2 and 3A4 to the active metabolite, monoethylglycinexylidide (MEGX) and has been used as an adulterant in illicit drugs.

Neuromuscular Blocking Agents

Neuromuscular blocking agents block neuromuscular transmission at the neuromuscular junction, resulting in paralysis. These are most often used in anesthesia to assist in intubation. The use of these agents in the clinical setting, while the patient is being artificially ventilated, should not result in death. **The presence of these agents outside of a clinical setting, in a non-ventilated patient, can result in death at any concentration**.

Common neuromuscular blocking agents include: atracurium, cisatracurium, doxacurium, gallamine, mivacurium, pancuronium, pipecuronium, rapacurium, rocuronium, succinylcholine, tubocurarine, and vecuronium.

Succinylcholine deserves an additional note, because it

- Can be difficult to find in postmortem cases due to short half-life.
- Absorbs onto glassware during storage.
- Is rapidly hydrolyzed to succinylmonocholine, choline, and succinic acid, all of which are found endogenously.

Metals and Metalloids

Humans are exposed to metals and elements through the environment, food and water, smoking, and certain occupations or hobbies. Some metals have also been used not only medicinally but also as poisons, including being components of insecticides or pesticides. The concentrations of metals seen in blood and tissues are often extremely variable due to diet, environment, and occupation, making interpretation of postmortem metal concentrations extremely difficult; it is recommended that such interpretation be done with great skepticism and reflection.

Metals tend to be eliminated by and accumulate in the kidneys, so renal tissue is often the preferred tissue when testing for an acute overdose. Chronic exposure can often be delineated by testing of the hair and/or fingernails. Tables 2.5 and 2.6 outline reported metal concentrations.

Numerous procedures can be utilized to test for metals, including inductively coupled plasma mass spectrophotometry (ICP), atomic absorption spectroscopy (AAS), atomic emission spectrophotometry (AES), and x-ray defraction. Be certain to contact the testing laboratory for any specific requirements.

The following metals deserve special consideration:

Aluminum
- Classic exposure was through dialysis; no longer common.
- Blocks incorporation of calcium into bone.
- Associated with elevated calcium concentrations.

Arsenic
- Is a metalloid. Used medicinally for years.
- A known carcinogen.
- Elemental arsenic (As^o) is not toxic; can be found in shellfish and seafood.
- Arsenate (As^{+5}), arsenite (As^{+3}), and arsine gas (AsH_3) are toxic— $As^{+5} < As^{+3} < AsH_3$.
- Can cause white lines across the nails, known as Mees lines or leukonychia striata.

Barium
- Often used in medical procedures as 40%–80% suspension (e.g., Entero-H and Barotrast).
- Overdose can cause hypokalemia.

Cadmium
- Most common exposure is from smoking and fish consumption.
- Inhalation of cadmium fumes can cause fatal pneumonitis.

Table 2.5 Nontoxic Concentrations of Common Metals

Metal	λ	Blood (mg/L)	Liver (mg/kg)	Kidney (mg/kg)	Brain (mg/kg)	Cardiac Muscle (mg/kg)	Skeletal Muscle (mg/kg)	Lung (mg/kg)	Other (mg/kg)
Aluminum	8 h–8 yr	0.004–0.4	0.6–2	0.07–0.4	0.2–0.9		0.07–0.9		Bone 1–12
Antimony	Unknown	0.002–0.06	0.01–0.07	0.01–0.1	0.01–0.1	0.01–0.1	0.01–0.1	0.03–0.2	Hair 0.1–2 Nail 0.2–2
Arsenic	10–30 h	0.003–0.3	0.02–0.09	0.02–0.1	0.02–0.1	0.02–0.06	0.04–0.1	0.05–0.1	Bone 0.05–0.2 Nail 0.9 Hair 0.02–8
Barium	10–80 h	0.001–0.1	0.003	0.01–0.09	0.004	0.009		0.16	
Bismuth	5–11 d	0.003–0.5	0.01–7	3	0.6			0.9	
Cadmium	10–30 yr	0.001–0.1	0.7–23	1–166	0.02–0.2	0.06–0.3	0.07–1	0.2–2	Bone 0.02–0.1 Hair 527–967
Copper	15–25 d	0.7–1.8	2–23	1–13	2–8	2–12	0.4–3	0.8–2	Spleen 4 Bone 3
Iron	3–6 h	0.3–1.5	29–479	7–160	8–96	6–73	11–59	112–280	Spleen 57–600
Lead	Blood 1–2 mo Bone >20 yr	0.003–0.5	0.2–4	0.1–2	0.02–0.8	0.01–1	0.02–0.5	0.05–2	Bone 0.2–4 Hair 0.1–20 Nail 0.06–1.5
Lithium	**See page 124**								
Mercury	14–50 d	0.002–0.2	0.002–1	0.2–3	0.04–0.2	0.001–0.1	0.02–0.2	0.02–0.3	Bone 0.05–0.07 Hair 1–15 Nail 0.06–0.8
Thallium	3–30 d	0.002–0.08	0.1–0.9	0.001–0.08	0.001–0.02				Hair 0.005–0.01

Table 2.6 Toxic and Lethal Concentrations of Common Metals

Metal	Toxic Blood (mg/L)	Blood (mg/L)	Liver (mg/kg)	Kidney (mg/kg)	Brain (mg/kg)	Spleen (mg/kg)	Lung (mg/kg)	Hair (mg/kg)	Other (mg/kg)
Aluminum	0.02–0.2	0.4–24	5–90	3–32	1–5				Bone 1–30
Antimony	0.05–210	4.6	45	32	6	6	6		Cardiac muscle 4
Arsenic	0.02–3	0.1–10	2–400	0.2–100	0.2–20	0.5–200		10–200	Nail 50–67 Skeletal muscle 12
Barium	0.3–27	0.2–23	2–141	7–162	0.4–31	23–26	15–24		Vitreous 26–50 Cardiac muscle 17–22
Bismuth	0.05–2	1–100			3–25				
Cadmium	0.01–0.05	0.1–1	11–200	70–5980	0.5–3		1–4		Heart 8–12
Copper	1–13	2–74	8–1410	9–61	1–11				
Iron	3–26	2–50[a]	1504	982	483				
Lead	0.1–6	1–5	8–34	8–24	7–74				Bone 2–2680
Lithium	See page 124								
Mercury	0.05–6	0.2–12	1–217	2–284	1–35	1–100	3–23	400–1600	Cardiac muscle 1–17
Thallium	0.05–8	0.2–11	1–54	1–37	2–55		0.5–1	10–14	Skeletal muscle 6–13 Cardiac muscle 2–13

[a] Serum concentrations.

Lead
- Associated with blood smear basophilic stippling.
- Can cause Burton's lines (thin blue lines along the gums at the dental margin).
- Causes hypochromic microcytic anemia.

Mercury
- Previously used medicinally and as dental amalgam fillings.
- Component of cinnabar pigment.
- In fish, may be found in elevated concentrations.
- Associated with acrodynia.
- Is found in three forms: elemental, inorganic, and organic. Inorganic forms of mercury are the most toxic.

Thallium
- May also cause Mees line and alopecia.
- Toxicity may be misdiagnosed as Guillain Barre syndrome.

Novel Psychoactive Substances

A novel psychoactive substance is a new term used to describe a large group of drugs that are meant to mimic the effects of more commonly known drugs such as amphtemaines, cocaine, opiates, or delta-9-tetrahydrocannabinol (THC). With many new identifications appearing monthly, the number of these drugs has grown significantly in recent years. Therapeutic, toxic, and/ or lethal concentrations overlap, and drug interactions are not well known. Caution should be used when interpreting their potential role in deaths, taking into account the circumstances surrounding death.

Novel psychoactive substances can be sedating, stimulating, or halluci-nogenic compounds. The main classes of these drugs can be separated into synthetic cannabinoids, synthetic stimulants and hallucinogens, and syn-thetic opioids.

Synthetic Cannabinoids

Synthetic cannabinoids are a class of drugs manufactured to mimic the effects of delta-9-tetrahydrocannabinol, the active ingredient in marijuana. Similar to THC, synthetic cannabinoids bind to cannabinoid receptors. However, it is important to note that THC is a weak partial agonist at these receptors, while synthetic cannabinoids are full agonists. In addition, their affinity for the receptors is greatly increased allowing them to have increased adverse effects. Some adverse effects can include seizures, agitation, irritation, anxi-ety, confusion, paranoia, tachycardia, hypertension, chest pain, hypokale-mia, hallucinations, tremors, delusions, nausea, and vomiting.

In vitro stability of some synthetic cannabinoids has been shown to be short; therefore, it is best to keep samples frozen and test as soon as possible. There are hundreds of synthetic cannabinoids, and new drugs are developed regularly. Table 2.7 is a non-comprehensive list of some common synthetic cannabinoids that have been implicated in causing toxicities.

Synthetic Opioids

Synthetic opioids are a class of drugs that bind to opioid receptors, much like opiates (codeine, morphine) and semi-synthetic opioids (hydrocodone, oxyco-done) and as such, they cause pain relief and anesthesia. In addition to pain relief and anesthesia, much like other opiates and opioids, these drugs can cause sedation, respiratory depression, and drowsiness, which can lead to coma and death.

Table 2.8 is a non-comprehensive list of synthetic opioids that have been implicated in causing toxicities.

Table 2.7   Synthetic Cannabinoids Implicated in Causing Toxicities

5F-AB-001	ADBICA	CUMYL-	JWH-122	MO-CHMINACA
5F-ADB	ADB-PINACA	THPINACA	JWH-133	NM-2201
5F-ADBICA	AF-AMB	EG-2201	JWH-200	NNE1
5F-ADB-PINACA	AM-1248	FUB-144	JWH-210	PB-22
5F-AMB	AM-2201	FUB-AKB-48	JWH-250	PX1/PX-1
5F-APICA	AM-2233	FUB-AMB	JWH-251	PX2/PX-2
5F-APINACA	AM-679	FUBIMINA	JWH-260	RCS-4
5F-MN-A8	AM-694	FUB-JWH-018	MAB-	RCS-4-C4
5F-PB-22	AMB	FUB-PB-22	CHMINACA	RCS-8
A-796260	AMB-	HU-210	MDMB-	THJ-018
AB-CHMINACA	FUBINACA	JWH-015	CHMCZCA	THJ-2201
ABDICA	APICA	JWH-018	MDMB-	UR-144
AB-FUBINACA	APINACA	JWH-018-5-	CHMINACA	WIN 55-212
AB-PINACA	APP-	Chloropentyl	MDMB-	XLR-11
ADB-	CHMINACA	JWH-019	FUBINACA	
CHMINACA	BB-22	JWH-022	MDMB-	
ADB-FUBINACA	CP 47-,497	JWH-073	CHMICA	
	CP-55,940	JWH-081	MMB-	
			CHMICA	
			MMB-	
			CHMINACA	
			MN-18	
			MN-25	

Table 2.8   Synthetic Opioids Implicated in Causing Toxicities

3-Methylfentanyl	p-Fluorobutyrylfentanyl
4-ANPP	p-Fluorofentanyl
4-Fluorobutyrfentanyl	Furanylfentanyl
4-Methoxy-butyryl fentanyl	Isobutyryl fentanyl
4-Methylphenethyl acetylfentanyl	Methoxyacetyl fentanyl
α-ME fentanyl	MT 45 (1-cyclohexyl-4-(1,2-diphenylethyl)piperazine)
Acetylfentanyl	Ocfentanyl
Acrylfentanyl	Ortho-fluorofentanyl
Acryloylfentanyl	Para-fluorofentanyl
AH7921	Sufentanil
Alfentanyl	Tetrahydrofuranyl fentanyl
Alpha-methylfentanyl	Thiafentanil
Beta-hydroxythiofentanyl	U-47700 (3,4-dichloro-*N*-[2-(dimethylamino)
Butyrylfentanyl	cyclohexyl]-*N*-methylbenzamide)
Carfentanil	U-48800
Cyclopropylfentanyl	U-49900 (trans-3,4-dichloro-*N*-[2-(diethylamino)
Despropionyl fentanyl	cyclohexyl]-*N*-methyl-benzamide)
FIBF (Para-Fluoro-Isobutyryl	U-50488 (*rel*-3,4-dichloro-*N*-methyl-*N*-[(1R,2R)-2-
Fentanyl)	(1-pyrrolidinyl)cyclohexyl]-benzeneacetamide)
	Valerylfentanyl

Synthetic Stimulants and Hallucinogens

Synthetic stimulants and hallucinogens mimic other more commonly known stimulants and hallucinogens such as methamphetamine, cocaine, and lysergic acid diethylamide (LSD). Similarly, they act on monoamines by inhibiting their transport and/or inducing their release. Synthetic stimulants are generally amphetamines, cathinones, tryptamines, phenethylamines, piperazines, piperidines, or related substances. Some adverse effects can include tachycardia, restlessness, anxiety, agitation, hypertension, nausea, vomiting, and diarrhea among others.

In vitro stability of some synthetic drugs has been shown to be short, therefore, it is best to keep samples frozen and test as soon as possible. Table 2.9 includes non-comprehensive lists of some common synthetic stimulants and hallucinogens that have been implicated in causing toxicities.

Volatiles

Volatiles as a class of drugs are considered forensically when they are intentionally inhaled with the intent of obtaining psychoactive effects; they are also referred to as *inhalants*. Volatiles are commonly constituents of fuel gases, propellants, solvents, anesthetics, automotive fuels, refrigerants, paint thinner, glues, and dry-cleaning agents. These compounds most commonly include aromatic and halogenated hydrocarbons and fluorocarbons. They are known to be cardiotoxic and are associated with lethal arrhythmias; they can also cause death by oxygen exclusion.

Common volatile compounds include benzene, butane, carbon tetrachloride, chloroform, diethyl ether, enflurane, ether, ethyl ether, fluothane, freon, gasoline, helium, isoflurane, methyl ether, nitrous oxide, oxybismethane, perchloroethylene, propane, tetrachloroethene, tetrafluoroethane, toluene, trichloroethylene, trichloroethane, trichloromethane, trifluoroethane, and xylene.

Volatiles are highly lipophilic, so in addition to blood, the brain is often a good secondary source. In fact, 1,1-difluoroethane has been detected in cerebral material approximately 50 hours after exposure and prolonged hospitalization.

Diagnosis of volatile or inhalant toxicity usually depends upon the circumstances of death and the presence of such a substance in the blood or tissue samples, regardless of concentration of the substance. However, concentrations in fatal cases have been reported and are described in Table 2.10.

(Continued)

Table 2.9 Synthetic Stimulants and Hallucinogens Implicated in Causing Toxicities

2 AI (2-Aminoindane)	3,4 DMMC (3,4 Dimethylmethcathinone)
2 DPMP (2-Diphenylmethylpiperidine)	3,4 MDPBP (3,4 Methylenedioxy-alpha-pyrrolidinobutiophenone)
2 MAPB (1-(benzofuran-2-yl)-N-methylpropan-2-amine)	3,4 MDPV (3,4-Methylenedioxypyrovalerone)
2 Methoxydiphenidine	4 CAB (4-Chlorophenylisobutylamine)
2 Methyl PPP (2-methyl-alpha-pyrrolidinopropiophenone)	4 Fluoroamphetamine
2 MMC (2-Methylmethcathinone)	4 MBC (4-Methylbenzylidene camphor)
25 B NBOMe	4 MEC (4-Methylethcathinone)
25 C NBOMe	4 MeO PCP (4-Methoxyphencyclidine)
25 H NBOMe	4 Methylamphetamine
25 I NBOMe	4 Methylthioamphetamine
2C B (4-Bromo-2,5-dimethoxphenethylamine)	4 MPBP (4-Methyl-2-pyrrolidinoburyrophenone)
2C B FLY (8-Bromo-2,3,6,7-tetrahydrobenzo[1,2-b:4,5-b']difuran-4-ethanamine)	4 MTA (4-Methylthioampheatmine)
2C C (2,5-Dimethoxy-4-chlorophenethylamine)	4 OH DET (4-Hydroxy diethyltryptamine)
2C E (2,5-Dimethoxy-4-iodophenethylamine)	5 APDI (5-(2-Aminopropyl)-2,3-dihydro-1H-indene
2C H (2,5-Dimethoxyphenethylamine)	5 APB (5-(2-Aminopropyl)benzofuran)
2C I (2,5-Dimethoxy-4-iodophenethylamine)	5 APDB (5-(2-Aminopropyl)-2,3-dihydrobenzofuran)
2C N (2,5-Dimethoxy-4-nitrophenethylamine)	5 IAI (5-Iodo-2-aminoindane)
2C P (2,5-Dimethoxy-4-propylphenethylamine)	5 IT (5-(2-Aminopropyl)indole)
2C T (2,5-Dimethoxy-4-methylthiophenethylamine)	5 MAPB (5-(2-Methylaminopropyl)benzofuran)
2C T2 (2,5-Dimethoxy-4-ethylthiophenethylamine)	5 MeO AMT (5-Methoxy-alpha-methyltryptamine)
2C T4 (2,5-Dimethoxy-4-isopropylthiophenethylamine)	5 MeO DALT (N,N-Diallyl-5-Methoxytryptamine)
2C T7 (2,5-Dimethoxy-4-propylthiophenethylamine)	5 MeO DiPT (5-Methoxy-N,N-diisopropyltryptamine)
3 FMC (3 Fluoromethcathinone)	5 MeO DMT (5-Methoxy-N,N-dimethyltryptamine)
3 MeO PCP (3-Methoxy-phencyclidine)	5 MeO MiPT (5-Methoxy-N-methyl-N-isopropyltryptamine)
3 MMC (3 Methylmethcathinone)	6 APB (6-(2-Aminopropyl)benzofuran)
	6 IT (6-(2-Aminopropyl)indole)

Table 2.9 (*Continued*) Synthetic Stimulants and Hallucinogens Implicated in Causing Toxicities

Alpha PBP (alpha-Pyrrolidinobutiophenone)	DMA (2,5 Dimethoxyamphetamine)
Alpha PHP (2-(1-pyrrolidinyl)-hexanophenone)	DMAA (Methylhexanamine)
Alpha-PHPP (alpha-Pyrrolidinopentiophenone)	DMT (*N, N*-Dimethyltryptamine)
Alpha PPP (alpha-pyrrolidinopropiophenone)	DOB (4 Bromo 2,5 dimethoxyamphetamine)
Alpha PVP (alpha Pyrrolodinopentiophenone)	DOC (4 Chloro 2,5 dimethoxyamphetamine)
Alpha PVT (alpha-pyrrolidinopentiothiophenone)	DOET (2,5 Dimethoxy 4 ethylamphetamine)
AMT (alpha methyltryptamine)	DOI (4 Iodo 2,5-dimethoxyamphetamine)
BCP (Benocyclidine)	DOM (2,5 Dimethoxy 4 methylamphetamine)
BDB (Benzodioxole-5-butanamine)	DPT (Dipropyltryptamine)
Brephedrone	EEC (Ethylethcathinone)
Brolamfetamine	Escaline
Bromo dragon FLY	Ethcathinone
Buphedrone	Ethylamphetamine
Butylone	Ethylcathinone
BZP (Benzylpiperazine)	Ethylethcathinone
CathinoneD2PM (Diphenyl-2-pyrrolidinemethanol)	Ethylone
DBZP (1,4-Dibenzylpiperazine)	Ethylphenidate
DET (*N,N*-Diethyltryptamine)	Eutylone
Dibutylone	Fenethylline
Dimethylcathinone	Flephedone
Dimethylone	Fluoromethamphetamine
DiPT (*N, N*-diisopropyltryptamine)	FMC (Fluoromethcathinone)

(Continued)

Table 2.9 (*Continued*) Synthetic Stimulants and Hallucinogens Implicated in Causing Toxicities

MBDB (*N*-Methyl-1,3-Berzodioxolylbutanamine)	Methylone
MBZP (Methylbenzylpiperazine)mCPP (1-(3-Chlorophenyl)piperazine)	MMC (Methylmethcathinone)
MDAI (5,6-Methylenedioxy2-aminoindane)	MPHP (Methyl-alpha-pyrrolidinohexanophenone)
MDEA (Methylenedioxyethylamphetamine)	MXE (Methoxetamine)
MDPPP (Methylenedioxy-alpha-pyrrolidinopropiophenone)	MXP (Methoxphenidine)
MeOPP (1-(4-Methoxyphenyl)piperazine)	*N*-Ethylpentylone
MeOPPP (4-Methoxy-alpha-pyrrolidinopropiophenone)	Naphyrone
Mephedrone	NEB (N-Ethylbuphedone)
Mephentermine	Pentedrone
Methcathinone	Pentylone
Methcopropamine	PMA (Phorbol 12-myristate 13-acetate) PMMA
Methedrone	(para-Methoxymethamphetamine)
Methiopropamine	Pyrovalerone
Methoxetamine	TFMPP (1-(m-Trifluoromethylphenyl)piperazine)
Methoxyamphetamine	TMA (Trimethoxyamphetamine)
Methoxymethamphetamine	WIN 35428 (beta-Carbomethoxy-3-beta-(4-fluorophenyl)tropane)

Table 2.10 Lethal Concentrations of Selected Volatile Substances

Volatile	Blood (mg/L)	Vitreous (mg/L)	Liver (mg/kg)	Kidney (mg/kg)	Brain (mg/kg)	Lung (mg/kg)	Adipose Tissue (mg/kg)	Skeletal Muscle (mg/kg)	Cardiac Muscle (mg/kg)
Benzene	0.9–120		2.6–379	5.5–75	14–179	22	22–120		
Butane	0.05–129		0.5–147	0.4–78	0.4–288	0.03–128	1.8–234	5.4–112	
Carbon tetrachloride	57–260	170	59–142	150	175–243	39–127		71	78–188
Chloroform	29–834		26–298	38–124	21–133	14–92	79–128		
Difluoroethane (Freon 152a)	3.2–380	2.6–200	88		118	60	236		
Trichloro-fluoromethane (Freon 11)	0.6–63		45–74	50	61–109	32–149			407
Chlorodifluoro-methane (Freon 22)	26–560	0.7–1	4.4–381	33–75	2.8–414	1.6–80			
Trichloro-trifluoroethane (Freon 113)	0.4–32		2.9–81	476	0.5–1370	0.05–3.5	5.4	8.8	
Propane	0.2–69		0.3–33	0.2–75	1–128	0.2–55	0.9–1276	0.3–213	1.7–34
Toluene (methyl-benzene)	1–114		3.6–433	39	19–740	6.6–100	12		63
Trichloro-ethane	0.1–720		4.9–220	2.6–120	3.2–1230	1.8–22		2.6–49	
Trichloro-ethylene	1.1–210		2.5–747	12–78	32–809	9.3–21			
Xylene (dimethyl-benzene)	4.9–110		3.6–29		6.1–19		7.1		12

Selected Sources

Adelson L. (1974). Chapter XIII murder by poison, in *The Pathology of Homicide*, C. C. Thomas (Ed.), Springfield, Geneseo, IL, pp. 725–875.

Berman E. (1980). *Toxic Metals and Their Analysis*. Heyden, Philadelphia, PA.

Bexar County Medical Examiner's Office data 1996–2015.

Broussard L. (2002). Chapter 19 inhalants, in *Principles of Forensic Toxicology*, B. Levine (Ed.), American Association for Clinical Chemistry, Washington, DC, pp. 345–353.

Dart RC (Ed). (2004). *Section 10 Metals in Medical Toxicology* (3rd ed.), Lippincott Williams & Wilkins, Philadelphia, PA, pp. 1387–1474.

EXTOXNET (Extension Toxicology Network) Cholinesterase Inhibition accessed at http://extoxnet.orst.edu/tibs/cholines.htm on June 1, 2008.

Gerostamoulos D, Elliott S, Walls C, Peters FT, Lynch M, Drummer OH. (2016). To measure or not to measure? That is the NPS question, *J Anal Toxicol*, 40(4): 318–320.

Huestis MA, Brandt SD, Rana S, Auwarter V, Baumann MH. (2017). Impact of novel psychoactive substances on clinical and forensic toxicology and global public health, *Clin Chem*, 63: 10.

Ivanenko NB, Ivanenko AA, Solovyev ND, Zeimal AE, Navolotskii DV, Drobyshev EJ. (2013). Biomonitoring of 20 trace elements in blood and urine of occupationally exposed workers by sector field inductively coupled plasma mass spectrometry, *Talanta*, 116: 764–769.

Karinen R, Johnsen L, Andresen W, Christophersen AS, Vindenes V, Oiestad EL. (2013). Stability study of fifteen synthetic cannabinoids of aminoalkylindole type in whole blood, stored in vacutainer evacuated glass tubes, *J Forensic Toxicol Pharmacol*, 2: 1.

Katz KD, Leonetti AL, Bailey BC, Surmaitis RM, Eustice ER, Kacinko S, Wheatley SM. (2016). Case series of synthetic cannabinoid intoxication from one toxicology center, *West J Emerg Med*, 17(3): 290–294.

Kemp AM, Clark, MS, Dobbs T et al. (2016). Top 10 facts you need to know about synthetic cannabinoids: Not so nice spice, *Am J Med*, 129: 240–244.

Knight B. (1991). *Forensic Pathology*. Oxford University Press. New York, pp. 530–532.

Logan BK, Mohr ALA, Friscia M et al. (2017). Reports of adverse events associated with use of novel psychoactive substances, 2013–2016: A review, *J Anal Toxicol*, 41: 573–610.

Mari M, Nadal M, Schuhmacher M et al. (2014). Human exposure to metals: Levels in autopsy tissues of individuals living near a hazardous waste incinerator, *Biol Trace Elem Res*, 159(1–3): 15–21.

Stephens BG. (2004). Chapter XXII investigation of deaths from drug abuse, in *Spitz and Fisher's Medicolegal Investigation of Death*, (4th ed.), W. U. Spitz and C. C. Thomas (Eds.), Springfield, Geneseo, IL, pp. 1166–1217.

Sumino K, Hayakawa K, Shibata T, Kitamura S. (1975). Heavy metals in normal Japanese tissues. Amounts of 15 heavy metals in 30 subjects, *Arch Environ Health*, 30(10): 487–494.

Toxicological Profile for Antimony and Compounds. (1992). Agency for Toxic Substances and Disease Registry, U.S. Public Health Service, available at https://www.atsdr.cdc.gov/toxprofiles/tp23.pdf.

Versieck J. (1985). Trace elements in human body fluids and tissues, *Crit Rev Clin Lab Sci*, 22(2): 97–184.

Yukawa M, Amano K, Suzuki-Yasumoto M, Terai M. (1980). Distribution of trace elements in the human body determined by neutron activation analysis, *Arch Environ Health*, 35(1): 36–44.

Alphabetical Listing of Drugs

3

Acetaminophen

Brand names: Tylenol and Paracetamol
Classification: Analgesic
λ: 1–3 h
V_d: 0.8–1 L/kg
Usual dosage: 325–1000 mg q 4–6 h

Source	Therapeutic/Nontoxic	Toxic	Lethal
Blood	5–26 mg/L	30–981 mg/L	160–1280 mg/L
Vitreous			779–878 mg/L
Liver			220–3260 mg/kg
Kidney			93–188 mg/kg
Brain			220 mg/kg
Skeletal muscle	18–55 mg/kg		179–220 mg/kg

Comments

- Metabolized by CYP 1A2 and 2E1
- Overdoses treated with *N*-acetylcysteine
- Causes hepatic necrosis; death usually occurs 3–5 days after ingestion

- Concentration is interpreted based on time since ingestion
  - Concentrations above the line are indicative of probable hepatotoxicity
  - Concentrations below the line indicate a low risk for hepatotoxicity

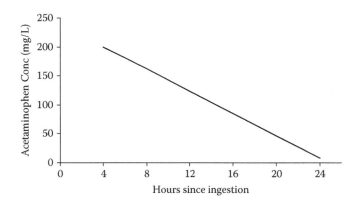

Hours since ingestion

Selected Sources

Bexar County Medical Examiner's Office data 1996–2015.

Dart RC, Rumack BH. (2004). Chapter 126 acetaminophen (Paracetamol), in *Medical Toxicology* (3rd ed.), R. C. Dart (Ed.), LWW, Philadelphia, PA.

Singer PP, Jones GR, Bannach BG, Denmark L. (2007). Acute fatal acetaminophen overdose without liver necrosis, *J Forensic Sci*, 52(4): 992–994.

Acetone

Brand names: Component of nail polish remover and industrial solvents
Classification: Solvent
λ: 17–27 h
V_d: 0.4–0.6 L/kg
Usual dosage: Not applicable

Source	Nontoxic	Toxic	Lethal
Blood	8–460 mg/L	1000–4000 mg/L	2570–5500 mg/L
Vitreous	80–500 mg/L		
Skeletal muscle	300–900 mg/kg		

Comments

- Metabolite of isopropanol
- Can be used as an inhalant
- Can be detected/present in diabetic/fasting states, ranging from:
  - 120–1950 mg/L blood
  - 180–2100 mg/L vitreous

Selected Sources

Ashley DL, Bonin MA, Cardinali FL, McCraw JM, Wooten JV. (1994). Blood concentrations of volatile compounds in a nonoccupationally exposed US population and in groups with suspected exposure, *Clin Chem*, 40(7 Pt 2): 1401–1404.

Bexar County Medical Examiner's Office data 1996–2015.

DiMaio VJ, DiMaio D. (2001). *Forensic Pathology*, (2nd ed.), CRC Press, Boca Raton, FL, p. 536.

Ernstgard L, Sjogren B, Warholm M, Johanson G. (2003) Sex differences in the toxicokinetics of inhaled solvent vapors in humans 2. 2-propanol, *Toxicol Appl Pharmacol*, 193(2): 158–167.

Jones AW. (2000). Elimination half-life of acetone in humans: Case reports and review of the literature. *J Anal Toxicol*, 24(1): 8–10.

Kostusiak V, Bekkal R, Mateu P. (2003). Survival after drinking lethal doses of acetone, *Intensive Care Med*, 29(2): 339.

Schulz M, Schmoldt A. (2003). Therapeutic and toxic blood concentrations of more than 800 drugs and other xenobiotics, *Pharmazie*, 58(7): 447–474.

Wang G, Mannelli G, Perbellini L, Rainier E, Brugnane F. (1994). Blood acetone concentration in normal people and in exposed workers 16 hours after the end of the workshift, *Intl Arch Occup Environ Health*, 65(5): 285–289.

Acetylsalicylic Acid

Brand names: Aspirin (Bayer and Ecotrin)
Classification: Non-steroidal anti-inflammatory (NSAID)
λ: 15–20 min
V_d: 0.1–0.2 L/kg
Usual dosage: 325–650 mg q 4–6 h

Source	Therapeutic/Nontoxic[a]	Toxic[a]	Lethal[a]
Blood	45–300 mg/L	300–1100 mg/L	400–7320 mg/L
Vitreous	93–228 mg/L		228 mg/L
Liver			258–1000 mg/kg
Kidney			300–1200 mg/kg
Brain			131–700 mg/kg
Skeletal muscle	28–400 mg/kg		440–1175 mg/kg

[a] All concentrations given are for salicylic acid.

Comments

- Rapidly metabolized to salicylic acid (λ 2–19 h; V_d 0.1–0.2 L/kg)
- May cause sudden death in asthmatics, regardless of concentration
- May cause Reye's syndrome in children

Selected Sources

Bexar County Medical Examiner's Office data 1996–2015.
Caplan YH, Ottinger WE, Crooks CR. (1983). Therapeutic and toxic drug concentrations in post mortem blood: A six year study in the State of Maryland, *J Anal Toxicol*, 7(5): 225–230.
Irey NS, Froede RC. (1974). Evaluation of deaths from drug overdose. A clinicopathologic study, *Am J Clin Path*, 61(6): 778–784.
Levy G. (1978). Clinical pharmacokinetics of aspirin, *Pediatrics*, 62(5: 2 Suppl): 867–872.
Paterson SC. (1985). Drug levels found in cases of fatal self-poisoning, *Forensic Sci Intl*, 27(2): 129–133.
Rainsford KD. (1984). *Aspirin and the Salicylates*. Butterworths, Boston, FL.
Rehling CJ. (1967). Poison residues in human tissues, in *Progress in Chemical Toxicology* Vol 3. A. Stolman (Ed.), Academic Press, London, UK, pp. 363–386.
Rumble RH, Brooks PM, Roberts MS. (1980). Metabolism of salicylate during chronic aspirin therapy, *Br J Clin Pharm*, 9(1): 41–45.

Albuterol

Brand names: Proventil and Ventolin
Alternate name: Salbutamol
Classification: β agonist
λ: 2–6 h
V_d: 1–3 L/kg
Usual dosage:
  Inhaled: two inhalations q 4–6 h
  oral: 2–4 mg t/qid
  0.1–0.2 mg/kg/dose3

Source	Therapeutic/Nontoxic	Toxic	Lethal
Blood	0.001–0.06 mg/L	0.02–0.45 mg/L	See comments

Comments

- Fatalities usually attributed to asthma rather than drug overdose

Selected Sources

Bexar County Medical Examiner's Office data 1996–2015.
Couper FJ, Drummer OH. (1999). Postmortem stability and interpretation of β_2 agonist concentrations, *J Forensic Sci*, 44(3): 523–526.
Lewis LD, Essex E, Volans GN, Cochrane GM. (1993). A study of self poisoning with oral salbutamol—Laboratory and clinical features, *Hum Exper Tox*, 12(5): 397–401.
Lewis LD, McLaren M, Essex E, Cochrane GM. (1990). Plasma concentrations of salbutamol in acute severe asthmatics, *Australian & New Zealand J Med*, 20(3): 204–207.
Medical Economics. (2007). *Physicians' Desk Reference*, (61st ed.), Thomson PDR, Montvale, NJ, p. 3055.

Alprazolam

Brand name: Xanax
Classification: Benzodiazepine
λ: 6–27 h
V_d: 1–1.5 L/kg
Usual dosage: 0.25–0.5 mg tid

Source	Therapeutic/Nontoxic	Toxic	Lethal
Blood	0.002–0.7 mg/L	0.04–0.6 mg/L	0.2–2.1 mg/L
Vitreous			0.6 mg/L
Liver			2.4–9.2 mg/kg
Kidney			3.8 mg/kg
Brain	0.007–0.1 mg/kg		
Skeletal muscle	0.05–0.2 mg/kg		

Comments

- Tolerance can develop and should be considered when interpreting drug concentrations
- Sudden withdrawal can cause seizures and death
- Metabolized by CYP 3A

Selected Sources

Bexar County Medical Examiner's Office data 1996–2015.
Glue P, Fang A, Gandelman K, Klee B. (2006). Pharmacokinetics of an extended release formulation of alprazolam (Xanax XR) in healthy normal adolescent and adult volunteers, *Am J Ther*, 13(5): 418–422.
Jenkins AJ, Levine B, Locke JL, Smialek JE. (1997). A fatality due to alprazolam intoxication, *J Anal Toxicol*, 21(3): 218–220.
Medical Economics. (2007) *Physicians' Desk Reference*, (61st ed.) Thomson PDR. Montvale, NJ, pp. 3092–3096.
Skov L, Holm KMD, Johansen SS, Linnet K. (2016). Postmortem brain and blood reference concentrations of alprazolam, bromazepam, chlordiazepoxide, diazepam, and their metabolites and a review of the literature, *J Anal Toxicol*, 40(7): 529–536.
Wolf BC, Lavezzi WA, Sullivan LM, Middleberg RA, Flannagan LM. (2005). Alprazolam-related deaths in Palm Beach County, *Am J Forensic Med Path*, 26(1): 24–27.
Wright CE, Sisson TL, Fleishaker JC, Antal EJ. (1997). Pharmacokinetics and psychomotor performance of alprazolam: Concentration-effect relationship, *J Clin Pharmacol*, 37(4): 321–329.

Amanitin

Brand name: Not applicable
Classification: Poison
λ: Unknown
V_d: ~1 L/kg
Usual dosage: Not applicable

Source	Nontoxic	Toxic	Lethal
Blood	No data available		0.008–0.19 mg/L

Comments

- Found in *Amanita*, *Galerina*, and *Conocyte* ("death cap") mushrooms
- Generally found in blood for 1–1.5 days, 4 days in urine, and 5 days in the liver or kidney
- Symptoms or signs of toxicity include nausea/vomiting/diarrhea, renal failure, and hepatic necrosis
- Symptoms start 5–15 hours after ingestion

Selected Sources

Jaeger A, Jehl F, Flesch F, Sauder P, Kopferschmitt J. (1993). Kinetics of amatoxins in human poisoning: Therapeutic implications, *J Tox Clin Tox*, 31(1): 63–80.
Vesconi S, Langer M, Iapichino G, Costantino D, Busi C, Fiume L. (1985). Therapy of cytotoxic mushroom intoxication, *Crit Care Med*, 13(5): 402–406.

Amantadine

Brand name: Symmetrel
Classification: Antiviral/anti-Parkinson's
λ: 9–31 h
V_d: 3–11 L/kg
Usual dosage: 100–200 mg bid/qd

Source	Therapeutic/Nontoxic	Toxic	Lethal
Blood	0.06–1 mg/L	1.5–13 mg/L	4–48 mg/L
Liver			135 mg/kg

Comments

- May prolong QT interval

Selected Sources

Bexar County Medical Examiner's Office data 1996–2015.
Cook PE, Dermer SW, McGurk T. (1986). Fatal overdose with amantadine, *Can J Psychiatry*, 31(8): 757–758.
Deleu D, Northway MG, Hanssens Y. (2002). Clinical pharmacokinetic and pharmacodynamic properties of drugs used in the treatment of Parkinson's disease, *Clin Pharmacokinet*, 41(4): 261–309.
Fahn S, Craddock G, Kumin G. (1971). Acute toxic psychosis from suicidal overdosage of amantadine, *Arch Neurol*, 25(1): 45–48.
Ing TS, Daugirdes JT, Soung LS. (1979). Toxic effects of amantadine in patients with renal failure, *Can Med Assoc J*, 120: 695–698.
Kwon SK, Ellsworth H, Lintner CP, Stellpflug SJ, Cole JB. (2011). Massive amantadine overdose resulting in status epilepticus and death, *Clin Tox*, 49: 614–615.
Reynolds PC, Van Meter S. (1984). A death involving amantadine, *J Anal Toxicol*, 8: 100.
Schwartz M, Schwartz MD, Patel MM, Kazzi ZN, Morgan BW. (2008). Cardiotoxicity after massive amantadine overdose, *J Med Toxicol*, 4(3): 173–179.

Amisulpride

Brand names: Socian and Solian
Classification: Antipsychotic
λ: 11–27 h
V_d: 5–6 L/kg
Usual dosage: 50–400 mg/d

Source	Therapeutic/Nontoxic	Toxic	Lethal
Blood	0.05–0.4 mg/L	9.6–4671 mg/L	13–140 mg/L

Comments

- Not available in the United States

Selected Sources

Barcelo YC. (2008). QT prolongation after acute amisulpride poisoning, *Clin Tox*, 46(5): 365.

Isbister GK. (2006). Amisulpride deliberate self-poisoning causing severe cardiac toxicity including QT prolongation and torsades de pointes, *Med J Aust*, 184(7): 354–356.

Kratzsch C, Peters FT, Kraemer T, Weber AA, Maurer HH. (2003). Screening, library-assisted identification and validated quantification of fifteen neuroleptics and three of their metabolites in plasma by liquid chromatography/ mass spectrometry with atmospheric pressure chemical ionization, *J Mass Spectrum*, 38(3): 283–295.

Rosenzweig P, Canal M, Patat A, Bergougnan L, Zieleniuk I, Bianchetti G. (2002). A review of the pharmacokinetics, tolerability and pharmacodynamics of amisulpride in healthy volunteers, *Hum Psychopharmacol*, 17(1): 1–13.

Tracqui A, Mutter-Schmidt C, Kintz P, Berton C, Mangin P. (1995). Amisulpride poisoning: A report on two cases, *Hum Exp Tox*, 14(3): 294–298.

Amitriptyline

Brand names: Elavil, Vanatrip, and Endep
Classification: Antidepressant (TCA)
λ: 8–50 h
V_d: 12–18 L/kg
Usual dosage: 75–150 mg qd

Source	Therapeutic/Nontoxic	Toxic	Lethal
Blood	0.02–0.24 mg/L	0.5–2.2 mg/L	1.8–86 mg/L
Vitreous			0.8–6 mg/L
Liver	3.2–10 mg/kg	>50 mg/kg	26–518 mg/kg
Kidney			5–98 mg/kg
Brain			4.8–22 mg/kg
Skeletal muscle	0.08–1 mg/kg		1.2–11 mg/kg

Comments

- Active metabolite: Nortriptyline
- Metabolized by CYP 2D6, 3A, 1A2, and 2C19
- May prolong QT interval; associated with cardiac arrhythmias

Selected Sources

Apple FS. (1989). Postmortem tricyclic antidepressant concentrations: Assessing cause of death using parent drug to metabolite ratio, *J Anal Toxicol*, 13(4): 197–198.

Bailey DN, Shaw RF. (1980). Interpretation of blood and tissue concentrations in fatal self-ingested overdose involving amitriptyline: An update, *J Anal Toxicol*, 4(5): 232–236.

Bexar County Medical Examiner's Office data 1996–2015.

Biggs JT, Spiker DG, Petit JM, Ziegler VE. (1977). Tricyclic antidepressant overdose: Incidence of symptoms, *JAMA*, 238(2): 135–138.

Langford AM, Pounder DJ. (1997). Possible markers for postmortem drug redistribution, *J Forensic Sci*, 42(1): 88–92.

Margalho C. (2007). Massive intoxication involving unusual high concentration of amitriptyline, *Hum Exp Toxicol*, 26(8): 667–670.

Tracqui A, Kintz P, Ritter-Lohner S, Mangin P, Lugnier A, Chaumont A. (1990). Toxicological findings after fatal amitriptyline self-poisoning, *Hum & Exper Tox*, 9(4): 257–261.

Vasiliades J, Bush KC. (1976). Gas liquid chromatographic determination of therapeutic and toxic levels of amitriptyline in human serum with a nitrogen-sensitive detector, *Anal Chem*, 48(12): 1708–1714.

Amlodipine

Brand name: Norvasc
Classification: Calcium channel blocker
λ: 32–44 h
V_d: 17–25 L/kg
Usual dosage: 2.5–10 mg qd

Source	Therapeutic/Nontoxic	Toxic	Lethal
Blood	0.001–0.4 mg/L	0.07–0.14 mg/L	0.2–2.7 mg/L
Liver			8.7–91 mg/kg
Kidney			40 mg/kg
Brain			5.4 mg/kg
Skeletal muscle			2.9 mg/kg

Selected Sources

Adams BD, Browne WT. (1998). Amlodipine overdose causes prolonged calcium channel blocker toxicity, *Am J Emer Med*, 16(5): 527–528.

Bexar County Medical Examiner's Office data 1996–2015.

Cosbey SH, Carson DJ. (1997). A fatal case of amlodipine poisoning, *J Anal Toxicol*, 21(3): 221–222.

Faulkner JK, McGibney D, Chasseaud LF, Perry JL, Taylor IW. (1986). The pharmacokinetics of amlodipine in healthy volunteers after single intravenous and oral doses and after 14 repeated oral doses given once daily, *Brit J Clin Pharm*, 22(1): 21–25.

Johansen SS, Genner J. (2003). A fatal case of amlodipine poisoning, *J Clin Forensic Med*, 10: 169–172.

Lehmann G, Reiniger G, Beyerle A, Rudolph W. (1993). Pharmacokinetics and additional anti-ischaemic effectiveness of amlodipine, a once-daily calcium antagonist, during acute and long-term therapy of stable angina pectoris in patients pre-treated with a beta-blocker, *Eur Heart J*, 14(11): 1531–1535.

Poggenborg RP, Videbaek L, Jacobsen IA. (2006). A case of amlodipine overdose, *Basic Clin Pharm Tox*, 99(3): 209–212.

Sklerov JH, Levine B, Ingwersen KM, Aronica-Pollack PA, Fowler D. (2006). Two cases of fatal amlodipine overdose, *J Anal Toxicol*, 30(5): 346–351.

Stanek EJ, Nelson CE, DeNofrio D. (1997). Amlodipine overdose, *Ann Pharmacotherapy*, 31(7–8): 853–856.

Amoxapine

Brand name: Asendin
Classification: Antidepressant (TCA)
λ: 8 h
V_d: Unknown
Usual dosage: 150–400 mg qd

Source	Therapeutic/Nontoxic	Toxic	Lethal
Blood	0.03–0.4 mg/L	0.3–2 mg/L	0.8–18 mg/L
Vitreous			0.2 mg/L
Liver			17–150 mg/kg
Brain			2.5–52 mg/kg

Comments

- Active metabolites: 8-hydroxyamoxapine (λ 30 h) and 7-hydroxy-amoxapine
- Metabolite of loxapine
- May prolong QT interval

Selected Sources

Beierle FA, Hubbard RW. (1983). Liquid chromatographic separation of antidepressant drugs: II. Amoxapine and maprotiline, *Ther Drug Monit*, 5(3): 293–301.

Bexar County Medical Examiner's Office data 1996–2015.

Kinney JL, Evans RK Jr. (1982). Evaluation of amoxapine, *Clin Pharm*, 1(5): 417–424.

Sedgwick P, Spiehler VR, Lowe DR. (1982). Toxicological findings in amoxapine overdose, *J Anal Toxicol*, 6(2): 82–84.

Taylor RL, Crooks CR, Caplan YH. (1982). The determination of amoxapine in human fatal overdoses, *J Anal Toxicol*, 6(6): 309–311.

Winek CL, Wahba WW, Rozin L. (1984). Amoxapine fatalities: Three case studies, *Forensic Sci Intl*, 26(1): 33–38.

Amphetamine

Brand names: Adderall, Dexedrine, Dextrostat, and Vyvanase (prodrug)
Street names: Bennies, Uppers, Speed, Pep Pills, and Co-pilots
Classification: Stimulant
λ: 9–12 h
V_d: 3–6 L/kg
Usual dosage: 2.5–20 mg bid

Source	Therapeutic/Nontoxic	Toxic	Lethal
Blood	0.02–0.7 mg/L	0.2–3 mg/L	0.5–41 mg/L
Liver			4.3–45 mg/kg
Kidney			3.8–48 mg/kg
Brain			2.8–41 mg/kg
Skeletal muscle			4 mg/kg

Comments

- Deaths are due to cardiovascular and central nervous system effects
  - Minimal concentration for central nervous system effects = 0.005 mg/L
  - Minimal concentration for cardiovascular effect = 0.02 mg/L
- Metabolized by CYP 2D6
- Metabolite of benzphetamine, clobenzorex, famprofazone, fenethylline, fenproporex, mefenorex, mesocarb, prenylamine, and lisdexamfetamine

Selected Sources

Adjutantis G, Coutselinis A, Dimopoulos G. (1975). Fatal intoxication with amphetamines, *Med Sci and Law*, 15(1): 62–63.
Angrist B, Corwin J, Bartlik B, Cooper T. (1987). Early pharmacokinetics and clinical effects of oral D-amphetamine in normal subjects, *Biol. Psychiatry*, 22(11): 1357–1368.
Bexar County Medical Examiner's Office data 1996–2015.
Heinemann A, Miyaishi S, Iwersen S, Schmoldt A, Püschel K. (1998). Body-packing as cause of unexpected sudden death, *Forensic Sci Intl*, 92(1): 1–10.
Meyer E, Van Bocxlaer JF, Dirinck IM, Lambert WE, Thienpont L, De Leenheer AP. (1997). Tissue distribution of amphetamine isomers in a fatal overdose, *J Anal Toxicol*, 21(3): 236–239.

Aripiprazole

Brand name: Abilify
Classification: Antipsychotic
λ: 47–75 h
V_d: 5 L/kg
Usual dosage: 10–30 mg qd

Source	Therapeutic/Nontoxic	Toxic	Lethal
Blood	0.03–0.9 mg/L	0.72–1.4 mg/L	1.9[a]–2.1[b] mg/L

[a] Co-intoxicant methadone 1.5 mg/L.
[b] Co-intoxicant not listed.

Comments

- Active metabolite: Dehydro-aripiprazole
- Metabolized by CYP 2D6 and 3A

Selected Sources

Carstairs SD, Williams SR. (2005). Overdose of aripiprazole, a new type of antipsychotic, *J Emerg Med*, 28(3): 311–313.
Mallikaarjun S, Salazar DE, Bramer SL. (2004). Pharmacokinetics, tolerability, and safety of aripiprazole following multiple oral dosing in normal healthy volunteers, *J Clin Pharmacol*, 44(2): 179–187.
Medical Economics. (2006). *Physicians' Desk Reference*, (60th ed.), Thomson PDR, Montvale, NJ, pp. 2472–2478.
Seifert SA, Schwartz MD, Thomas JD. (2005). Aripiprazole (Abilify) overdose in a child, *Clin Tox*, 43(3): 193–196.
Söderberg C, Wernvik E, Tillmar A, Spigset O, Kronstrand R, Reis M, Jönsson AK, Druid H. (2016). Antipsychotics—Postmortem fatal and non-fatal reference concentrations, *Forensic Sci Int*, 266: 91–101.
Skov L, Johansen SS, Linnet K. (2015). Postmortem femoral blood reference concentrations of aripiprazole, chlorprothixene and quetiapine, *J Anal Toxicol*, 39(1): 41–44.

Asenapine

Brand name: Saphris
Classification: Antipsychotic
λ: 24 h
V_d: 20–25 L/kg
Usual dosage: 5–10 mg bid

Source	Therapeutic/Nontoxic	Toxic	Lethal
Blood	0.001–0.02 mg/L	No data available	0.04[a]–0.7[b] mg/L
Liver			0.4[a]–42[b] mg/kg

[a] Co-intoxicants ethanol 0.16 g/dL, fluoxetine 2.6 mg/L, quetiapine 1.4 mg/L, hydrocodone 0.11 mg/L.

[b] Suffocation due to plastic bag and co-intoxicants quetiapine 2.9 mg/L, alprazolam 0.16 mg/L.

Comments

- Metabolized by CYP1A2

Selected Sources

Miller C, Pleitez O, Anderson D, Mertens-Maxham D, Wade N. (2013). Asenapine (Saphris®): GC-MS method validation and the postmortem distribution of a new atypical antipsychotic medication, *J Anal Toxicol*, 37(8): 559–564.

Taylor JE, Chandrasena RD. (2013). A case of intentional asenapine overdose, *Prim Care Companion CNS Disord*, 15(6).

US Food and Drug Administration. Drug Approvals and Databases. Saphris (asenapine) Sublingual Tablets (NDA 22–117) Background letter. www.fda.gov/downloads/AdvisoryCommittees/CommitteesMeetingMaterials/Drugs/PsychopharmacologicDrugsAdvisoryCommittee/UCM173876.pdf. Accessed November 11, 2014.

Atenolol

Brand name: Tenormin
Classification: β-blocker
λ: 5–8 h
V_d: 0.7–0.8 L/kg
Usual dosage: 50–200 mg qd

Source	Therapeutic/Nontoxic	Toxic	Lethal
Blood	0.04–0.7 mg/L	2.5–9.4 mg/L	No data available

Selected Sources

Amery A, De Plaen JF, Lijnen P, McAinsh J, Reybrouck T. (1977). Relationship between blood level of atenolol and pharmacologic effect, *Clin Pharm Thera*, 21(6): 691–699.

Czendlik CH, Sioufi A, Preiswerk G, Howald H. (1997). Pharmacokinetic and pharmacodynamic interaction of single doses of valsartan and atenolol, *Eur J Clin Pharm*, 52(6): 451–459.

DeLima LG, Kharasch ED, Butler S. (1995). Successful pharmacologic treatment of massive atenolol overdose: Sequential hemodynamics and plasma atenolol concentrations, *Anesthesiology*, 83(1): 204–207.

Gerkin R, Curry S. (1987). Signigicant bradycardia following acute self-poisoning with atenolol, *Vet Hum Tox*, 29: 479.

Montgomery AB, Stager MA, Schoene RB. (1985). Marked suppression of ventilation while awake following massive ingestion of atenolol, *Chest*, 88(6): 920–921.

Saitz R, Williams BW, Farber HW. (1991). Atenolol-induced cardiovascular collapse treated with hemodialysis, *Crit Care Med*, 19(1): 116–118.

Atomoxetine

Brand name: Strattera
Classification: Norepinephrine reuptake inhibitor
λ: 5 h
V_d: 1–2 L/kg
Usual dosage: 0.3–1.2 mg/kg bid/qd

Source	Therapeutic/Nontoxic	Toxic	Lethal
Blood	0.04–0.9 mg/L	No data available	5.4–8.3 mg/L[a]
Vitreous			0.96 mg/L[a]
Liver			29 mg/kg[a]

[a] Co-intoxicant venlafaxine 100 mg/L.

Comments

- Metabolized by CYP 2D6
- May prolong QT interval

Selected Sources

Garside D, Ropero-Miller JD, Riemer EC. (2006). Postmortem tissue distribution of atomoxetine following fatal and nonfatal doses—Three case reports, *J Forensic Sci*, 51(1): 179–182.
Sauer JM, Ring BJ, Witcher JW. (2005). Clinical Pharmacokinetics of Atomoxetine, *Clin Pharmacokinet*, 44(6): 571–590.

Atropine

Brand names: AtroPen and Sal-Tropine
Classification: Antimuscarinic
λ: 2–3 h
V_d: 1–3 L/kg
Usual dosage: 0.4–0.6 mg q 4–6 h

Source	Therapeutic/Nontoxic	Toxic	Lethal
Blood	0.006–0.3 mg/L	0.02–0.2 mg/L	0.2–3.1 mg/L
Liver			0.7 mg/kg

Comments

- Used to treat organophosphate poisoning
- Physostigmine is antidote to atropine poisoning

Selected Sources

Berghem L, Bergman U, Schildt B, Sorbo B. (1980). Plasma atropine concentrations determined by radioimmunoassay after single-dose i.v. and i.m. administration, *Br J Anaesth*, 52(6): 597–601.

Bogan R, Zimmermann T, Zilker T, Eyer F, Thiermann H. (2009). Plasma level of atropine after accidental ingestion of *Atropa belladonna*, *Clin Toxicol (Phila)*, 47(6): 602–604.

Hayden PW, Larson SM, Lakshminarayanan S. (1979). Atropine clearance from human plasma, *J Nucl Med*, 20(4): 366–367.

Kehe CR, Lasseter KC, Miller NC, Wick KA, Shamblen EC, Ekholm BP, Sandahl JH, Chang SF, Goldlust MB, Kvam DC. (1992). Comparative absorption of atropine from a metered-dose inhaler and an intramuscular injection, *Ther Drug Monit*, 14(2): 132–134.

Matsuda K, Morinaga M, Okamoto M, Miyazaki S, Isimaru T, Suzuki K, Tohyama K. (2006). Toxicological analysis of a case of *Datura stramonium* poisoning, *Rinsho Byori*, 54(10): 1003–1007.

Schneider F, Lutun P, Kintz P, Astruc D, Flesch F, Tempe JD. (1996). Plasma and urine concentrations of atropine after the ingestion of cooked deadly nightshade berries, *J Tox Clin Tox*, 34(1): 113–117.

Baclofen

Brand names: Lioresal and Kemstro
Classification: Muscle relaxant
λ: 2–8 h
V_d: 0.7–0.9 L/kg
Usual dosage: 5–15 mg tid

Source	Therapeutic/Nontoxic	Toxic	Lethal
Blood	0.05–0.6 mg/L	0.4–6 mg/L	17–106 mg/L

Selected Sources

Chapple D, Johnson D, Connors R. (2001). Baclofen overdose in two siblings, *Ped Emer Care*, 17(2): 110–112.

De Giovanni N, d'Aloja E. (2001). Death due to baclofen and dipyrone ingestion, *Forensic Sci Intl*, 123(1): 26–32.

Fraser AD, MacNeil D, Isner AF. (1991). Toxicological analysis of a fatal baclofen (Lioresal®) ingestion, *J Forensic Sci*, 36: 1596–1602.

Perry HE, Wright RO, Shannon MW, Woolf AD. (1998). Baclofen overdose: Drug experimentation in a group of adolescents, *Pediatrics*, 1(6): 1045–1048.

Wall GC, Wasiak W, Hicklin GA. (2006). An initially unsuspected case of baclofen overdose (Clinical Report), *Am J Crit Care*, 15(6): 611–613.

Wiersma HE, van Boxtel CJ, Butter JJ, van Aalderen WM, Omari T, Benninga MA. (2003). Pharmacokinetics of a single oral dose of baclofen in pediatric patients with gastroesophageal reflux disease, *Thera Drug Monitoring*, 25(1): 93–98.

Wu VC, Lin SL, Lin SM, Fang CC. (2005). Treatment of baclofen overdose by haemodialysis: A pharmacokinetic study, *Nephrol Dial Transplant*, 20(2): 441–443.

Benzphetamine

Brand name: Didrex
Classification: Stimulant/anorectic
λ: Unknown
V_d: Unknown
Usual dosage: 25–50 mg tid/bid/qd

Source	Therapeutic/Nontoxic	Toxic	Lethal
Blood	0.02–0.5 mg/L	No data available	14 mg/L
Vitreous			21 mg/L
Liver			106 mg/kg
Kidney			38 mg/kg
Brain			31 mg/kg

Comments

- Metabolized to d-amphetamine and d-methamphetamine

Selected Sources

Brooks JP, Phillips M, Stafford DT, Bell JS. (1982). A case of benzphetamine poisoning, *Am J Forensic Med Path*, 3(3): 245–257.
Cody JT, Valtier S. (1998). Detection of amphetamine and methamphetamine following administration of benzphetamine, *J Anal Toxicol*, 22(4): 299–309.
Kraemer T, Maurer HH. (2002). Toxicokinetics of amphetamines: metabolism and toxicokinetic data of designer drugs, amphetamine, methamphetamine, and their N-alkyl derivatives, *Ther Drug Monit*, 24(2): 277–289.

Benztropine

Brand name: Cogentin
Classification: Anti-Parkinson's agent
λ: Unknown
V_d: Unknown
Usual dosage: 1–2 mg qd

Source	Therapeutic/Nontoxic	Toxic	Lethal
Blood	0.004–0.4 mg/L	0.05–0.1 mg/L	0.2–1.1 mg/L
Vitreous			0.3 mg/L
Liver			1.6–9.6 mg/kg

Comments

• Metabolized by CYP 2D6

Selected Sources

Fahy P, Arnold P, Curry SC, Bond R. (1989). Serial serum drug concentrations and prolonged anticholinergic toxicity after benztropine (cogentin) overdose, *Am J Emer Med*, 7(2): 199–202.

Jindal SP, Lutz T, Hallstrom C, Vestergaard P. (1981), A stable isotope dilution assay for the antiparkinsonian drug benztropine in biological fluids, *Clin Chim Acta*, 112(3): 267–273.

Lynch MJ, Kotsos A. (2001). Fatal benztropine toxicity, *Med Sci Law*, 41(2): 155–158.

McIntyre IM, Mallett P, Burton CG, Morhaime J. (2014). Acute benztropine intoxication and fatality, *J Forensic Sci*, 59(6): 1675–1678.

Rosano TG, Meola JM, Wolf BC, Guisti LW, Jindal SP. (1994). Benztropine identification and quantitation in a suicidal overdose, *J Anal Toxicol*, 18(6): 348–353.

Bromazepam

Brand names: Compendium and Lectopam
Classification: Benzodiazepine
λ: 18–65 h
V_d: 1–1.5 L/kg
Usual dosage: 1.5–3 mg qHS

Source	Therapeutic/Nontoxic	Toxic	Lethal
Blood	0.01–0.5 mg/L	0.3–0.4 mg/L	0.8–7.7 mg/L
Brain	0.003–0.49 mg/kg		

Comments

- Tolerance can develop and should be considered when interpreting drug concentrations

Selected Sources

Escande M, Monjanel-Mouterde S, Diadema B, Coassolo P, Orluc A, Aubert C, Durand A, Cano JP. (1989). Determination of the optimal dose of bromazepam in the elderly, *Therapie*, 44(3): 219–222.

Fujii J, Inotsume N, Nakano M. (1990). Effect of food on the bioavailability of bromazepam following oral administration in healthy volunteers, *J Pharm Dyn*, 13(5): 269–271.

Laurito TL, Mendes GD, Santagada V, Caliendo G, de Moraes ME, De Nucci G. (2004). Bromazepam determination in human plasma by high-performance liquid chromatography coupled to tandem mass spectrometry: A highly sensitive and specific tool for bioequivalence studies, *J Mass Spect*, 39(2): 168–176.

Marrache F, Megarbane B, Pirnay S, Rhaoui A, Thuong M. (2004). Difficulties in assessing brain death in a case of benzodiazepine poisoning with persistent cerebral blood flow, *Hum Exp Tox*, 23(10): 503–505.

Michaud K, Romain N, Giroud C, Brandt C, Mangin P. (2001). Hypothermia and undressing associated with non-fatal bromazepam intoxication, *Forensic Sci Intl*, 124(2–3): 112–114.

Skov L, Dollerup Holm KM, Johansen SS, Linnet K. (2016). Postmortem brain and blood reference concentrations of alprazolam, bromazepam, chlordiazepoxide, diazepam and their metabolites and a review of the literature, *J Anal Toxicol*, 40(7): 529–536.

Bromphenirame

Brand names: Component of BroveX, Dallergy, Lodrane, Dimetapp, and Bromfed
Classification: Antihistamine
λ: 12–35 h
V_d: 9–15 L/kg
Usual dosage: 4 mg q 4–6 h

Source	Therapeutic/Nontoxic	Toxic	Lethal
Blood	0.004–0.3 mg/L	No data available	0.4–1 mg/L[a]
Liver			4.2 mg/kg[a]
Skeletal muscle			2.3 mg/kg[a]

[a] Co-intoxicant phenylpropanolamine 6.3 mg/L blood.

Selected Sources

Bruce RB, Pitts JE, Pinchbeck FM. (1968). Determination of brompheniramine in blood and urine by gas–liquid chromatography, *Anal Chem*, 40(8): 1246–1250.
Jumbelic MI, Hanzlick R, Cohle S. (1997). Alkylamine antihistamine toxicity and review of pediatric toxicology registry of the National Association of Medical Examiners, Report 4: Alkylamines, *Am J Forensic Med Path*, 18(1): 65–69.
Sen A, Akin A, Craft KJ, Canfield DV, Chaturvedi AK. (2007). First generation H1 anitihistamines found in pilot fatalities of civil aviation accidents, 1990–2005, *Aviat Space Environ Med*, 78(5): 514–522.
Simons FE, Frith EM, Simons KJ. (1982). The pharmacokinetics and antihistaminic effects of brompheniramine, *J Allergy Clin Immunol*, 70(6): 458–464.

Buprenorphine

Brand names: Buprenex, Subutex, Sublocade, and Suboxone (with naloxone)
Classification: Opiate agonist–antagonist
λ: 3–44 h
V_d: 1–1.5 L/kg
Usual dosage: 2–16 mg qd

Source	Therapeutic/Nontoxic	Toxic	Lethal
Blood	0.001–0.02 mg/L	0.02–0.2 mg/L	0.14–100 mg/L
Brain			6.4 mg/kg

Comments

- Interacts with HIV protease inhibitors and antifungals (azoles) resulting in increased buprenorphine concentrations
- Metabolized by CYP 3A4

Selected Sources

Compton P, Ling W, Moody D, Chiang N. (2006). Pharmacokinetics, bioavailability and opioid effects of liquid versus tablet buprenorphine, *Drug Alcohol Depend*, 82(1): 25–31.

Elkader A, Sproule B. (2005). Buprenorphine: Clinical pharmacokinetics in the treatment of opioid dependence, *Clin Pharmacokinet*, 44(7): 661–680.

Gaulier JM, Marquet P, Lacassie E, Dupuy JL, Lachatre G. (2000). Fatal intoxication following self-administration of a massive dose of buprenorphine, *J Forensic Sci*, 45(1): 226–228.

Jensen ML, Foster DJR, Upton RN, Kristensen K, Hansesn SH, Jensen NH, Nielsen BN, Skram U, Villesen HH, Christrup L. (2007). Population pharmacokinetics of buprenorphine following a two-stage intravenous infusion in healthy volunteers, *Eur J Clin Pharmacol*, 63(12): 1153–1159.

Kintz P. (2002). A new series of 13 buprenorphine-related deaths, *Clin Biochem*, 35(7): 513–516.

Seiden T, Ahlner J, Druid H, Dronstrand R. (2012). Toxicological and pathological findings in a series of buprenorphine related deaths. Possible risk factors for fatal outcome, *Forensic Sci Int*, 220(1–3): 284–290.

Tracqui A, Kintz P, Ludes B (1998). Buprenorphine-related deaths among drug addicts in France: a re-report on 20 fatalities, *J Anal Toxicol*, 22: 43.

Bupropion

Brand names: Wellbutrin and Zyban
Classification: Antidepressant
λ: 12–30 h
V_d: 17–20 L/kg
Usual dosage: 100 mg bid/tid

Source	Therapeutic/Nontoxic	Toxic	Lethal
Blood	0.01–0.6 mg/L	0.28–1.4 mg/L	1.5–21 mg/L
Vitreous			1.6 mg/L
Liver			12–14 mg/kg
Kidney			1.2 mg/kg
Skeletal muscle	0.08–0.2 mg/kg		

Comments

- Has multiple active metabolites
- Metabolized by CYP 2B6

Selected Sources

Daviss WB, Perel JM, Birmaher B, Rudolph GR, Melhem I, Axelson DA, Brent DA. (2006). Steady-state clinical pharmacokinetics of bupropion extended-release in youths, *J Am Academy Child Adol Psych*, 45(12): 1503–1509.

Friel PN, Logan BK, Fligner CL. (1993). Three fatal drug overdoses involving bupropion, *J Anal Toxicol*, 17(7): 436–438.

Harris CR, Gualtieri J, Stark G. (1997). Fatal bupropion overdose, *J Tox Clin Tox*, 35(3): 321–324.

Linder MW, Keck PE. (1998). Standards of laboratory practice: Antidepressant drug monitoring. National Academy of Clinical Biochemistry, *Clin Chem*, 44(5): 1073–1084.

Preskorn SH. (1983). Antidepressant response and plasma concentrations of bupropion, *J Clin Psych*, 44(5 Pt 2): 137–139.

Rohrig TP, Ray NG. (1992). Tissue distribution of bupropion in a fatal overdose, *J Anal Toxicol*, 16(5): 343–345.

Schmit G, de Boosere E, Vanhaebost J, Caproon A. (2017). Bupropion overdose resulted in a pharmacobezoar in a fatal Bupropion (Wellbutrin) sustained-release overdose: Postmortem distribution of bupropion and its major metabolites, *J Forensic Sci*, 62(6): 1674–1676.

Thorpe EL, Pizon AF, Lynch MJ, Boyer J. (2010). Bupropion induced serotonin syndrome: A case report, *J Med Toxicol*, 6(2): 168–171.

White RS, Langford JR. (2002). Sustained release bupropion: Overdose and treatment, *Am J Emer Med*, 20(4): 388–389.

Buspirone

Brand name: Buspar
Classification: Anxiolytic
λ: 2–6 h
V_d: 3–8 L/kg
Usual dosage: 15–30 mg qd

Source	Therapeutic/Nontoxic	Toxic	Lethal
Blood	0.0002–0.01 mg/L	No data available	2–7.3 mg/L

Comments

- Active metabolite: 6-hydroxybuspirone

Selected Sources

Dockens RC, Salazar DE, Fulmor IE, Wehling M, Arnold ME, Croop R. (2006). Pharmacokinetics of a newly identified active metabolite of buspirone after administration of buspirone over its therapeutic dose range, *J Clin Pharm*, 46(11): 1308–1313.
Mahmood I, Sahajwalla C. (1999). Clinical pharmacokinetics and pharmacodynamics of buspirone, an anxiolytic drug, *Clin Pharmacokinet*, 36(4): 277–287.
Roman M, Kronstrand R, Lindstedt D, Josefsson M. (2008). Quantitation of seven low-dosage antipsychotic drugs in human postmortem blood using LC-MS-MS, *J Anal Toxicol*, 32(2): 147–155.
Salazar DE, Frackiewicz EJ, Dockens R, Kollia G, Fulmor IE, Tigel PD, Uderman HD, Shiovitz TM, Sramek JJ, Cutler NR. (2001). Pharmacokinetics and tolerability of buspirone during oral administration to children and adolescents with anxiety disorder and normal healthy adults, *J Clin Pharmacol*, 41: 1351–1358.

Butalbital

Brand names: Bupap, Esgic, Floricet (w/ acetaminophen, caffeine), and
    Fiorinal (w/ caffeine)
Classification: Barbiturate
λ: 30–40 h
V_d: Unknown
Usual dosage: 50–100 mg per dose

Source	Therapeutic/Nontoxic	Toxic	Lethal
Blood	0.2–11 mg/L	7.0–40 mg/L	13–50 mg/L
Liver	0.5–24 mg/kg		50 mg/kg
Kidney	0.2–11 mg/kg		
Brain	0.2–0.6 mg/kg		
Skeletal muscle	0.1–7.1 mg/kg		
Cardiac muscle	0.2–8.7 mg/kg		

Comments

- Tolerance can develop and should be considered when interpreting
  drug concentrations

Selected Sources

Baselt RC, Cravey RH. (1977). A compendium of therapeutic and toxic concentra-
    tions of toxicologically significant drugs in human biofluids, *J Anal Toxicol*, 1:
    81–103.
Bexar County Medical Examiner's Office data 1996–2015.
Lewis RJ, Johnson RD, Southern TL, Canfield DV. (2003). Distribution of butal-
    bital in postmortem tissues and fluids from non-overdose cases, *J Anal Toxicol*,
    27(3): 145–148.

Butorphanol

Brand name: Stadol
Classification: Opiate agonist–antagonist
λ: 2–8 h
V_d: 7–11 L/kg
Usual dosage: 1 mg iv; 2 mg im; 1–2 mg intranasal q3–4 h

Source	Therapeutic/Nontoxic	Toxic	Lethal
Blood	0.0009–0.004 mg/L	No data available	4–9 mg/L

Selected Sources

Davis GA, Rudy AC, Archer SM, Wermeling DP. (2004). Pharmacokinetics of butorphanol tartrate administered from single-dose intranasal sprayer, *Am J Health Syst Pharm*, 61(3): 261–266.

Ramsey R, Higbee M, Maesner J, Wood J. (1988). Influence of age on the pharmacokinetics of butorphanol, *Acute Care*, 12(Suppl 1): 8–16.

Schulz M, Schmoldt A. (2003). Therapeutic and toxic blood concentrations of more than 800 drugs and other xenobiotics, *Pharmazie*, 58(7): 447–474.

Caffeine

Brand name: Cafcit
Classification: Methylxanthine (stimulant)
λ: 2–10 h
V_d: 0.5–0.9 L/kg
Usual dosage: 5 mg/kg qd

Source	Therapeutic/Nontoxic	Toxic	Lethal
Blood	2–34 mg/L	15–80 mg/L	33–1040 mg/L
Vitreous			100–159 mg/L
Liver			58–670 mg/kg
Kidney			13–352 mg/kg
Brain			75–188 mg/kg

Comments

- Metabolized by CYP 1A2
- Common sources of caffeine: 12 oz soda, ~40 mg; cup of coffee, ~150 mg; and energy drink, ~50–200 mg

Selected Sources

Alstott RL, Miller AJ, Forney RB. (1973). Report of a human fatality due to caffeine, *J Forensic Sci*, 18(2): 135–137.
Bexar County Medical Examiner's Office data 1996–2015.
Dimaio VJ, Garriott JC. (1974). Lethal caffeine poisoning in a child, *J Forensic Sci*, 3(3): 275–278.
Garriott JC, Simmons LM, Poklis A, Mackell MA. (1985). Five cases of fatal overdose from caffeine-containing "look-alike" drugs, *J Anal Toxicol*, 9(3): 141–143.
Jones AW. (2017). Review of caffeine related fatalities along with postmortem blood concentrations in 51 poisonings, *J Anal Toxicol*, 41: 167–172.
Kerrigan S, Lindsey T. (2005). Fatal caffeine overdose: Two case reports, *Forensic Sci Intl*, 153(1): 67–69.
Magdalan J, Zawadzki M, Skowronek R, Magdalan J, Zawadzki M, Skowronek R, Czuba M, Porębska B, Sozański T, Szpot P. (2017). Nonfatal and fatal intoxications with pure caffeine—Report of three different cases, *Forensic Sci Med Pathol*, 13: 355–368.
Medical Economics. (2007). *Physicians' Desk Reference*, (61st ed.), Thomson PDR, Montvale, NJ, pp. 1886–1889.
Winek CL, Wahba W, Williams K, Blenko J, Janssen J. (1985). Caffeine fatality: A case report, *Forensic Sci Intl*, 29(3–4): 207–211.

Carbamazepine

Brand names: Tegretol, Carbatrol, Equetro, and Epitol
Classification: Anticonvulsant
λ: 12–65 h
V_d: 0.8–1.4 L/kg
Usual dosage: 200–800 mg bid

Source	Therapeutic/Nontoxic	Toxic	Lethal
Blood	1.9–19 mg/L	10–55 mg/L	20–73 mg/L
Liver	2.2 mg/kg		123 mg/kg
Kidney			72 mg/kg
Brain			78–86 mg/kg
Cardiac muscle			64 mg/kg
Skeletal muscle	6.9–9.7 mg/kg		

Comments

- Metabolized by CYP 3A

Selected Sources

Bexar County Medical Examiner's Office data 1996–2015.

Denning DW, Matheson L, Bryson SM, Streete J, Berry DJ, Henry JA. (1985). Death due to carbamazepine self-poisoning: Remedies reviewed, *Hum Tox*, 4(3): 255–260.

Druid H, Holmgren P. (1997). A compilation of fatal and control concentrations of drugs in postmortem femoral blood, *J Forensic Sci*, 42(1): 79–87.

Fisher RS, Cysyk BJ. (1988). A fatal overdose of carbamazepine: Case report and review of literature, *J Tox Clin Tox*, 26(7): 477–486.

Goktas U, Kati I, Yuce HH. (2010). Management of a severe carbamazepine overdose with continuous venovenous hemodiafiltration, *Am J Emerg Med*, 28(2): 260e.1–260e.2.

Graves NM, Brundage RC, Wen Y, Cascino G, So E, Ahman P, Rarick J, Krause S, Leppik IE. (1998). Population pharmacokinetics of carbamazepine in adults with epilepsy, *Pharmacotherapy*, 18(2): 273–281.

Medical Economics. (2007). *Physicians' Desk Reference*, (61st ed.), Thomson PDR, Montvale, NJ.

Rawlins MD, Collste P, Bertilsson L, Palmer L. (1975). Distribution and elimination kinetics of carbamazepine in man, *Eur J Clin Pharmacol*, 8(2): 91–96.

Spiller HA, Carlisle RDJ. (2001). Timely antemortem and postmortem concentrations in a fatal carbamazepine overdose, *Forensic Sci*, 46(6): 510–512.

Carbinoxamine

Brand names: Palgic and Pediox
Classification: Antihistamine
λ: 10–20 h
V_d: Unknown
Usual dosage: 4–24 mg qd

Source	Therapeutic/Nontoxic	Toxic	Lethal
Blood	0.002–0.2 mg/L	No data available	0.25[a]–15 mg/L
Liver	2.5 mg/kg		

[a] Infant.

Comments

• Elevated concentrations may be associated with SIDS in infants

Selected Sources

Bexar County Medical Examiner's Office data 1996–2015.
Hoffman DJ, Leveque MJ, Thomson T. (1983). Capillary GLC assay for carbinoxamine and hydrocodone in human serum using nitrogen-sensitive detection, *J Pharm Sci*, 72(11): 1342–1344.
Schulz M, Schmoldt A. (2003). Therapeutic and toxic blood concentrations of more than 800 drugs and other xenobiotics, *Pharmazie*, 58(7): 447–474.
Stockis A, Deroubaix X, Jeanbaptiste B, Lins R, Allemon AM, Laufen H. (1995). Relative bioavailability of carbinoxamine and phenylephrine from a retard capsule after single and repeated dose administration in healthy subjects, *Arzneimittelforschung*, 45(9): 1009–1012.
Stockis A, Lebacq E, Deroubaix X, Allemon AM, Laufen H. (1992). Relative bioavailability of carbinoxamine and phenylpropanolamine from a retard suspension after single dose administration in healthy subjects, *Arzneimittelforschung*, 42(12): 1478–1481.

Carbon Monoxide

Brand name: Not applicable
Classification: Gas (combustion product of organic material)
λ: 5–6 h (21% O_2); 30–90 min (100% O_2)
V_d: Unknown
Usual dosage: Not applicable

Source	Nontoxic	Toxic	Lethal
Blood	0%–3% nonsmoker	10% SOB, headache	33%–72%
	3%–8% smoker	15%–30% impaired judgment	
	0.5%–4.7% infant	40%–50% confusion	
	10% hemolytic anemia	60%–70% unconsciousness	
Spleen	<10%	30%–50%	29%–72%

Environmental CO Concentration	Symptoms
100–200 ppm	Headache and dizziness after 2–3 h exposure; decreased judgment
400 ppm	Headache and dizziness after 1–2 h exposure
800 ppm	Dizziness and nausea after 45 min exposure; unconscious after 2 h exposure
1600 ppm	Headache, tachycardia, dizziness after 20 min exposure; death <2 h exposure
3200 ppm	Headache, tachycardia, dizziness after 5–10 min exposure; death 30 min exposure
6400 ppm	Headache, tachycardia, dizziness after 1–2 min exposure; death <20 min exposure
12800 ppm	Unconsciousness after 2–3 breaths; death in minutes

Selected Sources

Bexar County Medical Examiner's Office data 1996–2015.
Hampson NB. (2007). Carboxyhemoglobin elevation due to hemolytic anemia, *J Emer Med*, 33(1): 17–19.
Levine B (Ed). (2002). *Principles of Forensic Toxicology*. American Association for Clinical Chemistry, Washington, DC, pp. 330–337.

Carisoprodol

Brand name: Soma and Vanadom
Classification: Muscle relaxant
λ: 1–8 h
V_d: Unknown
Usual dosage: 350 mg tid

Source	Therapeutic/Nontoxic	Toxic	Lethal
Blood	10–40 mg/L	30–50 mg/L	39–110 mg/L
Liver	21–45 mg/kg		127 mg/kg
Kidney			110 mg/kg
Skeletal muscle	8.9–50 mg/kg		103 mg/kg

Comments

- Active metabolite: Meprobamate
- Metabolized by CYP 2C19
- Tolerance can develop and should be considered when interpreting drug concentrations

Selected Sources

Backer RC, Zumwalt R, McFeeley P, Veasey S, Wohlenberg N. (1990). Carisoprodol concentrations from different anatomical sites: Three overdose cases, *J Anal Toxicol*, 14(5): 332–334.

Bexar County Medical Examiner's Office data 1996–2015.

Davis GG, Alexander CB. (1998). A review of carisoprodol deaths in Jefferson County, Alabama, *South Med J*, 91(8): 726–730.

Maes R, Hodnett N, Landesman H, Kananen G, Finkle B, Sunshine I. (1969). The gas chromatographic determination of selected sedatives (Ethchlorvynol, paraldehyde, meprobamate, and carisoprodol) in biological material, *J Forensic Sci*, 14(2): 235–254.

Olsen H, Koppang E, Alvan G, Mørland J. (1994). Carisoprodol elimination in humans, *Ther Drug Monit*, 16(4): 337–340.

Cetirizine

Brand name: Zyrtec
Classification: Antihistamine
λ: 5.5–9 h
V_d: 0.4–0.6 L/kg
Usual dosage: 2.5–10 mg qd

Source	Therapeutic/Nontoxic	Toxic	Lethal
Blood	0.1–1 mg/L	2.4[a] mg/L	No data available

[a] Child (18 months).

Comments

- Xyzal (levocetirizine) is R-enantiomer of cetirizine and *laboratories usually do not differentiate between cetirizine and levocetirizine*

Selected Sources

Lefebvre RA, Rosseel MT, Bernheim J. (1988). Single dose pharmacokinetics of cetirizine in young and elderly volunteers, *Int J Clin Pharmacol Res*, 8(6): 463–470.
Pandya KK, Bangaru RA, Gandhi TP, Modi IA, Modi RI, Chakravarthy BK. (1996). High-performance thin-layer chromatography for the determination of cetirizine in human plasma and its use in pharmacokinetic studies, *J Pharm Pharmacol*, 48(5): 510–513.
Ridout SM, Tariq SM. (1997). Cetirizine overdose in a young child, *J Allergy Clin Immunol*, 99(6 Pt 1): 860–861.
Wood SG, John BA, Chasseaud LF, Yeh J, Chung M. (1987). The metabolism and pharmacokinetics of 14C-cetirizine in humans, *Ann Allergy*, 59(6 Pt 2): 31–34.

Chloral Hydrate

Brand names: Somnote, Aquachloral, and Noctec
Classification: Sedative/hypnotic
λ: 3–4 min
V_d: 0.3–1 L/kg
Usual dosage: 500–2000 mg tid/qid

Source	Therapeutic/Nontoxic[a]	Toxic[a]	Lethal[a]
Blood	1.5–15 mg/L	40–50 mg/L	60–1700 mg/L
Vitreous			73 mg/L

[a] All concentrations are for trichloroethanol.

Comments

- Active metabolite: Trichloroethanol (λ 8–30 h)

Selected Sources

Benson R. (2000). *Concise International Chemical Assessment Document No, 25: Choral Hydrate International Programme on Chemical Safety.* World Health Organization, Geneva, Switzerland.

Benson R. (2000). *Toxicological Review of Chloral Hydrate (CAS No.302-17-0).* U.S. EPA, Washington, DC.

Bexar County Medical Examiner's Office data 1996–2015.

Gaulier JM, Merle G, Lacassie E, Courtiade B, Haglund P, Marquet P, Lachâtre GJ. (2001). Fatal intoxications with chloral hydrate, *Forensic Sci*, 46(6): 1507–1509.

Heller PF, Goldberger BA, Caplan YH. (1992). Chloral hydrate overdose: Trichloroethanol detection by gas chromatography/mass spectrometry, *Forensic Sci Intl*, 52(2): 231–234.

Levine B, Park J, Smith TD, Caplan YH. (1985). Chloral hydrate: Unusually high concentrations in a fatal overdose, *J Anal Toxicol*, 9(5): 232–233.

Chlordiazepoxide

Brand names: Librium and Librax (with Clidinium)
Street name: Lib
Classification: Benzodiazepine
λ: 24–48 h
V_d: 0.3–0.6 L/kg
Usual dosage: 5–10 mg tid/qid

Source	Therapeutic/Nontoxic	Toxic	Lethal
Blood	1–10 mg/L	3–60 mg/L	7.7[a]–20 mg/L
Liver			10 mg/kg
Brain	0.003–1.85 mg/kg		
Skeletal muscle	0.9–1.5 mg/kg		

[a] Ethanol was co-intoxicant 0.19 g/dL.

Comments

- Tolerance can develop and should be considered when interpreting drug concentrations
- Active metabolite: Nordiazepam (λ 38–135 h) and temazepam (λ 7–18 h)

Selected Sources

Bexar County Medical Examiner's Office data 1996–2015.
Cate JC, Jatlow PI. (1973). Chlordiazepoxide overdose: Interpretation of serum drug concentrations, *Clin Tox*, 6(4): 533–561.
Druid H, Holmgren P. (1997). A compilation of fatal and control concentrations of drugs in postmortem femoral blood, *J Forensic Sci*, 42(1): 79–87.
Rada RT, Kellner R, Buchanan JG. (1975). Chlordiazepoxide and alcohol: A fatal overdose, *J Forensic Sci*, 20(3): 544–547.
Skov L, Holm KM, Johansen SS, Linnet K. (2016). Postmortem brain and blood reference concentrations of alprazolam, bromazepam, chlordiazepoxide, diazepam and their metabolites and a review of the literature, *J Anal Toxicol*, 40(7): 529–536.
Stanski DR, Greenblatt DJ, Selwyn A, Shader RI, Franke K, Koch-Weser J. (1976). Plasma and cerebrospinal fluid concentrations of chlordiazepoxide and its metabolites in surgical patients, *Clin Pharmacol Ther*, 20(5): 571–578.
Wallace JE, Blum K, Singh JM. (1974). Determination of drugs in biological specimens—A review, *J Tox Clin Tox*, 7(5): 477–495.

Chloroquine

Brand name: Aralen
Classification: Antimalarial/antiarthritic
λ: 72–300 h
V_d: 116–285 L/kg
Usual dosage: 150–600 mg qd

Source	Therapeutic/Nontoxic	Toxic	Lethal
Blood	0.02–2.3 mg/L	0.5–1.0 mg/L	3–460 mg/L
Vitreous			5.3 mg/L
Liver	2.9–58 mg/kg		16–1307 mg/kg
Kidney	0.6–5.8 mg/kg		11–1690 mg/kg
Brain	0.7–7.3 mg/kg		1–100 mg/kg
Skeletal muscle			10–132 mg/kg
Cardiac muscle			23–24 mg/kg

Comments

• Prolongs QT interval

Selected Sources

Bexar County Medical Examiner's Office data 1996–2015.
Gustafsson LL, Walker O, Alván G, Beermann B, Estevez F, Gleisner L. (1983). Disposition of chloroquine in man after single intravenous and oral doses, *Br J Clin Pharm*, 15(4): 471–479.
Keller T, Schneider A, Lamprecht R, Aderjan R, Tutsch-Bauer E, Kisser W. (1998). Fatal chloroquine intoxication, *Forensic Sci Intl*, 96(1): 21–28.
Kuhlman JJ, Mayes RW, Levine B, Jones R, Wagner GN, Smith ML. (1991). Cloroquine distribution in postmortem cases, *J Forensic Sci*, 36(5): 1572–1579.
Muhm M, Stimpfl T, Malzer R, Mortinger H, Binder R, Vycudilik W, Berzlanovich A, Bauer G, Laggner AN. (1996). Suicidal chloroquine poisoning: Clinical course, autopsy findings, and chemical analysis, *J Forensic Sci*, 41(6): 1077–1079.
Noirfalise A. (1978). Chloroquine intoxication: Two case reports, *J Forensic Sci*, 11(3): 177–179.

Chlorpheniramine

Brand names: Component of over-the-counter (OTC) cold medications
    including: Tylenol Cold, Vicks 44, Tussionex, Chlor-trimeton
Classification: Antihistamine
λ: 12–43 h
V_d: 2.5–3.8 L/kg
Usual dosage: 4 mg q 4–6 h

Source	Therapeutic/Nontoxic	Toxic	Lethal[a]
Blood	0.01–0.3 mg/L	0.5 mg/L	1.1 mg/L
Liver	0.5–2.5 mg/kg		6.6 mg/kg
Kidney			1.4 mg/kg
Brain			2.5 mg/kg
Lung			5.2 mg/kg
Skeletal muscle	0.07–0.08 mg/kg		5.0 mg/kg

[a] Co-intoxicant ethanol 0.12 g/dL and diazepam/nordiazepam combined concentration 0.2 mg/L.

Selected Sources

Bexar County Medical Examiner's Office data 1996–2015.
Huang SM, Athanikar NK, Sridhar K, Huang YC, Chiou WL. (1982). Pharmacokinetics of chlorpheniramine after intravenous and oral administration in normal adults, *Eur J Clin Pharm*, 22(4): 359–365.
Reed D. (1981). A fatal case involving chlorpheniramine, *Clin Tox*, 18(8): 941–943.
Sen A, Akin A, Craft KJ, Canfield DV, Chaturvedi AK. (2007). Fist generation H1 antihistamines found in pilot fatalities of civil aviation accidents, 1990–2005, *Aviat Space Environ Med*, 78(5): 514–522.
Soper JW, Chaturvedi AK, Canfield DV. (2000). Prevalence of chlorpheniramine in aviation accident pilot fatalities, 1991–1996, *Aviat Space Environ Med*, 71(12): 1206–1209.

Chlorpromazine

Brand names: Thorazine, Largactil, and Ormazine
Classification: Antipsychotic
λ: 23–37 h
V_d: 10–35 L/kg
Usual dosage: 300–800 mg qd

Source	Therapeutic/Nontoxic	Toxic	Lethal
Blood	0.01–5 mg/L	0.5–3 mg/L	3–43 mg/L
Liver	3.5–17 mg/kg		45–2110 mg/kg
Kidney			4–740 mg/kg
Brain			125–200 mg/kg
Skeletal muscle	1 mg/kg		12 mg/kg

Comments

- Prolongs QT interval
- Metabolized by CYP 2D6

Selected Sources

Algeri EJ, Katsas GG, McBay AJ. (1959). Toxicology of some new drugs: Glutethimide, meprobamate and chlorpromazine, *J Forensic Sci*, 4: 111–135.

Bailey DN, Guba JJ. (1979). Gas-chromatographic analysis for chlorpromazine and some of its metabolites in human serum, with use of a nitrogen detector, *Clin Chem*, 25(7): 1211–1215.

Bexar County Medical Examiner's Office data 1996–2015.

Bonnichsen R, Geertinger P, Maehly AC. (1970). Toxicological data on phenothiazine drugs in autopsy cases, *Zeitschrift für Rechtsmedizin/J Legal Med*, 67(3): 158–169.

Coutselinis A, Dimopoulos G, Dritsas C. (1974). Fatal intoxication with chlorpromazine with special regard to the influence of putrefaction on its toxicological analysis, *J Forensic Sci*, 4(2): 191–194.

Dahl SG, Strandjord RE. (1977). Pharmacokinetics of chlorpromazine after single and chronic dosage, *Clin Pharm Ther*, 21(4): 437–448.

Citalopram

Brand names: Celexa and Lexapro (escitalopram)
Classification: Antidepressant (SSRI)
λ: 12–37 h
V_d: 10–18 L/kg
Usual dosage: 20–60 mg qd (escitalopram 10–20 mg qd)

Source	Therapeutic/Nontoxic	Toxic	Lethal
Blood	0.01–1.7 mg/L	0.48–5.9 mg/L	3.2–49 mg/L
Vitreous	0.1–0.2 mg/L		0.3 mg/L
Liver	0.4–21 mg/kg		12–55 mg/kg
Kidney			13 mg/kg
Brain			2–22 mg/kg
Skeletal muscle	0.06–1.1 mg/kg		

Comments

- Prolongs QT interval
- Metabolized by CYP 2C19, 2D6, and 3A
- Escitalopram is the s-enantiomer of citalopram and *laboratories usually do not differentiate between escitalopram and citalopram*

Selected Sources

Anastos N, McIntyre IM, Lynch MJ, Drummer OH. (2002). Postmortem concentrations of citalopram, *J Forensic Sci*, 47(4): 882–884.
Bexar County Medical Examiner's Office data 1996–2015.
Jonasson B, Saldeen T. (2002). Citalopram in fatal poisoning cases, *Forensic Sci Intl*, 126(1): 1–6.
Liotier J, Coudore F. (2011). Drug monitoring of a case of citalopram overdose, *Drug Chem Toxicol*, 34(4): 420–423.
Luchini D, Morabito G, Centini F. (2005). Case report of a fatal intoxication by citalopram, *Am J Forensic Med Path*, 26(4): 352–354.
Oström M, Eriksson A, Thorson J, Spigset O. (1996). Fatal overdose with citalopram, *Lancet*, 348(9023): 339–340.
Segura LJ, Bravo B. (2004). Postmortem citalopram concentrations: Alone or along with other compounds, *J Forensic Sci*, 49(4): 814–819.
Tarabar AF, Hoffman RS, Nelson L. (2008). Citalopram overdose: Late presentation of torsades de pointes (TdP) with cardiac arrest, *J Med Toxicol*, 4(2): 101–105.
Worm K, Dragsholt C, Simonsen K, Kringsholm B. (1998). Citalopram concentrations in samples from autopsies and living persons, *Intl J Legal Med*, 111(4): 188–190.

Clobazam

Brand names: Frisium and Urbanyl
Classification: Benzodiazepine
λ: 10–40 h
V_d: 1 L/kg
Usual dosage: 5–15 mg qd

Source	Therapeutic/Nontoxic	Toxic	Lethal
Blood	0.14–0.41 mg/L	No data available	3.9 mg/L
Liver			2.4 mg/kg
Kidney			5.3 mg/kg

Comments

- Active metabolite: Desmethylclobazam
- Not available in the United States
- Tolerance can develop and should be considered when interpreting drug concentrations

Selected Sources

Monjanel-Mouterde S, Antoni M, Bun H, Botta-Frindlund D, Gauthier A, Durand A, Cano JP. (1994). Pharmacokinetics of a single oral dose of clobazam in patients with liver disease, *Pharmacol Toxicol*, 74(6): 345–350.

Proença P, Teixeira H, Pinheiro J, Marques EP, Vieira DN. (2004). Forensic intoxication with clobazam: HPLC/DAD/MSD analysis, *Forensic Sci Intl*, 143(2–3): 205–209.

Rouini M, Ardakani YH, Hakemi L, Mokhberi M, Badri G. (2005). Simultaneous determination of clobazam and its major metabolite in human plasma by a rapid HPLC method, *J Chromatogr B Analyt Technol Biomed Life Sci*, 823(2): 167–171.

Clomipramine

Brand name: Anafranil
Classification: Antidepressant (TCA)
λ: 19–37 h
V_d: 9–25 L/kg
Usual dosage: 25 mg qd

Source	Therapeutic/Nontoxic	Toxic	Lethal
Blood	0.2–0.4 mg/L	0.6–1.6 mg/L	1.7–3.3 mg/L
Liver	7–20 mg/kg		12–320 mg/kg
Brain			4.9–8 mg/kg

Comments

- Can cause serotonin syndrome
- Active metabolite: N-desmethylclomipramine
- Metabolized by CYP 1A2, 2D6, 3A, and 2C19
- May prolong QT interval

Selected Sources

Bexar County Medical Examiner's Office data 1996–2015.
Druid H, Holmgren P. (1997). A compilation of fatal and control concentrations of drugs in postmortem femoral blood, *J Forensic Sci*, 42(1): 79–87.
Gex-Fabry M, Haffen E, Paintaud G, Bizouard P, Sechter D, Bechtel PR, Balant LP. (2000). Population pharmacokinetics of clomipramine, desmethylclomipramine and hydroxylated metabolites in patients with depression receiving chronic treatment: Model evaluation, *Ther Drug Monit*, 22(6): 701–711.
McIntyre IM, King CV, Cordner SM, Drummer OH. (1994). Postmortem clomipramine: Therapeutic or toxic concentrations? *J Forensic Sci*, 39(2): 486–493.
Meatherall RC, Guay DR, Chalmers JL, Keenan JR. (1983). A fatal overdose with clomipramine, *J Anal Toxicol*, 7(4): 168–171.
Stolk LM, van der Geest S. (1998). Plasma concentrations after a clomipramine intoxication, *J Anal Toxicol*, 22(7): 612–613.

Clonazepam

Brand name: Klonopin
Classification: Benzodiazepine
λ: 19–60 h
V_d: 1.5–4.4 L/kg
Usual dosage: 0.25–5 mg bid

Source	Therapeutic/Nontoxic	Toxic	Lethal
Blood	0.004–0.2 mg/L	0.1–0.6 mg/L	0.7–1.4 mg/L

Comments

- Tolerance can develop and should be considered when interpreting drug concentrations

Selected Sources

Berlin A, Dahlström H. (1975). Pharmacokinetics of the anticonvulsant drug clonazepam evaluated from single oral and intravenous doses and by repeated oral administration, *Eur J Clin Pharmacol*, 9(2–3): 155–159.

Bexar County Medical Examiner's Office data 1996–2015.

Burrows DL, Hagardorn AN, Harlan GC, Wallen ED, Ferslew KE. (2003). A fatal drug interaction between oxycodone and clonazepam, *J Forensic Sci*, 48(3): 683–686.

Greenblatt DJ, Blaskovich PD, Nuwayser ES, Harmatz JS, Chen G, Zinny MA. (2005). Clonazepam pharmacokinetics: Comparison of subcutaneous microsphere injection with multiple-dose oral administration, *J Clin Pharmacol*, 45(11): 1288–1293.

Welch TR, Rumack BH, Hammond K. (1977). Clonazepam overdose resulting in cyclic coma, *Clin Tox*, 10(4): 433–436.

Clozapine

Brand names: Clozaril and FazaClo
Classification: Antipsychotic
λ: 4–66 h
V_d: 4.6–5 L/kg
Usual dosage: 300–450 mg qd

Source	Therapeutic/Nontoxic	Toxic	Lethal
Blood	0.04–1.7 mg/L	0.9–7.0 mg/L	1.3–13 mg/L
Vitreous			1.3 mg/L
Liver	0.8–1.5 mg/kg	5.9–17 mg/kg	6.5–85 mg/kg
Skeletal muscle	1.7 mg/kg		

Comments

- Prolongs QT interval
- Metabolized by CYP 1A2, 3A4, and 2D6
- Active metabolite: Desmethylclozapine

Selected Sources

Bexar County Medical Examiner's Office data 1996–2015.
Druid H, Holmgren P. (1997). A compilation of fatal and control concentrations of drugs in postmortem femoral blood, *J Forensic Sci*, 42(1): 79–87.
Flanagan RJ, Spencer EP, Morgan PE, Barnes TR, Dunk L. (2005). Suspected clozapine poisoning in the UK/Eire, 1992–2003, *Forensic Sci Intl*, 155(2–3): 91–99.
Ishii A, Mizoguchi K, Kageoka M, Seno H, Kumazawa T, Suzuki O. (1997). Nonfatal suicidal intoxication by clozapine, *J Tox Clin Tox*, 35(2): 195–197.
Keller T, Miki A, Binda S, Dirnhofer R. (1997). Fatal overdose of clozapine, *Forensic Sci Intl*, 86(1–2): 119–125.
Kratzsch C, Peters FT, Kraemer T, Weber AA, Maurer HH. (2003). Screening, library-assisted identification and validated quantification of fifteen neuroleptics and three of their metabolites in plasma by liquid chromatography/mass spectrometry with atmospheric pressure chemical ionization, *J Mass Spectrum*, 38(3): 283–295.
Meeker JE, Herrmann PW, Som CW, Reynolds PC. (1992). Clozapine tissue concentrations following an apparent suicidal overdose of clozaril, *J Anal Toxicol*, 16(1): 54–56.
Medical Economics. (2007). *Physicians' Desk Reference*, (61st ed.), Thomson PDR, Montvale, NJ, pp. 2184–2189.
Worm K, Kringsholm B, Steentoft A. (1993). Clozapine cases with fatal, toxic or therapeutic concentrations, *Int J Legal Med*, 106(3): 115–118.

Cocaine

Brand name: Cocaine hydrochloride
Street names: Coke, Snow, and Crack; w/ heroin: Dynamite and Belushi,
  Eightball, Moonrock, and Speedball; w/ PCP: Jim Jones, Parachute,
  and Spaceball
Classification: Local anesthetic (ENT)/stimulant
λ: 0.7–1.5 h
V_d: 1.7–2.7 L/kg
Usual dosage: 1%–10% solutions used topically; 1–2 mg/kg/dose

Source	Therapeutic/Nontoxic	Toxic	Lethal
Blood	0.1–15 mg/L	0.1–5 mg/L	0.1–330 mg/L
Vitreous			0.8–13 mg/L
Liver			0.2–393 mg/kg
Kidney			3.8–28 mg/kg
Brain			0.04–74 mg/kg
Skeletal muscle	0.1 mg/kg		0.1–48 mg/kg

Comments

- Can be metabolized *in vitro* (and *in vitro*) to ecgonine methyl ester and benzoylecgonine
- Active metabolites: Cocaethylene, and norcocaine
- Metabolized by CYP 3A

Selected Sources

Amon CA, Tate LG, Wright RK, Matusiak W. (1986). Sudden death due to ingestion of cocaine, *J Anal Toxicol*, 10(5): 217–218.
Bexar County Medical Examiner's Office data 1996–2015.
Ellefsen KN, Concheiro M, Pirard S, Gorelick DA, Huestis MA. (2016). Pharmacodynamic effects and relationships to plasma and oral fluid pharmacokinetics after intravenous cocaine administration, *Drug Alchol Depen*, 163: 116–125.
Jenkins AJ, Levine B, Titus J, Smialek JE. (1999). The interpretation of cocaine and benzoylecgonine concentrations in postmortem cases, *Forensic Sci Intl*, 101(1): 17–25.
Poklis A, Maginn D, Barr JL. (1987). Tissue disposition of cocaine in man: A report of five fatal poisonings, *Forensic Sci Intl*, 33(2): 83–88.
Winek CL, Wahba WW, Rozin L, Janssen JK. (1987). An unusually high blood cocaine concentration in a fatal case, *J Anal Toxicol*, 11(1): 43–46.

Codeine

Brand names: Often combined with acetaminophen or aspirin (ASA) (Tylenol w/ codeine, Empirin w/ codeine)
Classification: Opiate
λ: 1.1–4 h
V_d: 2.2–4.7 L/kg
Usual dosage: 15–60 mg q 4 h

Source	Therapeutic/Nontoxic	Toxic	Lethal
Blood	0.03–0.4 mg/L	0.5–1 mg/L	1–48 mg/L
Vitreous	0.02–0.4 mg/L		0.6–1.2 mg/L
Liver	0.6 mg/kg		13–128 mg/kg
Kidney			2.3–36 mg/kg
Brain			2–33 mg/kg
Skeletal muscle	0.06–1 mg/kg		1.9 mg/kg
Adipose tissue			2.1 mg/kg

Comments

- Metabolized to morphine by CYP 2D6
- Tolerance can develop and should be considered when interpreting drug concentrations

Selected Sources

Bexar County Medical Examiner's Office data 1996–2015.

Gerostamoulos J, Burke MP, Drummer OH. (1996). Involvement of codeine in drug-related deaths, *Am J Forensic Med Path*, 17(4): 327–335.

Guay DR, Awni WM, Findlay JW, Halstenson CE, Abraham PA, Opsahl JA, Jones EC, Matzke GR. (1988). Pharmacokinetics and pharmacodynamics of codeine in end-stage renal disease, *Clin Pharmacol Ther*, 43(1): 63–71.

Kim I, Barnes AJ, Oyler JM, Schepers R, Joseph RE Jr, Cone EJ, Lafko D, Moolchan ET, Huestis MA. (2002). Plasma and oral fluid pharmacokinetics and pharmacodynamics after oral codeine administration, *Clin Chem*, 48(9): 1486–1496.

Kintz P, Tracqui A, Mangin P. (1991). Codeine concentrations in human samples in a case of fatal ingestion, *Int J Legal Med*, 104(3): 177–178.

Pearson MA, Poklis A, Morrison RR. (1979). A fatality due to the ingestion of (methyl morphine) codeine, *Clin Tox*, 15(3): 267–271.

Peat MA, Sengupta A. (1977). Toxicological investigations of cases of death involving codeine and dihydrocodeine, *J Forensic Sci*, 9(1): 21–32.

Cyanide

Brand names: Component of some insecticides
Classification: Poison
λ: 1 h
V_d: 0.4 L/kg
Usual dosage: Not applicable

Source	Therapeutic/Nontoxic	Toxic	Lethal
Blood	<0.25 mg/L	0.25–5 mg/L	1–249 mg/L
Vitreous			0.5–1.4 mg/L
Liver			0.1–43 mg/kg
Kidney			0.5–55 mg/kg
Brain			0.6–30 mg/kg

Comments

- Associated with bright red lividity and musculature at autopsy
- Distinct bitter almond smell
- Can be created by microorganisms; best to test blood immediately
- Can be found in fire deaths: 0.2–2 mg/L survivors; 1–5 mg/L fatalities

CN concentration	Symptoms
<0.2 mg/L	Usually none
0.5–1.0 mg/L	Flushing, tachycardia
1–2.5 mg/L	Stupor and agitation
>2.5 mg/L	Coma

Selected Sources

Adelson L. (1974). Chapter XIII murder by poison, in *The Pathology of Homicide*, Charles C Thomas (Ed.), Springfield, IL, pp. 725–875.
Bexar County Medical Examiner's Office data 1996–2015.
Hall AH, Doutre WH, Ludden T, Kulig KW, Rumack BH. (1987). Nitrite/thiosulfate treated acute cyanide poisoning: estimated kinetics after antidote, *J Tox Clin Tox*, 25(1–2): 121–133.
Levine B (Ed). (2002). *Principles of Forensic Toxicology*. American Association for Clinical Chemistry, Washington, DC, pp. 337–344.
Rhee J, Jung J, Yeom H, Lee H, Lee S, Park Y, Chung H. (2011). Distribution of cyanide in heart blood, peripheral blood and gastric contents in 21 cyanide related fatalities, *Forensic Sci Int*, 210: e12–e15.
Stoll S, Roider G, Keil W. (2017). Concentrations of cyanide in blood smaples of corpses after smoke inhlataion of varying origin, *Int J Legal Med*, 131: 123–129.

Cyclizine

Brand name: Marezine
Classification: Antihistamine
λ: 7–24 h
V_d: 13–21 L/kg
Usual dosage: 50 mg q 4–6 h

Source	Therapeutic/Nontoxic	Toxic	Lethal
Blood	0.01–0.3 mg/L	0.75–1 mg/L	15–80 mg/L
Liver			37 mg/kg
Brain			3 mg/kg

Selected Sources

Backer RC, McFeeley P, Wohlenberg N. (1989). Fatality resulting from cyclizine overdose, *J Anal Toxicol*, 13(5): 308–309.
Battista HJ, Henn R, Schnabel F. (1978). Clinical course, morphological and toxicological findings in a fatal case of cyclizine poisoning in a child, *Beitrage zur Gerichtlichen Medizin*, 36: 429–431.
Griffin DS, Baselt RC. (1984). Blood and urine concentrations of cyclizine by nitrogen-phosphorus gas-liquid chromatography, *J Anal Toxicol*, 8(2): 97–99.
Land G, Dean K, Bye A. (1981). Determination of cyclizine and norcyclizine in plasma and urine using gas-liquid chromatography with nitrogen selective detection, *J Chromatogr*, 222(1): 135–140.
Schulz M, Schmoldt A. (2003). Therapeutic and toxic blood concentrations of more than 800 drugs and other xenobiotics, *Pharmazie*, 58(7): 447–474.

Cyclobenzaprine

Brand names: Flexeril, Amrix, and Fexmid
Classification: Muscle relaxant
λ: 8.3–47 h
V_d: Unknown
Usual dosage: 5 mg tid

Source	Therapeutic/Nontoxic	Toxic	Lethal
Blood	0.002–0.5 mg/L	No data available	0.7–1.8 mg/L
Liver			3.1–120 mg/kg
Skeletal muscle	0.16–0.5 mg/kg		0.6 mg/kg

Comments

- Metabolized by CYP 1A2

Selected Sources

Bexar County Medical Examiner's Office data 1996–2015.
Spiller HA, Cutino L. (2003). Fatal cyclobenzaprine overdose with postmortem values, *J Forensic Sci*, 48(4): 883–884.
Winchell GA, King JD, Chavez-Eng CM, Constanzer ML, Korn SH. (2002). Cyclobenzaprine pharmacokinetics, including the effects of age, gender and hepatic insufficiency, *J Clin Pharmacol*, 42(1): 61–69.

Cyproheptadine

Brand name: Periactin
Classification: Antihistamine
λ: 8.6 h
V_d: Unknown
Usual dosage: 4 mg tid

Source	Therapeutic/Nontoxic	Toxic	Lethal
Blood	0.003–0.03 mg/L	No data available	0.5[a]–0.6[b] mg/L
Liver			7.6[b] mg/kg
Kidney			1.8[b] mg/kg

[a] Co-intoxicant citalopram 2.3 mg/L.
[b] Blood ethanol 0.09 g/dL.

Selected Sources

Bexar County Medical Examiner's Office data 1996–2015.
Gunja N, Collins M, Graudins A. (2004). A comparison of the pharmacokinetics of oral and sublingual cyproheptadine, *J Tox Clin Tox*, 42(1): 79–83.
Levine B, Green-Johnson D, Hogan S, Smialek JE. (1998). A cyproheptadine fatality, *J Anal Toxicol*, 22(1): 72–74.

Desipramine

Brand name: Norpramin
Classification: Antidepressant (TCA)
λ: 12–28 h
V_d: 24–60 L/kg
Usual dosage: 75–150 mg qd

Source	Therapeutic/Nontoxic	Toxic	Lethal
Blood	0.04–0.6 mg/L	0.4–1.8 mg/L	3–36 mg/L
Vitreous	0.04 mg/L		
Liver			50–140 mg/kg
Skeletal muscle	0.08 mg/kg		10 mg/kg

Comments

- Metabolite of imipramine
- Prolongs QT interval
- Metabolized by CYP 2D6

Selected Sources

Amitai Y, Frischer H. (2004). Excess fatality from desipramine and dosage recommendations, *Ther Drug Monit*, 26(5): 468–473.

Bexar County Medical Examiner's Office data 1996–2015.

Burke MJ, Harvey AT, Preskorn SK. (1996). Pharmacokinetics of the newer antidepressants, *Am J Med*, 100(1): 119–121.

Chaturvedi AK, Hidding JT, Rao NG, Smith JC, Bredehoeft SJ. (1987). Two tricyclic antidepressant poisonings: Levels of amitriptyline, nortriptyline and desipramine in post-mortem biological samples, *Forensic Sci Intl*, 33(2): 93–101.

Linder MW, Keck PE. (1998). Standards of laboratory practice: Antidepressant drug monitoring, National Academy of Clinical Biochemistry, *Clin Chem*, 44(5): 1073–1084.

Sawyer WT, Caudill JL, Ellison MJ. (1984). A case of severe acute desipramine overdose, *Am J Psychiatry*, 141(1): 122–123.

Desloratadine

Brand name: Clarinex
Classification: Antihistamine
λ: 27–36 h
V_d: 49 L/kg
Usual dosage: 2.5–10 mg qd

Source	Therapeutic/Nontoxic	Toxic	Lethal
Blood	0.003–0.006 mg/L	No data available	

Comments

- May prolong QT interval
- Active metabolite: 3-hydroxydesloratadine

Selected Sources

Affrime M, Banfield C, Gupta S, Cohen A, Boutros T, Thonoor M, Cayen M. (2002). Comparison of pharmacokinetics and metabolism of desloratadine, fexofenadine, levocetirizine and mizolastine in humans, *Clin Pharmacokinet*, 41(Suppl 1): 21–28.

Devillier P, Roche N, Faisy C. (2008). Clinical pharmacokinetics and pharmacodynamics of desloratadine, fexofenadine and levocetirizine: A comparative review, *Clin Pharmacokinet*, 47(4): 217–230.

Molimard M, Diquet B, Benedetti MS. (2004). Comparison of pharmacokinetics and metabolism of desloratadine, fexofenadine, levocetirizine and mizolastine in humans, *Fundam Clin Pharmacol*, 18(4): 399–411.

Desvenlafaxine

Brand name: Pristiq
Classification: Antidepressant (SNRI)
λ: 8–14 h
V_d: 3–4 L/kg
Usual dosage: 50–100 mg qd

Source	Therapeutic/Nontoxic	Toxic	Lethal
Blood	0.06–0.3 mg/L	No data available	

Comments

- Metabolite of venlafaxine

Selected Sources

Baird-Bellaire S, Behrle JA, Parker VD, Patat A, Paul J, Nichols AI. (2013). An open-label, single-dose, parallel-group study of the effects of chronic hepatic impairment on the safety and pharmacokinetics of desvenlafaxine, *Clin Ther*, 35(6): 782–794.

Nichols AI, Focht K, Jiang Q, Preskorn SH, Kane CP. (2011). Pharmacokinetics of venlafaxine extended release 75 mg and desvenlafaxine 50 mg in healthy CYP2D6 extensive and poor metabolizers: A randomized, open-label, two-period, parallel-group, crossover study, *Clin Drug Investig*, 31(3): 155–167.

Dexfenfluramine

Brand name: Redux
Classification: Anorectic
λ: 13–20 h
V_d: 10–14 L/kg
Usual dosage: 15 mg bid

Source	Therapeutic/Nontoxic	Toxic	Lethal
Blood	0.013–0.05 mg/L	0.15–0.8 mg/L	3.3 mg/L[a]

[a] Postmortem sample in suicide case; exact cause of death not given.

Comments

- No longer available in the United States
- Associated with pulmonary hypertension and cardiac valve disease
- Active metabolite: Nordexfenfluramine
- Metabolized by CYP 2D6 and 1A2

Selected Sources

Cheymol G, Weissenburger J, Poirier JM, Gellee C. (1995). The pharmacokinetics of dexfenfluramine in obese and non-obese subjects, *Br J Clin Pharm*, 39(6): 684–7.

LoVecchio F, Curry SC. (1998). Dexfenfluramine overdose, *Ann Emer Med*, 32(1): 102–103.

Redux™ package insert (1996). Wyeth-Ayerst Laboratories.

Dextromethorphan

Brand names: Common component of OTC cough medicines including Balamine, Tylenol Cold, and Vicks
Classification: Antitussive
λ: 3–4 h
V_d: 5–6 L/kg
Usual dosage: 10–30 mg q 4 h

Source	Therapeutic/Nontoxic	Toxic	Lethal
Blood	0.005–0.8 mg/L	0.1–2.8 mg/L	1.3–18 mg/L
Vitreous			0.7 mg/L
Liver			19–230 mg/kg
Skeletal muscle	0.07–0.5 mg/kg		

Comments

• Metabolized by CYP 2D6 and 3A4

Selected Sources

Bexar County Medical Examiner's Office data 1996–2015.
Ganetsky M, Babu KM, Boyer EW. (2007). Serotonin syndrome in dextromethorphan ingestion responsive to propofol therapy, *Pediatr Emerg Care*, 23(11): 829–831.
Logan BK, Goldfogel G, Hamilton R, Kuhlman J. (2009). Five deaths resulting from abuse of dextromethorphan sold over the internet, *J Anal Toxicol*, 33(2): 99–103.
Majlesi N, Lee DC, Ali SS. (2011). Dextromethorphan abuse masquerading as a recurrent seizure disorder, *Pediatr Emerg Care*, 27(3): 210–211.
Rammer L, Holmgren P, Sandler H. (1988). Fatal intoxication by dextromethorphan: A report on two cases, *Forensic Sci Intl*, 37(4): 233–236.
Schadel M, Wu D, Otton SV, Kalow W, Sellers EM. (1995). Pharmacokinetics of dextromethorphan and metabolites in humans: Influence of the CYP2D6 phenotype and quinidine inhibition, *J Clin Psychopharmacol*, 15(4): 263–269.
Schwartz AR, Pizon AF, Brooks DE. (2008) Dextromethorphan-induced serotonin syndrome, *Clin Toxicol (Phila)*, 46(8): 771–773.
Vetticaden SJ, Cabana BE, Prasad VK, Purich ED, Jonkman JH, de Zeeuw R. (1989). Phenotypic differences in dextromethorphan metabolism, *Pharm Res*, 6(1): 13–19.
Yoo Y, Chung H, Kim E, Kim M. (1996). Fatal zipeprol and dextromethorphan poisonings in Korea, *J Anal Toxicol*, 20(3): 155–158.

Diazepam

Brand names: Valium and Valrelease
Street name: V
Classification: Benzodiazepine
λ: 30–66 h
V_d: 1–2 L/kg
Usual dosage: 2–20 mg bid

Source	Therapeutic/Nontoxic	Toxic	Lethal
Blood	0.02–4 mg/L	3–20 mg/L	1.2–30 mg/L
Liver			16 mg/kg
Brain	0.002–0.6 mg/kg		
Skeletal muscle	0.1–1 mg/kg		

Comments

- Sudden withdrawal can lead to anxiety, seizures, and death
- Tolerance can develop and should be considered when interpreting drug concentrations
- Metabolized by CYP 2C19 and 3A4
- Active metabolite: Nordiazepam (λ 38–135 h) and temazepam (λ 7–18 h)

Selected Sources

Cardauns H, Iffland R. (1973). Fatal intoxication of a young drug addict with diazepam, *Archiv für Toxikologie*, 31(2): 147–151.

Finkle BS, McCloskey KL, Goodman LS. (1979). Diazepam and drug-associated deaths. A survey in the United States and Canada, *JAMA*, 242(5): 429–434.

Greenblatt DJ, Harmatz JS, Friedman H, Locniskar A, Shader RI. (1989). A large-sample study of diazepam pharmacokinetics, *Ther Drug Mon*, 11(6): 652–657.

Jönsson AK, Söderberg C, Espnes KA, Ahlner J, Eriksson A, Reis M, Druid H. (2014). Sedative and hypnotic drugs—fatal and non-fatal reference blood concentrations, *Forensic Sci Int*, 236: 138–145.

Tada K, Moroji T, Sekiguchi R, Motomura H, Noguchi T. (1985). Liquid-chromatographic assay of diazepam and its major metabolites in serum, and application to pharmacokinetic study of high doses of diazepam in schizophrenics, *Clin Chem*, 31(10): 1712–1715.

Vukcević NP, Ercegović GV, Segrt Z, Djordjević S, Stosić JJ. (2016). Benzodiazepine poisoning in elderly, *Vojnosanit Pregl*, 73(3): 234–238.

Dicyclomine

Brand names: Bentyl, Byclomine, and Dibent
Classification: Antimuscarinic/antispasmotic
λ: 1.8 h
V_d: 3.6 L/kg
Usual dosage: 10–20 mg qid

Source	Therapeutic/Nontoxic	Toxic	Lethal
Blood	0.02–0.6 mg/L	0.2 mg/L	0.2–0.5 mg/L[a]
Vitreous			0.1 mg/L[a]

[a] Infant deaths.

Selected Sources

Bexar County Medical Examiner's Office data 1996–2015.
Garriott JC, Rodriquez R, Norton LE. (1984). Two cases of death involving dicyclomine in infants. Measurement of therapeutic and toxic concentrations in blood, *J Tox Clin Tox*, 22(5): 455–462.
Medical Economics. (2006). *Physicians' Desk Reference*, (60th ed.), Thomson PDR, Montvale, NJ, pp. 724–726.

Digitoxin

Brand name: Digitaline
Classification: Cardiac glycoside
λ: 6–12 d
V_d: 0.5–0.8 L/kg
Usual dosage: 0.05–0.2 mg qd

Source	Therapeutic/Nontoxic	Toxic	Lethal
Blood	0.006–0.03 mg/L	0.03–0.6 mg/L	0.2–0.8 mg/L

Comments

- Usually measured by immunoassays that may cross-react with oleander and digoxin
- Treated with digibind (digoxin immune fab)
- Found in several plant species including foxglove (*digitalis purpurea*)

Selected Sources

Kanji S, MacLean RD. (2012). Cardiac glycoside toxicity: More than 200 years and counting, *Crit Care Clin*, 28(4): 527–535.

Krappweis J, Petereit G, Justus J, Altmann E, Kirch W. (1996). Digitoxin intoxication with lethal outcome, *Eur J Med Res*, 1(12): 551–553.

MacFarland RT, Marcus FI, Fenster PE, Graves PE, Perrier D. (1984). Pharmacokinetics and bioavailability of digitoxin by a specific assay, *Eur J Clin Pharm*, 27(1): 85–89.

Ochs HR, Grube E, Greenblatt DJ, Arendt R, Bodem G. (1981). Pharmacokinetics and pharmacodynamics of intravenous digoxin and digitoxin, *Wien Klin Wochenschr*, 59(16): 889–897.

Schmitt K, Tulzer G, Häckel F, Sommer R, Tulzer W. (1994). Massive digitoxin intoxication treated with digoxin-specific antibodies in a child, *Ped Card*, 15(1): 48–49.

Woolf AD, Wenger T, Smith TW, Lovejoy FH. (1992). The use of digoxin-specific Fab fragments for severe digitalis intoxication in children, *NEJM*, 326(26): 1739–1744.

Digoxin

Brand names: Lanoxin, Lanoxicaps, and Digitalis
Classification: Cardiac glycoside
λ: 1.5–2 d
V_d: 4–8 L/kg
Usual dosage: 0.125–3 mg qd

Source	Therapeutic/Nontoxic	Toxic	Lethal
Blood	0.0008–0.01 mg/L	0.002–0.04 mg/L	0.003–1.3 mg/L
Vitreous	0.002–0.007 mg/L		0.003–0.05 mg/L
Liver	0.03–0.2 mg/kg		0.03–0.73 mg/kg
Kidney	0.05–0.4 mg/kg		0.1–1.7 mg/kg
Brain	0.003–0.3 mg/kg		0.009–0.05 mg/kg
Skeletal muscle	0.008–0.06 mg/kg		0.01–0.4 mg/kg
Cardiac muscle	0.03–0.5 mg/kg		0.04–1.2 mg/kg

Comments

- Causes increased potassium
- Usually measured by immunassays that may cross-react with olean-der and digitoxin
- Treated with digibind (digoxin immune fab)

Selected Sources

Bexar County Medical Examiner's Office data 1996–2015.
DiMaio VJ, Garriott JC, Putnam R. (1975). Digoxin concentrations in postmortem specimens after overdose and therapeutic use, *J Forensic Sci*, 20(2): 340–347.
Kanji S, MacLean RD. (2012). Cardiac glycoside toxicity: More than 200 years and counting, *Crit Care Clin*, 28(4): 527–535.
Rietbrock N, Wojahn H, Weinmann J, Hasford J, Kuhlmann J. (1978). Suicide with beta-methyldigoxin, *Dtsch Med Wochenschr*, 103(46): 1841–1844.
Ritz S, Harding P, Martz W, Schütz HW, Kaatsch HJ. (1992). Measurement of digi-talis-glycoside levels in ocular tissues: A way to improve postmortem diagno-sis of lethal digitalis-glycoside poisoning? I. Digoxin, *Intl J Legal Med*, 105(3): 149–154.
Selesky M, Spiehler V, Cravey RH, Elliot HW. (1977). Digoxin concentrations in fatal cases, *J Forensic Sci*, 22(2): 409–417.
Smolarz A, Roesch E, Lenz E, Neubert H, Abshagen P. (1985). Digoxin specific anti-body (Fab) fragments in 34 cases of severe digitalis intoxication, *J Tox Clin Tox*, 23(4–6): 327–340.

Dihydrocodeine

Brand names: Codicontin, Synalgos (w/ ASA and caffeine), Novahistine (w/ phenylephrine), and HydroTussin (w/ pseudoephedrine and chlorpheniramine)
Classification: Opioid
λ: 3–4.5 h
V_d: 1–1.5 L/kg
Usual dosage: 16–32 mg q 4 h

Source	Therapeutic/Nontoxic	Toxic	Lethal
Blood	0.03–0.3 mg/L	0.5–1 mg/L	0.4–166 mg/L
Liver			1.3 mg/kg
Kidney			11 mg/kg
Brain			0.8 mg/kg

Comments

- Metabolite of hydrocodone
- Active metabolite: Dihydromorphine
- Tolerance can develop and should be considered when interpreting drug concentrations

Selected Sources

Al-Asmari AI, Anderson RA. (2010). The role of dihydrocodeine (DHC) metabolites in dihydrocodeine-related deaths, *J Anal Toxicol*, 34(8): 476–490.
Klinder K, Skopp G, Mattern R, Aderjan R. (1999). The detection of dihydrocodeine and its main metabolites in cases of fatal overdose, *Intl J Legal Med*, 112(3): 155–158.
Rowell FJ, Seymour RA, Rawlins MD. (1983). Pharmacokinetics of intravenous and oral dihydrocodeine and its acid metabolites, *Eur J Clin Pharm*, 25(3): 419–424.
Schulz M, Schmoldt A. (2003). Therapeutic and toxic blood concentrations of more than 800 drugs and other xenobiotics, *Pharmazie*, 58(7): 447–474.
Skopp G, Klinder K, Pötsch L, Zimmer G, Lutz R, Aderjan R. (1998). Postmortem distribution of dihydrocodeine and metabolites in a fatal case of dihydrocodeine intoxication, *Forensic Sci Intl*, 95(2): 99–107.
Woodford N, Hawkins B, Forrest ARW. (2003). Dihydrocodeine-related deaths: A ten-year review. *Presented at the AAFS Annual Meeting*, Chicago, IL.

Diltiazem

Brand names: Cardizem and Tiazac
Classification: Calcium channel blocker
λ: 2–13 h; 28–40 h for ER
V_d: 3–11 L/kg
Usual dosage: 60–120 mg bid; 120–420 mg qd for ER

Source	Therapeutic/Nontoxic	Toxic	Lethal
Blood	0.05–1.4 mg/L	0.6–6.1 mg/L	3–42 mg/L
Vitreous	0.1 mg/L		3.5–5.5 mg/L
Liver	0.3–3 mg/kg		41–182 mg/kg
Kidney	0.8–1 mg/kg		49 mg/kg
Brain	0.5–0.8 mg/kg		33–76 mg/kg
Skeletal muscle	0.1–1.7 mg/kg		

Selected Sources

Belleflamme M, Hantson P, Gougnard T, Minon JM, Wittebole X, Laterre PF, Mairesse J, Dugernier T. (2012). Survival despite extremely high plasma diltiazem level in a case of acute poisoning treated by the molecular-adsorbent recirculating system, *Eur J Emerg Med*, 19(1): 59–61.

Bexar County Medical Examiner's Office data 1996–2015.

Cantrell FL, Williams SR. (2005). Fatal unintentional overdose of diltiazem with antemortem and postmortem values, *Clin Tox*, 43(6): 587–588.

Kaliciak HA, Huckin SN, Cave WS. (1992). A death attributed solely to diltiazem, *J Anal Toxicol*, 16(2): 102–103.

Kalin JR, Wood KM, Lee QJ. (1994). A possible suicide by diltiazem overdose, *J Anal Toxicol*, 18(3): 180–182.

Luomanmäki K, Tiula E, Kivistö KT, Neuvonen PJ. (1997). Pharmacokinetics of diltiazem in massive overdose, *Ther Drug Monit*, 19(2): 240–242.

Moriya F, Hashimoto Y. (2004). Redistribution of diltiazem in the early postmortem period, *J Anal Toxicol*, 28(4): 269–271.

Romano G, Barbera N, Rossitto C, Spadaro G. (2002). Lethal diltiazem poisoning, *J Anal Toxicol*, 26(6): 374–377.

Roper TA, Sykes R, Gray C. (1993). Fatal diltiazem overdose: Report of four cases and review of the literature, *Postgrad Med J*, 69(812): 474–476.

Diphenhydramine

Brand names: Benadryl, Nytol, Simply Sleep, Sominex, and Compoz
Classification: Antihistamine
λ: 2–13 h
V_d: 2–5 L/kg
Usual dosage: 25–50 mg q 4–6 h

Source	Therapeutic/Nontoxic	Toxic	Lethal
Blood	0.004–3.8 mg/L	1–19 mg/L	5–39 mg/L
Vitreous			6–15 mg/L
Liver	0.5–4 mg/kg		34–260 mg/kg
Kidney			50–114 mg/kg
Brain			8–32 mg/kg
Skeletal muscle	0.5–2 mg/kg		7–22 mg/kg

Comments

- May prolong QT interval
- Metabolized by CYP 2D6

Selected Sources

Abdelmalek D, Schwarz ES, Sampson C, Halcomb SE, McCammon C, Arroyo-Plasencia A, Stenger A, Krehbiel N, Mullins ME. (2014). Life-threatening diphenhydramine toxicity presenting with seizures and a wide complex tachycardia improved with intravenous fat emulsion, *Am J Ther*, 21(6): 542–544.

Abdi A, Rose E, Levine M. (2014). Diphenhydramine overdose with intraventricular conduction delay treated with hypertonic sodium bicarbonate and i.v. lipid emulsion, *West J Emerg Med*, 15(7): 855–858.

Aderjan R, Bösche J, Schmidt G. (1982). Poisoning by diphenhydramine—Forensic-toxicologic interpretation of analytic results, *Zeitschrift für Rechtsmedizin*, 88(4): 263–270.

Bexar County Medical Examiner's Office data 1996–2015.

Botch-Jones SR, Johnson R, Kleinschmidt K, Bashaw S, Ordonez J. (2014). Diphenhydramine's role in death investigations: An examination of diphenhydramine prevalence in 2 US geographical areas, *Am J Forensic Med Pathol*, 35(3): 181–185.

Hausmann E, Wewer H, Wellhöner HH, Weller JP. (1983). Lethal intoxication with diphenhydramine. Report of a case with analytical follow-up, *Arch Tox*, 53(1): 33–39.

Pragst F, Herre S, Bakdash A. (2006). Poisonings with diphenhydramine—A survey of 68 clinical and 55 death cases, *Forensic Sci Intl*, 161(2–3): 189–197.

Sen A, Akin A, Craft KJ, Canfield DV, Chaturvedi AK. (2007). First-generation H1 antihistamines found in pilot fatalities of civil aviation accidents, 1990–2005, *Aviat Space Environ Med*, 78(5): 514–522.

Dipyrone

Brand names: Analgin, Conmel, Novalgin, and Metamizole
Classification: NSAID
λ: 2–4 h
V_d: 1 L/kg
Usual dosage: 500–1000 mg tid

Source	Therapeutic/Nontoxic[a]	Toxic[a]	Lethal[a]
Blood	4–11 mg/L	20 mg/L	669 mg/L[b]

[a] Concentrations are of active metabolite, 4-methyl-amino-antipyrine (MAA).
[b] Co-intoxicant baclofen 106 mg/L.

Comments

- Not available in the United States
- May cause agranulocytosis or renal insufficiency
- Active metabolite: 4-methyl-amino-antipyrine (MAA)

Selected Sources

de Giovanni N, d'Aloja E. (2001). Death due to baclofen and dipyrone ingestion, *Forensic Sci Intl*, 123(1): 26–32.

Levy M, Zylber-Katz E, Rosenkranz B. (1995). Clinical pharmacokinetics of dipyrone and its metabolites, *Clin Pharmacokinet*, 28(3): 216–234.

Rizzoni G, Furlanut M. (1984). Cyanotic crises in a breast-fed infant from mother taking dipyrone, *Hum Tox*, 3(6): 505–507.

Sistovaris N, Pola W, Wolhoff H. (1983). Thin-layer chromatographic determination of major metamizole metabolites in serum and urine, *J Chromatography A*, 274: 289–298.

Vlahov V, Badian M, Verho M, Bacracheva N. (1990). Pharmacokinetics of metamizol metabolites in healthy subjects after a single oral dose of metamizol sodium, *Eur J Clin Pharm*, 38(1): 61–65.

Donepezil

Brand name: Aricept
Classification: Acetylcholinesterase inhibitor (Alzheimer treatment)
λ: 50–80 h
V_d: 10–12 L/kg
Usual dosage: 5–10 mg qd

Source	Therapeutic/Nontoxic	Toxic	Lethal
Blood	0.003–0.5 mg/L	0.55 mg/L	No data available
Liver	1.2–9.2 mg/kg		
Skeletal muscle	1–1.5 mg/kg		

Comments

- Toxicities treated with atropine
- Metabolized by CYP 2D6 and 3A4

Selected Sources

Bexar County Medical Examiner's Office data 1996–2015.

Nagasawa S, Torimitsu S, Chiba F, Kubo Y, Yajima D, Iwase H. (2015). Donepezil distribution in postmortem cases and potential for redistribution, *Forensic Sci Intl*, 251: 132–138.

Nagasawa S, Yajima D, Torimitsu S, Chiba F, Iwase H. (2015). Postmortem memantine concentration in a non-intoxication case, and the possibility of postmortem redistribution: A case report, *Forensic Sci Int*, 257: e12–e15.

Rogers SL, Cooper NM, Sukovaty R, Pederson JE, Lee JN, Friedhoff LT. (1998). Pharmacokinetic and pharmacodynamic profile of donepezil HCl following multiple oral doses, *Br J Clin Pharm*, 46(Suppl 1): 7–12.

Rogers SL, Friedhoff LT. (1998). Pharmacokinetic and pharmacodynamic profile of donepezil HCl following single oral doses, *Br J Clin Pharm*, 46(Suppl 1): 1–6.

Xie Z, Liao Q, Xu X, Yao M, Wan J, Liu D. (2006). Rapid and sensitive determination of donepezil in human plasma by liquid chromatography/tandem mass spectrometry: Application to a pharmacokinetic study, *Rapid Commun Mass Spectrom*, 20(21): 3193–3198.

Yano H, Fukuhara Y, Wada K, Kowa H, Nakashima K. (2003). A case of acute cholinergic adverse effects induced by donepezil overdose: A follow-up of clinical course and plasma concentration of donepezil, *Rinsho Shinkeigaku*, 43(8): 482–486.

Dothiepin

Brand names: Dosulepin and Prothiaden
Classification: Antidepressant (TCA)
λ: 11–24 h
V_d: 19–195 L/kg
Usual dosage: 75–300 mg bid/tid

Source	Therapeutic/Nontoxic	Toxic	Lethal
Blood	0.003–0.1 mg/L	0.8–5.5 mg/L	2.3–62 mg/L
Vitreous			0.3–0.9 mg/L
Liver			2–52 mg/kg
Kidney			3.1–10 mg/kg
Brain			2.8 mg/kg
Skeletal muscle			0.4–18 mg/kg
Cardiac muscle			2.9–17 mg/kg

Comments

- Active metabolite: Desmethyldothiepin

Selected Sources

Cirimele V, Kintz P, Tracqui A, Mangin P. (1995). A fatal dothiepin overdose, *Forensic Sci Intl*, 76(3): 205–209.

Ilett KF, Hackett LP, Dusci LJ, Paterson JW. (1991). Disposition of dothiepin after overdose: Effects of repeated-dose activated charcoal, *Ther Drug Monit*, 13(6): 485–489.

Keller T, Schneider A, Tutsch-Bauer E. (2000). Fatal intoxication due to dothiepin, *Forensic Sci Intl*, 109(2): 159–166.

Langford AM, Taylor KK, Pounder DJ. (1998). Drug concentration in selected skeletal muscles, *J Forensic Sci*, 43(1): 22–27.

Maguire KP, Burrows GD, Norman TR, Scoggins BA. (1981). Metabolism and pharmacokinetics of dothiepin, *Br J Clin Pharm*, 12(3): 405–409.

Paterson SC. (1985). Drug levels found in cases of fatal self-poisoning, *Forensic Sci Intl*, 27(2): 129–133.

Pounder DJ, Hartley AK, Watmough PJ. (1994). Postmortem redistribution and degradation of dothiepin. Human case studies and an animal model, *Am J Forensic Med Path*, 15(3): 231–235.

Robinson AE, Coffer AI, McDowall RD. (1974). Toxicology of some autopsy cases involving tricyclic antidepressant drugs, *Zeitschrift für Rechtsmedizin*, 74(4): 261–266.

Roelofsen EE, Wilhelm AJ, Sinjewel A, Franssen EJ. (2008). Toxicokinetics of dothiepin: 2 case reports, *Ther Drug Monit*, 30(5): 638–641.

Williams KR, Pounder DJ. (1997). Site-to-site variability of drug concentrations in skeletal muscle, *Am J Forensic Med Path*, 18(3): 246–250.

Doxepin

Brand names: Sinequan, Adapin, and Silenor
Classification: Antidepressant (TCA)
λ: 6–23 h
V_d: 17–31 L/kg
Usual dosage: 30–150 mg qd

Source	Therapeutic/Nontoxic	Toxic	Lethal
Blood	0.009–0.7 mg/L	0.2–6.7 mg/L	1–150 mg/L
Vitreous			3 mg/L
Liver			6–500 mg/kg
Kidney			3–70 mg/kg
Brain			2–42 mg/kg
Skeletal muscle			1–38 mg/kg
Cardiac muscle			3–16 mg/kg

Comments

- Metabolized by CYP 2D6 and 2C19
- May prolong QT interval
- Active metabolite: Desmethyldoxepin (nordoxepin)

Selected Sources

Bexar County Medical Examiner's Office data 1996–2015.

Caplan YH, Ottinger WE, Crooks CR. (1983). Therapeutic and toxic drug concentrations in post mortem blood: A six year study in the State of Maryland, *J Anal Toxicol*, 7(5): 225–230.

Cordonnier J, Heyndrickx A, Jordaens L, Brijs R, de Keyser R. (1983). A fatal intoxication due to doxepin, *J Anal Toxicol*, 7(4): 161–164.

de Groot G, Maes RAA, Hodnett CN, Kelly RC, Bost RO, Sunshine I. (1978). Four cases of fatal doxepin poisoning, *J Anal Toxicol*, 2: 18–20.

Frank RD, Kierdorf HP. (2000). Is there a role for hemoperfusion/hemodialysis as a treatment option in severa tricyclic intoxication, *Intl J Artif Org*, 23(9): 618–623.

Gronewold A, Dettling A, Haffner HT, Skopp G. (2009). Doxepin and nordoxepin concentrations in body fluids and tissues in doxepin associated deaths, *Forensic Sci Int*, 190(1–3): 74–79.

Koski A, Ojanperä I, Sistonen J, Vuori E, Sajantila A. (2007). A fatal doxepin poisoning associated with a defective CYP2D6 genotype, *Am J Forensic Med Pathol*, 28(3): 259–261.

Quai I, Fagarasan M, Fagarasan E, Usineviciu I. (1985). Tricyclic antidepressants: Clinical considerations, tissue concentrations and morphopathologic changes in the acute intoxication in man, *Acta Medicinae Legalis et Socialis*, 35(1): 107–109.

Doxylamine

Brand names: Bendectin and Unisom
Classification: Antihistamine
λ: 10–12 h
V_d: 2–3 L/kg
Usual dosage: 25–50 mg qHS

Source	Therapeutic/Nontoxic	Toxic	Lethal
Blood	0.05–4 mg/L	1–7.5 mg/L	1–165 mg/L
Liver	17–40 mg/kg		5–500 mg/kg
Kidney			22 mg/kg
Skeletal muscle			6.3 mg/kg

Selected Sources

Bexar County Medical Examiner's Office data 1996–2015.

Bockholdt B, Klug E, Schneider V. (2001). Suicide through doxylamine poisoning, *Forensic Sci Intl*, 119(1): 138.

Eckes L, Tsokos M, Herre S, Gapert R, Hartwig S. (2014). Post-mortem evidence of doxylamine in toxicological analyses, *Sci Justice*, 54(1): 61–65.

Köppel C, Tenczer J, Ibe K. (1987). Poisoning with over-the-counter doxylamine preparations: An evaluation of 109 cases, *Hum Toxicol*, 6(5): 355–359.

Mendoza FS, Atiba JO, Krensky AM, Scannell LM. (1987). Rhabdomyolysis complicating doxylamine overdose, *Clin Pediatr (Phila)*, 26(11): 595–597.

Sen A, Akin A, Craft KJ, Canfield DV, Chaturvedi AK. (2007). First-generation H1 antihistamines found in pilot fatalities of civil aviation accidents, 1990–2005, *Aviat Space Environ Med*, 78(5): 514–522.

Siek TJ, Dunn WA. (1993). Documentation of a doxylamine overdose death: quantitation by standard addition and use of three instrumental techniques, *J Forensic Sci*, 38(3): 713–720.

Wu Chen NB, Schaffer MI, Lin RL, Kurland ML, Donoghue ER, Stein RJ. (1983). The general toxicology unknown. II. A case report: doxylamine and pyrilamine intoxication, *J Forensic Sci*, 28(2): 398–403.

Duloxetine

Brand name: Cymbalta
Classification: Antidepressant (SNRI)
λ: 8–17 h
V_d: 16–23 L/kg
Usual dosage: 20–60 mg qd

Source	Therapeutic/Nontoxic	Toxic	Lethal
Blood	0.02–0.4 mg/L	0.4–2 mg/L	0.9–6 mg/L
Vitreous			0.6 mg/L
Liver	0.3–22 mg/kg		360 mg/kg

Comments

- Metabolized by CYP 2D6 and 1A2
- May cause liver failure

Selected Sources

Anderson D, Reed S, Lintemoot J, Kegler S, DeQuintana S, Sandberg M. (2006). A first look at duloxetine (Cymbalta) in a postmortem laboratory, *J Anal Toxicol*, 30(8): 576–580.
Bexar County Medical Examiner's Office data 2003–2015.
Hanje AJ, Pell LJ, Votolato NA, Frankel WL, Kirkpatrick RB. (2006). Case report: Fulminant hepatic failure involving duloxetine hydrochloride, *Clin Gastroenterol Hepatol*, 4(7): 912–917.
Isalberti C, Reed D. (2008). Case study: A fatality involving duloxetine, *Bull Intl Assoc Forensic Tox*, 38(2): 32–34.
Menchetti M, Gozzi BF, Saracino MA, Mercolini L, Petio C, Raggi MA. (2009). Non-fatal overdose of duloxetine in combination with other antidepressants and benzodiazepines, *World J Biol Psychiatry*, 10(4 Pt 2): 385–389.
Paulzen M, Hiemke C, Gründer G. (2009). Plasma levels and cerebrospinal fluid penetration by duloxetine in a patient with a non-fatal overdose during a suicide attempt, *Int J Neuropsychopharmacol*, 12(10): 1431–1432.
Scanlon KA, Stoppacher R, Blum LM, Starkey SJ. (2016). Comprehensive duloxetine analysis in a fatal overdose, *J Anal Toxicol*, 40(2): 167–170.
Vey EL, Kovelman I. (2010). Adverse events, toxicity and post-mortem data on duloxetine: Case reports and literature survey, *J Forensic Leg Med*, 17(4): 175–185.

Ephedrine

Brand names: Primatene and Rynatuss (w/ chlorpheniramine, phenylephrine, and carbetapentane)
Street names: Ma Huang, Herbal Ecstasy
Classification: Stimulant/decongestant
λ: 3–11 h
V_d: 2–4 L/kg
Usual dosage: 10–20 mg bid

Source	Therapeutic/Nontoxic	Toxic	Lethal
Blood	0.05–0.14 mg/L	0.11–23 mg/L	3.5–20 mg/L
Liver			15[a]–24 mg/kg
Kidney			14 mg/kg
Brain	<0.2 mg/kg		8.9 mg/kg

[a] Co-intoxicant caffeine 86 mg/L.

Comments

- Found in *Ephedra* species of plants
- No longer available in the United States

Selected Sources

Backer R, Tautman D, Lowry S, Harvey CM, Poklis A. (1997). Fatal ephedrine intox-
ication, *J Forensic Sci*, 42(1): 157–159.
Berlin I, Warot D, Aymard G, Acquaviva E, Legrand M, Labarthe B, Peyron I, Diquet
B, Lechat P. (2001). Pharmacodynamics and pharmacokinetics of single nasal
(5 mg and 10 mg) and oral (50 mg) doses of ephedrine in healthy subjects,
Eur J Clin Pharmacol, 57(6–7): 447–455.
Garriott JC, Simmons LM, Poklis A, Mackell MA. (1985). Five cases of fatal overdose
from caffeine-containing "look-alike" drugs, *J Anal Toxicol*, 9(3): 141–143.
Gurley BJ, Gardner SF, White LM, Wang PL. (1998). Ephedrine pharmacokinet-
ics after the ingestion of nutritional supplements containing *Ephedra Sinica*
(Ma Huang), *Ther Drug Monit*, 20(4): 439–445.
Haller CA, Benowitz NL. (2000). Adverse cardiovascular and central nervous sys-
tem events associated with dietary supplements containing ephedra alkaloids,
NEJM, 343(25): 1833–1838.
Marinetti L, Lehman L, Casto B, Harshbarger K, Kubiczek P, Davis J. (2005). Over-
the-counter cold medications-postmortem findings in infants and the rela-
tionship to cause of death, *J Anal Toxicol*, 29(7): 738–743.
Ryall JE. (2008). Caffeine and ephedrine fatality, *Bull Assoc Forensic Tox*, 17(3): 13.

Ethanol

Brand names: Drinking alcohol; ethyl alcohol
Classification: CNS depressant
λ: zero-order kinetics; 0.01–0.03 g/dL per hour
V_d: 0.4–0.6 L/kg
Usual dosage: Approximately 14 g of ethanol per beverage

Blood Ethanol Content	Findings
0.05 g/dL	Less alert with impaired coordination
0.08–0.1 g/dL	Impaired coordination and judgment, decreased reaction time, loss of concentration, emotional instability
0.1–0.2 g/dL	Disorientation, decreased balance and gait functioning, slurred speech, poor sensory perception, confusion
0.2–0.3 g/dL	Stupor, lack of response to stimuli, vomiting
0.3–0.45 g/dL	Unconsciousness, depressed reflexes, coma
>0.45 g/dL	Death

Lethal Concentrations

Blood	0.3–1.8 g/dL	Liver	0.2–1.2 g/100 g
Kidney	0.3–1.0 g/100 g	Brain	0.3–0.9 g/100 g

Comments

- Metabolized by CYP 2E1
- Can develop tolerance
- Specimen to whole blood ratios at equilibrium:
  - Serum, 1.1–1.35; saliva 1.1; vitreous 1.2; bile 1.0; CSF 1.1
  - Liver 0.6; kidney 0.7; brain 0.8
- Ethanol production is possible with decomposition (0.07–0.22 g/dL), especially in the setting of diabetes (up to 0.5 g/dL)

Selected Sources

Bexar County Medical Examiner's Office data 1996–2015.
Collison IB. (2005). Elevated postmortem ethanol concentrations in an insulin-dependent diabetic, *J Anal Toxicol*, 29: 762–764.
Levine B, Caplan YH. (2006). Chapter 11: Alcohol, in *Principles of Forensic Toxicology* (2nd ed.), B. Levine (Ed.), AACC Press, Washington, DC.

Ethylene Glycol

Brand name: Component of antifreeze
Classification: Alcohol
λ: 2–5 h
V_d: 0.5–0.8 L/kg
Usual dosage: Not applicable

Source	Nontoxic	Toxic	Lethal
Blood	94–182 mg/L	50–3860 mg/L	100–23400 mg/L
Vitreous			454–10280 mg/L
Liver			300–15120 mg/kg
Kidney			225–3900 mg/kg
Brain			135–1960 mg/kg
Skeletal muscle			643–3600 mg/kg
Cardiac muscle			58 mg/kg

Comments

- Associated with calcium oxalate crystal deposition in kidneys, brain, and blood vessels

Selected Sources

Bexar County Medical Examiner's Office data 1996–2015.
Bowen DA, Minty PS, Sengupta A. (1978). Two fatal cases of ethylene glycol poisoning, *Med Sci Law*, 18(2): 101–107.
Garg U, Frazee C 3rd, Johnson L, Turner JW. (2009). A fatal case involving extremely high levels of ethylene glycol without elevation of its metabolites or crystalluria, *Am J Forensic Med Pathol*, 30(3): 273–275.
Hantson P, Vanbinst R, Mahieu P. (2002). Determination of ethylene glycol tissue content after fatal oral poisoning and pathologic findings, *Am J Forensic Med Path*, 23(2): 159–161.
Harris LS. (1980). Case 38–1979: Ethylene glycol poisoning, *NEJM*, 302(8): 466.
Klendshoj NC, Rejent TA. (1966). Tissue levels of some poisoning agents less frequently encountered, *J Forensic Sci*, 11(1): 75–80.
Moreau CL, Kerns W, Tomaszewski CA, McMartin KE, Rose SR, Ford MD, Brent J. (1998). Glycolate kinetics and hemodialysis clearance in ethylene glycol poisoning, *J Toxicol Clin Toxicol*, 36: 659–666.
Verrilli MR, Deyling CL, Pippenger CE, Van Lente F, Vidt DG, Sivak ED. (1987). Fatal ethylene glycol intoxication. Report of a case and review of the literature, *Cleveland Clinic J Med*, 54(4): 289–295.
Viinamaki J, Sajantila A, Ojanpera I. (2015). Ethylene glycol and metabolite concentrations in fatal ethylene glycol poisonings, *J Anal Toxicol*, 39(6): 481–485.

Felbamate

Brand name: Felbatol
Classification: Anticonvulsant
λ: 18–23 h
V_d: 0.7–0.9 L/kg
Usual dosage: 300–600 mg tid/qid

Source	Therapeutic/Nontoxic	Toxic	Lethal
Blood	35–157 mg/L	111–200 mg/L	No data available
Brain	13–74 mg/kg		

Comments

- Associated with hepatic necrosis and aplastic anemia
- May prolong QT interval
- Metabolized by CYP 2E1 and 3A4

Selected Sources

Adusumalli VE, Wichmann JK, Kucharczyk N, Kamin M, Sofia RD, French J. (1994). Drug concentrations in human brain tissue samples from epileptic patients treated with felbamate, *Drug Metab Dispos*, 22(1): 168–170.
Meier KH, Olson KR, Olson JL. (2005). Acute felbamate overdose with crystalluria, *Clin Tox*, 43(3): 189–192.
Nagel TR, Schunk JE. (1995). Felbamate overdose: A case report and discussion of a new antiepileptic drug, *Ped Emer Care*, 11(6): 369–371.
Rengstorff DS, Milstone AP, L Seger DL, Meredith TJ. (2000). Felbamate overdose complicated by massive crystalluria and acute renal failure, *J Tox Clin Tox*, 38(6): 667–669.
Sachdeo R, Narang-Sachdeo SK, Shumaker RC, Perhach JL, Lyness WH, Rosenberg A. (1997). Tolerability and pharmacokinetics of monotherapy felbamate doses of 1,200–6,000 mg/day in subjects with epilepsy, *Epilepsia*, 38(8): 887–892.

Fenfluramine

Brand name: Pondimin
Classification: Anorectic
λ: 13–30 h
V_d: 12–16 L/kg
Usual dosage: 20 mg tid

Source	Therapeutic/Nontoxic	Toxic	Lethal
Blood	0.04–0.3 mg/L	0.5–2.5 mg/L	6–16 mg/L
Liver			31–136 mg/kg
Kidney			27 mg/kg
Brain			42 mg/kg
Skeletal muscle			16 mg/kg
Cardiac muscle			20 mg/kg

Comments

- Not available in the United States
- Associated with pulmonary hypertension and cardiac toxicity

Selected Sources

Bryant SM, Lozada C, Wahl M. (2005). A Chinese herbal weight loss product adulterated with fenfluramine, *Ann Emerg Med*, 46(2): 208.

Fleisher MR, Campbell DB. (1969). Fenfluramine overdosage, *Lancet*, 2: 1306–1307.

Gold RG, Gordon HE, da Costa RWD, Porteous IB, Kimber KJ. (1969). Fenfluramine overdosage, *Lancet*, 2: 1306.

Kintz P, Mangin P. (1992). Toxicological findings after fatal fenfluramine self-poisoning, *Hum Exp Tox*, 11(1): 51–52.

Namera A, Yashiki M, Liu J, Okajima K, Hara K, Imamura T. (2000). Simple and simultaneous analysis of fenfluramine, amphetamine and methamphetamine in whole blood by gas chromatography-mass spectrometry after headspace-solid phase microextraction and derivatization, *Forensic Sci Intl*, 109(3): 215–223.

Sun Y. (2000). Determination of fenfluramine in corpse using GC/NPD and GC/MS, *Fa Yi Xue Za Zhi*, 16(1): 21–23.

Von Mühlendahl KE, Krienke EG. (1979). Fenfluramine poisoning, *Clin Toxicol*, 14(1): 97–106.

Fentanyl

Brand names: Duragesic, Actiq, Ionsys, Sublimaze, and Fentora
Street names: China Girl, King Ivory, Goodfellas
Classification: Opioid
λ: 3–12 h
V_d: 3–8 L/kg
Usual dosage: 12.5–100 µg/h transdermal; 200–1600 µg self-titrated oral transmucosal

Source	Therapeutic/Nontoxic	Toxic	Lethal
Blood	0.0002–0.07 mg/L	0.003–0.02 mg/L	0.003–0.2 mg/L
Liver	0.008–0.2 mg/kg		0.004–0.4 mg/kg
Kidney			0.01–0.09 mg/kg
Brain	0.003–0.01 mg/kg		0.01–0.1 mg/kg
Cardiac muscle			0.1–0.2 mg/kg
Skeletal muscle	0.004–0.05 mg/kg		0.2–0.5 mg/kg

Comments

- Tolerance can develop and should be considered when interpreting drug concentrations
- Has shown tremendous variation in postmortem concentrations with significant postmortem redistribution
- Metabolized by CYP 3A4

Selected Sources

Andresen H, Gullans A, Veselinovic M, Anders S, Schmoldt A, Iwersen-Bergmann S, Mueller A. (2012). Fentanyl: Toxic or therapeutic? Postmortem and antemortem blood concentrations after transdermal fentanyl application, *J Anal Toxicol*, 36(3): 182–194.
Bexar County Medical Examiner's Office data 1996–2015.
Luckenbill K, Thompson J, Middleton O, Kloss J, Apple F. (2008). Fentanyl postmortem redistribution: Preliminary findings regarding the relationship among femoral blood and liver and heart tissue concentrations, *J Anal Toxicol*, 32(8): 639–643.
Palamalai V, Olson KN, Kloss J, Middleton O, Mills K, Strobl AQ, Thomas LC, Apple FS. (2013). Superiority of postmortem liver fentanyl concentrations over peripheral blood influenced by postmortem interval for determination of fentanyl toxicity, *Clin Biochem*, 46(7–8): 598–602.
Thompson JG, Baker AM, Bracey AH, Seningen J, Kloss JS, Strobl AQ, Apple FS. (2007). Fentanyl concentrations in 23 postmortem cases from the Hennepin County medical examiner's office, *J Forensic Sci*, 52(4): 978–981.

Fexofenadine

Brand name: Allegra
Classification: Antihistamine
λ: 8–18 h
V_d: 5–6.5 L/kg
Usual dosage: 30–180 mg q d/bid

Source	Therapeutic/Nontoxic	Toxic	Lethal
Blood	0.05–1.5 mg/L	No data available	

Selected Sources

Robbins DK, Castles MA, Pack DJ, Bhargava VO, Weir SJ. (1998). Dose proportionality and comparison of single and multiple dose pharmacokinetics of fexofenadine (MDL 16455) and its enantiomers in healthy male volunteers, *Biopharm Drug Dispos*, 19(7): 455–463.

Russell T, Stoltz M, Weir S. (1998). Pharmacokinetics, pharmacodynamics, and tolerance of single- and multiple-dose fexofenadine hydrochloride in healthy male volunteers, *Clin Pharm Ther*, 64(6): 612–621.

Simons FER, Simons KJ. (1999). Clinical pharmacology of new histamine H receptor antagonists, *Clin Pharmacokinet*, 36(5): 329–352.

Flecainide

Brand name: Tambocor
Classification: Antiarrhythmic
λ: 11–27 h
V_d: 5–9 L/kg
Usual dosage: 50–150 mg bid

Source	Therapeutic/Nontoxic	Toxic	Lethal
Blood	0.2–4.0 mg/L	1.0–11 mg/L	7–100 mg/L
Vitreous	1.4 mg/L		8–15 mg/L
Liver			18–550 mg/kg
Kidney			28–74 mg/kg

Comments

- Concentrations may increase postmortem

Selected Sources

Benijts T, Borrey D, Lambert WE, De Letter EA, Piette MH, Van Peteghem C, De Leenheer AP. (2003). Analysis of flecainide and two metabolites in biological specimens by HPLC: Application to a fatal intoxication, *J Anal Toxicol*, 27(1): 47–52.

Bexar County Medical Examiner's Office data 1996–2015.

Forrest ARW, Marsh I, Galloway JH. (1991). A rapidly fatal overdose with flecainide, *J Anal Toxicol*, 15: 41–43.

Levine B, Chute D, Caplan YH. (1990). Flecainide intoxication, *J Anal Toxicol*, 14: 335–336.

Lynch MJ, Gerostamoulos J. (2001). Flecainide toxicity: Cause and contribution to death, *Leg Med (Tokyo)*, 3(4): 233–236.

O'Sullivan JJ, McCarthy PT, Wren C. (1995). Differences in amiodarone, digoxin, flecainide and sotalol concentrations between antemortem serum and femoral postmortem blood, *Hum Exp Toxicol*, 14(7): 605–608.

Reynolds JC, Judge BS. (2015). Successful treatment of flecainide-induced cardiac arrest with extracorporeal membrane oxygenation in the ED, *Am J Emerg Med*, 33(10): 1542.

Rogers C, Anderson DT, Ribe JK, Sathyavagiswaran L. (1993). Fatal flecainide intoxication, *J Anal Toxicol*, 17(7): 434–435.

Romain N, Giroud C, Michaud K, Augsburger M, Mangin P. (1999). Fatal flecainide intoxication, *Forensic Sci Intl*, 106(2): 115–123.

Sivalingam SK, Gadiraju VT, Hariharan MV, Atreya AR, Flack JE, Aziz H. (2013). Flecainide toxicity—Treatment with intravenous fat emulsion and extra corporeal life support, *Acute Card Care*, 15(4): 90–92.

Yoshitome K, Miyaishi S, Yamamoto Y, Ishizu H. (2008). Postmortem increase of flecainide level in cardiac blood, *J Anal Toxicol*, 32(6): 451–453.

Flunitrazepam

Brand name: Rohypnol
Street names: Forget Me Not, Mexican Valium, Roofies, Rope
Classification: Benzodiazepine
λ: 9–24 h
V_d: 3–5.5 L/kg
Usual dosage: 1–2 mg/dose

Source	Therapeutic/Nontoxic	Toxic	Lethal
Blood	0.001–0.15 mg/L 0.02–0.05 mg/L 7-AF	0.05 mg/L	0.06–0.8 mg/L 0.1–1.6 mg/L 7-AF
Kidney			0.2–0.5 mg/kg
Brain			0.3 mg/kg
Cardiac muscle			0.04 mg/kg
Skeletal muscle			0.1 mg/kg

Comments

- Active metabolite: 7-aminoflunitrazepam (7-AF)
- Often not detected on routine (immunoassay) benzodiazepine screens

Selected Sources

Balmaceda-Harmelink U, Andresen H, Tsokos M. (2004). Suicidal monointoxication with flunitrazepam. Further comment on coloration phenomena of the upper gastrointestinal tract, *Archiv für Kriminologie*, 214(3–4): 93–98.

Boxenbaum HG, Posmanter HN, Macasieb T, Geitner KA, Weinfeld RE, Moore JD. (1978). Pharmacokinetics of flunitrazepam following single- and multiple-dose oral administration to healthy human subjects, *J Pharmacokinet Biopharm*, 6(4): 283–293.

Drummer OH, Syrjanen ML, Cordner SM. (1993). Deaths involving the benzodiazepine flunitrazepam, *Am J Forensic Med Path*, 14(3): 238–243.

Hasegawa K, Wurita A, Minakata K, Gonmori K, Nozawa H, Yamagishi I, Watanabe K, Suzuki O. (2015). Postmortem distribution of flunitrazepam and its metabolite 7-aminoflunitrazepam in body fluids and solid tissues in an autopsy case: Usefulness of bile for their detection, *Leg Med (Tokyo)*, 17(5): 394–400.

Heyndrickx B. (1987). Fatal intoxication due to flunitrazepam, *J Anal Toxicol*, 11(6): 278.

Jönsson AK, Söderberg C, Espnes KA, Ahlner J, Eriksson A, Reis M, Druid H. (2014). Sedative and hypnotic drugs—Fatal and non-fatal reference blood concentrations. *Forensic Sci Int*, 236: 138–145.

Fluoride

Brand name: Component of some insecticides or rodenticides
Classification: Element
λ: 2–9 h
V_d: 0.5–0.7 L/kg
Usual dosage: Not applicable

Source	Therapeutic/Nontoxic	Toxic	Lethal
Blood	0.01–0.6 mg/L	0.3–38 mg/L	3–300 mg/L
Vitreous			2.5–12 mg/L
Liver	0.7 mg/kg		1.6–81 mg/kg
Kidney	0.8 mg/kg		2–68 mg/kg
Brain	0.6 mg/kg		2.5–20 mg/kg
Lung			17.5–19 mg/kg
Cardiac muscle	0.6 mg/kg		14 mg/kg
Skeletal muscle			4.5–18 mg/kg

Comments

- Chronic exposure can lead to skeletal fluorosis
- A toxic component of sulfuryl fluoride, which is a colorless, odorless gas used as fumigant

Selected Sources

Adelson L. (1974). Chapter XIII: Murder by poison, in *The Pathology of Homicide*, C. C. Thomas, Springfield, IL, pp. 725–875.

Ekstrand J, Alván G, Boréus LO, Norlin A. (1977). Pharmacokinetics of fluoride in man after single and multiple oral doses, *Eur J Clin Pharm*, 12(4): 311–317.

Kaa E, Selvig K, Dybdahl H, Siboni A. (1986). A case of fluoride poisoning, *Am J Forensic Med Path*, 7(3): 266–267.

Martínez MA, Ballesteros S, Piga FJ, Sánchez de la Torre C, Cubero CA. (2007). The tissue distribution of fluoride in a fatal case of self-poisoning, *J Anal Toxicol*, 31(8): 526–533.

Menchel SM, Dunn WA. (1984). Hydrofluoric acid poisoning, *Am J Forensic Med Path*, 5(3): 245–248.

Poklis A, Mackell MA. (1989). Disposition of fluoride in a fatal case of unsuspected sodium fluoride poisoning, *Forensic Sci Intl*, 41(1–2): 55–59.

Speaker JH. (1976). Determination of fluoride by specific ion electrode and report of a fatal case of fluoride poisoning, *J Forensic Sci*, 21(1): 121–126.

Fluoxetine

Brand names: Prozac and Sarafem
Classification: Antidepressant (SSRI)
λ: 1–3 d
V_d: 20–45 L/kg
Usual dosage: 20–80 mg qd

Source	Therapeutic/Nontoxic	Toxic	Lethal
Blood	0.02–1 mg/L	0.9–2 mg/L	1.3–33 mg/L
Vitreous			5.2 mg/L
Liver	0.7–29 mg/kg		54–400 mg/kg
Kidney	0.2–9 mg/kg		
Brain	0.3–12 mg/kg		
Skeletal muscle	0.6–3 mg/kg		
Cardiac muscle	0.2–8 mg/kg		

Comments

- Metabolized by CYP 2D6, 3A4, 2C9, and 2C19
- Active metabolite: Norfluoxetine
- Prolongs QT interval

Selected Sources

Bexar County Medical Examiner's Office data 1996–2015.
Cantrell FL, Vance C, Schaber B, McIntyre I. (2009). Fatal fluoxetine intoxication with markedly elevated central blood, vitreous, and liver concentrations, J Anal Toxicol, 33(1): 62–64.
Compton R, Spiller HA, Bosse GM. (2005). Fatal fluoxetine ingestion with postmortem blood concentrations, Clin Tox, 43(4): 277–279.
Johnson RD, Lewis RJ, Angier MK. (2007). The distribution of fluoxetine in human fluids and tissues, J Anal Toxicol, 31(7): 409–414.
Kincaid RL, McMullin MM, Crookham SB, Rieders F. (1990). Report of a fluoxetine fatality, J Anal Toxicol, 14(5): 327–329.
Orsulak PJ, Kenney JT, Debus JR, Crowley G, Wittman PD. (1988). Determination of the antidepressant fluoxetine and its metabolite norfluoxetine in serum by reversed-phase HPLC with ultraviolet detection, Clin Chem, 34(9): 1875–1878.
Roettger JR. (1990). The importance of blood collection site for the determination of basic drugs: A case with fluoxetine and diphenhydramine overdose, J Anal Toxicol, 14(3): 191–192.

Fluphenazine

Brand names: Prolixin
Classification: Antipsychotic
λ: 11–28 h (HCl); 7–14 d (decanoate)
V_d: 11 L/kg
Usual dosage: 2.5–10 mg bid/qd

Source	Therapeutic/Nontoxic	Toxic	Lethal
Blood	0.002–0.02 mg/L	0.05–0.1 mg/L	See comments

Comments

- Fatalities have been reported due to neuroleptic malignant syndrome
- May prolong QT interval

Selected Sources

Aruna AS, Murungi JH. (2005). Fluphenazine-induced neuroleptic malignant syndrome in a schizophrenic patient, *Ann Pharmacother*, 39(6): 1131–1135.

Basu J. (1991). An unusual presentation of neuroleptic malignant syndrome, *J Indian Med Assoc*, 89(1): 16.

Kratzsch C, Peters FT, Kraemer T, Weber AA, Maurer HH. (2003). Screening, library-assisted identification and validated quantification of fifteen neuroleptics and three of their metabolites in plasma by liquid chromatography/ mass spectrometry with atmospheric pressure chemical ionization, *J Mass Spectrum*, 38(3): 283–295.

Midha KK, Hawes EM, Hubbard JW, Korchinski ED, McKay G. (1988). Variation in the single dose pharmacokinetics of fluphenazine in psychiatric patients, *Psychopharmacology (Berl)*, 96(2): 206–211.

Roman M, Kronstrand R, Lindstedt D, Josefsson M. (2008). Quantitation of seven low-dosage antipsychotic drugs in human postmortem blood using LC-MS-MS, *J Anal Toxicol*, 32(2): 147–155.

Totten VY, Hirschenstein E, Hew P. (1994). Neuroleptic malignant syndrome presenting without initial fever: A case report, *J Emerg Med*, 12(1): 43–47.

Flurazepam

Brand names: Dalmane and Dalmadorm
Classification: Benzodiazepine
λ: 1–3 h
V_d: 3–5 L/kg
Usual dosage: 15–30 mg qHS

Source	Therapeutic/Nontoxic	Toxic	Lethal
Blood	0.0005–0.16 mg/L	0.15–0.2 mg/L	0.5–5.5 mg/L
Vitreous			1.3 mg/L
Liver			2.7–130 mg/kg
Kidney			0.9 mg/kg
Brain			0.8 mg/kg

Comments

- Active metabolite: *N*-desalkylflurazepam (therapeutic: 0.03–0.15 mg/L; toxic > 0.05 mg/L)
- Tolerance can develop and should be considered when interpreting drug concentrations

Selected Sources

Bexar County Medical Examiner's Office data 1996–2015.

Ferrara SD, Tedeschi L, Marigo M, Castagna F. (1979). Concentrations of phenobarbital, flurazepam, and flurazepam metabolites in autopsy cases, *J Forensic Sci*, 24(1): 61–69.

Martello S, Oliva A, De Giorgio F, Chiarotti M. (2006). Acute flurazepam intoxication: A case report, *Am J Forensic Med Path*, 27(1): 55–57.

McIntyre IM, Syrjanen ML, Lawrence KL, Dow CA, Drummer OH. (1994). A fatality due to flurazepam, *J Forensic Sci*, 39(6): 1571–1574.

Medical Economics. (2007). *Physicians' Desk Reference* (61st ed.), Thomson PDR, Montvale, NJ, pp. 3342–3343.

Fluvoxamine

Brand names: Luvox, Faverin, and Dumyrox
Classification: Antidepressant (SSRI)
λ: 9–28 h
V_d: 25 L/kg
Usual dosage: 50–100 mg qd/bid

Source	Therapeutic/Nontoxic	Toxic	Lethal
Blood	0.02–0.5 mg/L	0.65–1.9 mg/L	2.2–11 mg/L
Vitreous	0.16–0.28 mg/L		1.9 mg/L

Comments

- Metabolized by CYP 2D6; minor pathway CYP 1A2

Selected Sources

Banerjee AK. (1988). Recovery from prolonged cerebral depression after fluvoxamine overdose, *Br Med J* (*Clinical Research Ed.*), 296: 1774.

Bexar County Medical Examiner's Office data 1996–2015.

Garnier R, Azoyan P, Chataigner D, Taboulet P, Dellattre D, Efthymiou ML. (1993). Acute fluvoxamine poisoning, *J Intl Med Research*, 21(4): 197–208.

Hahn I, Blancaflor G, Hoffman RS, Howland MA, Nelson LS. (2000). Fluvoxamine overdose producing status epilepticus, *Clin Tox*, 38(5): 573.

Kunsman GW, Rodriguez R, Rodriguez P. (1999). Fluvoxamine distribution in postmortem cases, *Am J Forensic Med Path*, 20(1): 78–83.

Oka H, Shirakawa Y, Koyama K, Maekawa S, Hirota M, Nishizaki O. (2002). A case of fluvoxamine overdose, *Chudoku Kenkyu*, 15(1): 53–57.

Sano R, Takahashi K, Kominato Y et al. (2011). A case of fatal drug intoxication showing a high-density duodenal content by postmortem computed tomography, *Leg Med* (*Tokyo*), 13(1): 39–40.

Spigset O, Ohman R. (1996). A case of fluvoxamine intoxication demonstrating nonlinear elimination pharmacokinetics, *J Clin Psychopharmacology*, 16(3): 254–255.

Wood DM, Rajalingam Y, Greene SL, Morgan PE, Gerrie D, Jones AL. (2007). Status epilepticus following intentional overdose of fluvoxamine: A case report with serum fluvoxamine concentration, *Clin Tox*, 45(7): 791.

Gabapentin

Brand names: Neurontin and Gabarone
Classification: Anticonvulsant
λ: 5–7 h
V_d: 0.5–0.9 L/kg
Usual dosage: 100–1800 mg tid

Source	Therapeutic/Nontoxic	Toxic	Lethal
Blood	2–20 mg/L	23–104 mg/L	32–180 mg/L
Vitreous	3–8 mg/L		32 mg/L
Liver	1–10 kg/kg		26–42 mg/kg
Skeletal muscle	1.6 mg/kg		

Selected Sources

Bexar County Medical Examiner's Office data 1996–2015.

Boyd RA, Türck D, Abel RB, Sedman AJ, Bockbrader HN. (1999). Effects of age and gender on single-dose pharmacokinetics of gabapentin, *Epilepsia*, 40(4): 474–479.

Gatti G, Ferrari AR, Guerrini R, Bonanni P, Bonomi I, Perucca E. (2003). Plasma gabapentin concentrations in children with epilepsy: Influence of age, relationship with dosage, and preliminary observations on correlation with clinical response, *Ther Drug Monit*, 25(1): 54–60.

Hamm CE, Gary RD, McIntyre IM. (2016).Gabapentin concentrations and postmortem distribution, *Forensic Sci Int*, 262: 201–203.

Jones H, Aguila E, Farber HW. (2002). Gabapentin toxicity requiring intubation in a patient receiving long-term hemodialysis, *Ann Int Med*, 137(1): 74.

Middleton O. (2011). Suicide by gabapentin overdose, *J Forensic Sci*, 56(5): 1373–1375.

Spiller HA, Dunaway MD, Cutino L. (2002). Massive gabapentin and presumptive quetiapine overdose, *Vet Hum Tox*, 44(4): 243–244.

Ramoo B, Tarau MC, Dudley M, Frazee CC, Garg U. (2014). Gabapentin related fatality: A case study, *ToxTalk*, 38(1): 19–21.

Verma A, St Clair EW, Radtke RA. (1999). A case of sustained massive gabapentin overdose without serious side effects, *Ther Drug Monit*, 21(6): 615–617.

Gamma-hydroxybutyrate (GHB)

Brand name: Xyrem
Street names: Liquid Ecstasy, Georgia Home Boy, Grievous Bodily Harm,
    Max (w/ amphetamine), Special K-lube (w/ ketamine and ETOH)
Classification: Sedative/hypnotic
λ: 0.5–1 h
V_d: 0.4–1 L/kg
Usual dosage: 2–6 g/dose

Source	Therapeutic/Nontoxic	Toxic	Lethal
Blood	0.08–197 mg/L	100–340 mg/L	220–4400 mg/L
Vitreous	0.2–39 mg/L		48–2856 mg/L
Liver			52–1080 mg/kg
Brain	10–50 mg/kg		102–711 mg/kg

Comments

• Endogeneous concentrations in postmortem blood measured to be
  <50 mg/L in the absence of decomposition
• Concentrations increase with decomposition

Selected Sources

Andresen-Streichert H, Jensen P, Kietzerow J, Schrot M, Wilke N, Vettorazzi E,
    Mueller A, Iwersen-Bergmann S. (2015). Endogenous gamma-hydroxybutyric
    acid (GHB) concentrations in post-mortem specimens and further recommen-
    dation for interpretative cut-offs, *Int J Legal Med*, 129(1): 57–68.
Bexar County Medical Examiner's Office data 1996–2015.
Kintz P, Villain M, Pélissier AL, Cirimele V, Leonetti G. (2005). Unusually high
    concentrations in a fatal GHB case, *J Anal Toxicol*, 29(6): 582–585.
Korb AS, Cooper G. (2014). Endogenous concentrations of GHB in postmortem
    blood from deaths unrelated to GHB use, *J Anal Toxicol*, 38(8): 582–588.
Knudsen K, Jonsson U, Abrahamsson J. (2010). Twenty-three deaths with gamma-
    hydroxybutyrate overdose in western Sweden between 2000 and 2007, *Acta
    Anaesthesiol Scand*, 54(8): 987–992.
Mazarr-Proo S, Kerrigan S. (2005). Distribution of GHB in tissues and fluids follow-
    ing a fatal overdose, *J Anal Toxicol*, 29(5): 398–400.
Sporer KA, Chin RL, Dyer JE, Lamb R. (2003). Gamma-hydroxybutyrate serum
    levels and clinical syndrome after severe overdose, *Ann Emer Med*, 42(1): 3–8.
Zvosec DL, Smith SW, Porrata T, Strobl AQ, Dyer JE. (2011). Case series of 226
    γ-hydroxybutyrate-associated deaths: Lethal toxicity and trauma, *Am J Emerg
    Med*, 29(3): 319–332.

Guaifenesin

Brand names: Hytuss, Organidin, Humibid, and Mucinex
Classification: Expectorant
λ: 1–5 h
V_d: 1 L/kg
Usual dosage: 200–400 mg q 4 h

Source	Therapeutic/Nontoxic	Toxic	Lethal
Blood	0.1–1.4 mg/L	No data available	25[a]–27[b] mg/L
Vitreous			7[b]–9[a] mg/L
Liver			25[a] mg/kg
Brain			17[a] mg/kg

[a] Co-intoxicant: Ethanol 0.12 g/dL.
[b] Co-intoxicant: Diphenhydramine 8.8 mg/L and chlorpheniramine 0.2 mg/L.

Selected Sources

Aluri JB, Stavchansky S. (1993). Determination of guaifenesin in human plasma by liquid chromatography in the presence of pseudoephedrine, *J Pharm Biomed Anal*, 11(9): 803–808.

Eichhold TH, McCauley-Myers DL, Khambe DA, Thompson GA, Hoke SH. (2007). Simultaneous determination of dextromethorphan, dextrorphan and guaifenesin in human plasma using semi-automated liquid/liquid extraction and gradient liquid chromatography tandem mass spectrometry, *J Pharm Biomed Anal*, 43(2): 586–600.

Maynard WR, Bruce RB. (1970). GLC determination of guaiacol glyceryl ether in blood, *J Pharm Sci*, 59(9): 1346–1348.

Okic M, Johnson T, Crifasi JA, Long C, Mitchell EK. (2013). Swift onset of central nervous system depression and asystole following an overdose of guaifenesin, *J Anal Toxicol*, 37 (5): 318–319.

Wogoman H, Steinberg M, Jenkins AJ. (1999). Acute intoxication with guaifenesin, diphenhydramine, and chlorpheniramine, *Am J Forensic Med Path*, 20(2): 199–202.

Haloperidol

Brand name: Haldol
Classification: Antipsychotic
λ: 13–23 h
V_d: 11–25 L/kg
Usual dosage: 0.5–10 mg bid/tid po; 2–5 mg/dose im

Source	Therapeutic/Nontoxic	Toxic	Lethal
Blood	0.005–0.1 mg/L	0.05–0.5 mg/L[a]	0.2–1.9 mg/L
Liver	5.0 mg/kg		44 mg/kg
Kidney	0.7 mg/kg		

[a] Children.

Comments

- Associated with malignant neuroleptic syndrome
- Prolongs QT interval particularly at higher doses
- Metabolized by CYP 3A4

Selected Sources

Bexar County Medical Examiner's Office data 1996–2015.

Froemming JS, Lam YW, Jann MW, Davis CM. (1989). Pharmacokinetics of haloperidol, *Clin Pharmacokinet*, 17(6): 396–423.

Kratzsch C, Peters FT, Kraemer T, Weber AA, Maurer HH. (2003). Screening, library-assisted identification and validated quantification of fifteen neuroleptics and three of their metabolites in plasma by liquid chromatography/mass spectrometry with atmospheric pressure chemical ionization, *J Mass Spectrum*, 38(3): 283–295.

Levine BS, Wu SC, Goldberger BA, Caplan YH. (1991). Two fatalities involving haloperidol, *J Anal Toxicol*, 15(5): 282–284.

Tonkin AL, Bochner F. (1994). Therapeutic drug monitoring and patient outcome. A review of the issues, *Clin Pharmacokinet*, 27(3): 169–174.

Tsujimoto A, Tsujimoto G, Ishizaki T, Nakazawa S, Ichihashi Y. (1982). Toxic haloperidol reactions with observation of serum haloperidol concentration in two children, *Dev Pharm Ther*, 4(1–2): 12–17.

Zaleon CR, Guthrie SK. (1994). Antipsychotic drug use in older adults, *Am J Hosp Pharm*, 51(23): 2917–2943.

Heroin

Brand name: Not applicable; diacetylmorphine
Street names: Brown Sugar, H, Horse, Junk, Smack; w/ cocaine: Belushi,
  Dynamite, Eightball, Speedball, and Moonrock; w/ cocaine & LSD:
  Frisco
Classification: Opioid
λ: 2–6 min (MAM 10–40 min)
V_d: 0.5–1.5 L/kg
Usual dosage: Not applicable

Source	Chronic Use/Nontoxic		Lethal	
	Morphine	MAM	Morphine	MAM
Blood	0.01–0.2 mg/L	0.001–0.02 mg/L	0.01–1.7 mg/L	0.001–0.5 mg/L
Vitreous			0.01–0.2 mg/L	0.004–0.2 mg/L
Liver			0.04–10 mg/kg	
Kidney			0.7–1.9 mg/kg	
Brain			0.02–0.7 mg/kg	
Skeletal muscle	0.01–0.2 mg/kg	0.001–0.06 mg/kg	0.14–1 mg/kg	0.01–0.35 mg/kg

Comments

- Metabolized to morphine and 6-monoacetylmorphine (MAM); the latter is considered specific for heroin
- Codeine and papaverine, components of the poppy seed, may also be present in small amounts in heroin deaths

Selected Sources

Bexar County Medical Examiner's Office data 1996–2015.
Girardin F, Rentsch KM, Schwab MA, Maggiorini M, Pauli-Magnus C, Kullak-Ublick GA. (2003). Pharmacokinetics of high doses of intramuscular and oral heroin in narcotic addicts, *Clin Pharm Thera*, 74(4): 341–352.
Moriya F, Hashimoto Y. (1997). Distribution of free and conjugated morphine in body fluids and tissues in a fatal heroin overdose: Is conjugated morphine stable in postmortem specimens?, *J Forensic Sci*, 42(4): 736–740.
Rook EJ, Huitema ADR, Ree JM, Beijnen JH. (2006). Pharmacokinetics and pharmacokinetix variability of heroin and its metabolites: Review of the literature, *Curr Clin Pharmacol*, 1: 109–118.
Wyman J, Bultman S. (2004). Postmortem distribution of heroin metabolites in femoral blood, liver, cerebrospinal fluid, and vitreous humor, *J Anal Toxicol*, 28(4): 260–263.

Hydrocodone

Brand names: Zohydro and Hysingla; component of Vicodin, Hycodan, Lortab, Norco, and Hycotuss
Classification: Opioid
λ: 3.5–6 h
V_d: 3–5 L/kg
Usual dosage: 5–10 mg q 4–6 h

Source	Therapeutic/Nontoxic	Toxic	Lethal
Blood	0.02–0.3 mg/L	0.1–0.2 mg/L	0.2–1.6 mg/L
Vitreous	0.02–0.4 mg/L		0.5–0.9 mg/L
Skeletal muscle	0.1–0.6 mg/kg		0.3–0.9 mg/kg

Comments

- Main active metabolite: Hydromorphone
- Metabolized by CYP 2D6
- Tolerance can develop and should be considered when interpreting drug concentrations

Selected Sources

Ackerman WE, Ahmad M. (2007). Effect of cigarette smoking on serum hydrocodone levels in chronic pain patients, *J Arkansas Med Soc*, 104(1): 19–21.
Baker DD, Jenkins AJ. (2008). A comparison of methadone, oxycodone, and hydrocodone related deaths in Northeast Ohio, *J Anal Toxicol*, 32(2): 165–171.
Barnhart JW, Caldwell WJ. (1977). Gas chromatographic determination of hydrocodone in serum, *J Chromatography*, 130: 243–249.
Bexar County Medical Examiner's Office data 1996–2015.
Medical Economics. (2007). *Physicians' Desk Reference*, (61st ed.), Thomson PDR, Montvale, NJ, pp. 535–536.
Molina DK, Hargrove VM. (2011). What is the lethal concentration of hydrocodone? *Am J Forensic Med Pathol*, 32(2): 108–111.
Park JI, Nakamura GR, Griesemer EC, Noguchi TT. (1982). Hydromorphone detected in bile following hydrocodone ingestion, *J Forensic Sci*, 27(1): 223–224.
Spiller HA. (2003). Postmortem oxycodone and hydrocodone blood concentrations, *J Forensic Sci*, 48(2): 429–431.

Hydrogen Sulfide

Brand name: Not applicable
Classification: Gas
λ: Unknown
V_d: Unknown
Usual dosage: Not applicable

Source	Nontoxic		Lethal	
	Sulfide	Thiosufate	Sulfide	Thiosufate
Blood	0–0.05 mg/L	0–0.3 mg/L	0.1–32 mg/L	0.01–137 mg/L
Liver	0.02–3 mg/kg		0.4 mg/kg	
Kidney	0.02–3.6 mg/kg		0.3 mg/kg	
Lung	0.02–0.7 mg/kg		0.4 mg/kg	9.3 mg/kg
Brain	0.1–0.5 mg/kg		1–2.7 mg/kg	5 mg/kg
Skeletal muscle	0.2–0.3 mg/kg		0.16 mg/kg	

Environmental H_2S concentration	Symptoms
0.02–0.1 ppm	Notice odor; headache, nausea
5–100 ppm	Irritation of mucous membranes; offensive odor
100–500 ppm	Olfactory fatigue/paralysis; pulmonary edema
500 ppm	Unconscious within 30–60 min of exposure
700–900 ppm	Rapidly unconscious; coma
>1000 ppm	Collapse of CNS; death

Comments

- A naturally occurring gas formed by the breakdown of organic material in the absence of oxygen; it smells like rotten eggs
- Exposure can cause black discoloration of coins in pockets and green discoloration of mucus membranes
- Can be produced during decomposition
    sulfide = 2–33 mg/L blood; 1.4–3.8 mg/kg lung; 0.9 mg/kg brain; 4–6 mg/kg skeletal muscle; 2–7 mg/kg liver; and 4–5 mg/kg kidney

Selected Sources

Barbera N, Montana A, Indorato F, Arbouche N, Romano G. (2017). Evaluation of the role of toxicological data in discriminating between H_2S femoral blood concentration secondary to lethal poisoning and endogenous H_2S putrefactive production, *J Forensic Sci*, 62(2): 390–394.

Gerasimon G, Bennett S, Musser J, Rinard J. (2007). Acute hydrogen sulfide poisoning in a dairy farmer, *Clin Tox*, 45(4): 420–423.

Kage S, Kashimura S, Ikeda H, Kudo K, Ikeda N. (2002). Fatal and nonfatal poisoning by hydrogen sulfide at an industrial waste site, *J Forensic Sci*, 47(3): 652–655.

Nagata T, Kage S, Kimura K, Kudo K, Noda M. (1990). Sulfide concentrations in postmortem mammalian tissues, *J Forensic Sci*, 35(3): 706–712.

Nogué S, Pou R, Fernández J, Sanz-Gallén P. (2011). Fatal hydrogen sulphide poisoning in unconfined spaces, *Occup Med (Lond)*, 61(3): 212–214.

Hydromorphone

Brand names: Dilaudid and Palladone
Classification: Opioid
λ: 2–3.5 h
V_d: 1–3 L/kg
Usual dosage: 1–4 mg q 4–6 h

Source	Therapeutic/Nontoxic	Toxic	Lethal
Blood	0.001–0.1 mg/L	0.1 mg/L	0.06–2.9 mg/L
Vitreous	0.02–0.04 mg/L		0.06–0.2 mg/L
Liver			0.07–0.8 mg/kg
Kidney			0.1–0.7 mg/kg
Brain			0.5 mg/kg

Comments

- Metabolite of hydrocodone and morphine
- Tolerance can develop and should be considered when interpreting drug concentrations

Selected Sources

Bexar County Medical Examiner's Office data 1996–2015.
Levine B, Saady J, Fierro M, Valentour J. (1984). A hydromorphone and ethanol fatality, *J Forensic Sci*, 29(2): 655–659.
Meatherall R, Lee C, Phillips S. (2011). Accidental death from hydromorphone ingestion, *J Forensic Sci*, 56(Suppl 1): S271–S274.
Medical Economics. (2007). *Physicians' Desk Reference*, (61st ed.), Thomson PDR, Montvale, NJ, pp. 440–446.
Wallage HR, Palmentier JPFP. (2006). Hydromorphone-related fatalities in Ontario, *J Anal Toxicol*, 30(3): 202–209.
Walls HC. (1976). Hydromorphone death, *Bull Intl Assoc Forensic Tox*, 12(3): 7–8.

Hydroxychloroquine

Brand names: Plaquenil and Quineprox
Classification: Aminoquinolone (antimalarial)
λ: 16–56 d
V_d: 580–815 L/kg
Usual dosage: 200–600 mg qd

Source	Therapeutic/Nontoxic	Toxic	Lethal
Blood	0.03–39 mg/L	3–26 mg/L	36–104 mg/L
Vitreous	1.4–1.5 mg/L		3.3 mg/L
Liver			71–500 mg/kg
Skeletal muscle	3.5–4.4 mg/kg		5–60.5 mg/kg

Comments

- It can be used chronically in high doses to treat autoimmune diseases

Selected Sources

Bexar County Medical Examiner's Office data 1996–2015.
Dalley RA, Hainsworth D. (1965). Fatal plaquenil poisoning, *J Forensic Sci Soc*, 5(2): 99–101.
Gunja N, Roberts D, McCoubrie D, Lamberth P, Jan A, Simes DC, Hackett P, Buckley NA. (2009). Survival after massive hydroxychloroquine overdose, *Anaesth Intensive Care*, 37(1): 130–133.
Jordan P, Brookes JG, Nikolic G, Le Couteur DG, Le Couteur D. (1999). Hydroxychloroquine overdose: Toxicokinetics and management, *J Toxicol Clin Toxicol*, 27(7): 861–864.
Molina DK. (2012). Postmortem hydroxychloroquine concentrations in nontoxic cases, *Am J Forensic Med Pathol*, 33: 41–42.
Villalobos D. (1991). Plaquenil (hydroxychloroquine) plasmaphereses (PPR) in an overdose, *Vet Hum Toxicol*, 33(4): 364.

Hydroxyzine

Brand names: Vistaril, Atarax, and Rezine
Classification: Antihistamine/anxiolytic
λ: 5–24 h
V_d: 13–28 L/kg
Usual dosage: 25–100 mg qid

Source	Therapeutic/Nontoxic	Toxic	Lethal
Blood	0.07–0.4 mg/L	0.1–1.4 mg/L	0.7–39 mg/L
Liver	0.9–4.9 mg/kg		15–414 mg/kg
Brain			0.5–163 mg/kg

Comments

- Active metabolite: Cetirizine
- May prolong QT interval

Selected Sources

Druid H, Holmgren P. (1997). A compilation of fatal and control concentrations of drugs in postmortem femoral blood, *J Forensic Sci*, 42(1): 79–87.

Johnson GR. (1982). A fatal case involving hydroxyzine, *J Anal Toxicol*, 6(2): 69–70.

Kintz P, Godelar B, Mangin P. (1990). Gas chromatographic identification and quantification of hydroxyzine: Application in a fatal self-poisoning, *Forensic Sci Intl*, 48(2): 139–143.

McIntyre IM, Mallett P, Trochta A, Morhaime J. (2013). Hydroxyzine distribution in postmortem cases and potential for redistribution, *Forensic Sci Int*, 231(1–3): 28–33.

Péhourcq F. (2004). A simple high-performance liquid chromatographic method for detection of hydroxyzine in human plasma after overdose, *J Pharm Tox Methods*, 50(1): 41–44.

Spiehler V, Fukumoto R. (1984). Another fatal case involving hydroxyzine, *J Anal Toxicol*, 8(5): 242–243.

Ibogaine

Brand name: Not applicable
Classification: Hallucinogen/stimulant
λ: 4–7 h
V_d: 13 L/kg
Usual dosage: 500–1000 mg/dose

Source	Nontoxic		Lethal	
	Ibogaine	Noribogaine	Ibogaine	Noribogaine
Blood	0.03–1.3 mg/L	0.02–1.2 mg/L	0.2–11 mg/L	11–22 mg/L
Liver			0.2–40 mg/kg	6–50 mg/kg
Kidney			0.3–7 mg/kg	4–5 mg/kg
Brain			12–19 mg/kg	19 mg/kg
Skeletal muscle			7.7 mg/kg	3.4 mg/kg

Comments

- It is an alkaloid from *Tabernanthe iboga* used to treat opiate withdrawal
- Active metabolite: Noribogaine
- Metabolized by CYP 2D6 as well as CYP 2C9 and 3A4
- Associated with cardiac arryhthymias

Selected Sources

Alper KR, Stajić M, Gill JR. (2012). Fatalities temporally associated with the ingestion of ibogaine, *J Forensic Sci*, 57(2): 398–412.

Cienki J, Mash D, Hearn W. (2001). Ibogaine fatalities, *Clin Tox*, 39(5): 547.

Kontrimaviciūte V, Mathieu O, Mathieu-Daudé J-C, Vainauskas P, Casper T, Baccino E. (2006). Distribution of ibogaine and noribogaine in a man following a poisoning involving root bark of the tabernanthe iboga shrub, *J Anal Toxicol*, 30(7): 434–440.

Maas U, Strubelt S. (2006). Fatalities after taking ibogaine in addiction treatment could be related to sudden cardiac death caused by autonomic dysfunction, *Med Hypotheses*, 67(4): 960–964.

Mazoyer C, Carlier J, Boucher A, Péoc'h M, Lemeur C, Gaillard Y. (2013). Fatal case of a 27-year-old male after taking iboga in withdrawal treatment: GC-MS/MS determination of ibogaine and ibogamine in iboga roots and postmortem biological material, *J Forensic Sci*, 58(6): 1666–1672.

Papadodima SA, Dona A, Evaggelakos CI, Goutas N, Athanaselis SA. (2013). Ibogaine related sudden death: A case report, *J Forensic Leg Med*, 20(7): 809–811.

Ibuprofen

Brand names: Advil and Motrin
Classification: NSAID
λ: 1.5–2.5 h
V_d: 0.1–0.2 L/kg
Usual dosage: 200–800 mg q 4–6 h

Source	Therapeutic/Nontoxic[a]	Toxic[a]	Lethal
Blood	10–60 mg/L	100–740 mg/L	81–1050 mg/L
Liver			74–942 mg/kg
Brain			284 mg/kg
Skeletal muscle	1–14 mg/kg		232 mg/kg

[a] Renal toxicity can occur in the therapeutic range.

Comments

- Metabolized by CYP 2C9 as well as 2C8, 2C19 and 3A4
- May cause renal failure

Selected Sources

Bexar County Medical Examiner's Office data 1996–2015.
Holubek W, Stolbach A, Nurok S, Lopez O, Wetter A, Nelson L. (2007). A report of two deaths from massive ibuprofen ingestion, *J Med Toxicol*, 3(2): 52–55.
Kunsman GW, Rohrig TP. (1993). Tissue distribution of ibuprofen in a fatal overdose, *Am J Forensic Med Path*, 14(1): 48–50.
Lee CY, Finkler A. (1986). Acute intoxication due to ibuprofen overdose, *Arch Path Lab Med*, 110(8): 747–749.
Levine M, Khurana A, Ruha AM. (2010). Polyuria, acidosis, and coma following massive ibuprofen ingestion, *J Med Toxicol*, 6(3): 315–317.
Lodise M, De-Giorgio F, Rossi R, d'Aloja E, Fucci N. (2012). Acute ibuprofen intoxication: Report on a case and review of the literature, *Am J Forensic Med Pathol*, 33(3): 242–246.
Seifert SA, Bronstein AC, McGuire T. (2000). Massive ibuprofen ingestion with survival, *J Tox Clin Tox*, 38(1): 55–57.
Wood DM, Monaghan J, Streete P, Jones AL, Dargan PI. (2006). Fatality after deliberate ingestion of sustained-release ibuprofen: A case report, *Critical Care*, 10(2): R44.

Imipramine

Brand name: Tofranil
Classification: Antidepressant (TCA)
λ: 7–18 h
V_d: 10–25 L/kg
Usual dosage: 75–300 mg qd

Source	Therapeutic/Nontoxic	Toxic	Lethal
Blood	0.1–0.4 mg/L	0.5–6 mg/L	1.2–28 mg/L
Vitreous			1.9 mg/L
Liver	9.7–17 mg/kg		24–293 mg/kg
Kidney			37–55 mg/kg
Brain			28–67 mg/kg
Skeletal muscle	0.1–0.4 mg/kg		9.6–24 mg/kg
Cardiac muscle			19–65 mg/kg

Comments

- Active metabolite: Desipramine
- May prolong QT interval
- Metabolized by CYP 2D6, 1A2, 2C19, and 3A4

Selected Sources

Apple FS. (1989). Postmortem tricyclic antidepressant concentrations: Assessing cause of death using parent drug to metabolite ratio, *J Anal Toxicol*, 13(4): 197–198.

Bexar County Medical Examiner's Office data 1996–2015.

Biggs JT, Spiker DG, Petit JM, Ziegler VE. (1977). Tricyclic antidepressant overdose: Incidence of symptoms, *JAMA*, 238(2): 135–138.

Hanzlick RL. (1984). Postmortem blood concentrations of parent tricyclic antidepressant (TCA) drugs in 11 cases of suicide, *Am J Forensic Med Path*, 5(1): 11–13.

Kinoshita H, Taniguchi T, Kubota A, Nishiguchi M, Ouchi H, Minami T. (2005). An autopsy case of imipramine poisoning, *Am J Forensic Med Path*, 26(3): 271–274.

Quai I, Fagarasan M, Fagarasan E, Usineviciu I. (1985). Tricyclic antidepressants: Clinical considerations, tissue concentrations and morphopathologic changes in the acute intoxication in man, *Acta Medicinae Legalis et Socialis*, 35(1): 107–109.

Sandeman DJ, Alahakoon TI, Bentley SC. (1997). Tricyclic poisoning—successful management of ventricular fibrillation following massive overdose of imipramine, *Anaesth Intensive Care*, 25(5): 542–545.

Insulin

Brand names: Novolog, Humalog, Lantus, Novolin, and Humulin
Classification: Hormone
λ: 0.5–24 h (depending upon formulation)
V_d: 0.2–0.4 L/kg
Usual dosage: 0.3–1.5 units/kg/d SC in divided doses

Source	Therapeutic/Nontoxic[a]	Toxic[a]	Lethal[a]
Blood	6–70 μunit/mL[b] 50–1100 μunit/mL[c]	300–7390 μunit/mL	297–7500 μunit/mL
Vitreous			29–103 μunit/mL
Kidney	See comments		384 μunit/g
Skeletal muscle			373 μunit/g
Adipose tissue	10–75 μunit/g		581–74000 μunit/g

[a] All concentrations are for free insulin.
[b] Nondiabetics.
[c] Insulin-dependent diabetics.

Comments

- Insulin is not found in significant concentrations in tissue (liver, brain, or kidney)
- Testing may be performed by immunoassay, but immunoassay cannot differentiate endogeneous vs exogeneous insulin
  - Not all immunoassays crossreact with all synthetic insulins
  - It can get interference from anti-insulin antibodies
- It can test for c-peptide to differentiate endogeneous and exogeneous insulin
  - Normal insulin:c-peptide ratio, <1 (0.1–0.5); exogeneous insulin ratio, >1
- Insulin concentrations may decrease postmortem due to degradation, particularly in hemolyzed samples

Selected Sources

Batalis NI, Prahlow JA. (2004). Accidental insulin overdose, *J Forensic Sci*, 49(5): 1117–1120.

Bauman WA, Yalow RS. (1981). Insulin as a lethal weapon, *J Forensic Sci*, 26(3): 594–598.

Hess C, Madea B, Daldrup T, Musshoff F. (2013). Determination of hypoglycaemia induced by insulin or its synthetic analogues post mortem, *Drug Test Anal*, 5(9–10): 802–807.

Matsumura M, Nakashima A, Tofuku Y. (2000). Electrolyte disorders following massive insulin overdose in a patient with type 2 diabetes, *Int Med*, 39(1): 55–57.

Palmiere C, Sabatasso S, Torrent C, Rey F, Werner D, Bardy D. (2015). Post-mortem determination of insulin using chemiluminescence enzyme immunoassay: Preliminary results, *Drug Test Anal*, 7(9): 797–803.

Shibutani Y, Ogawa C. (2000). Suicidal insulin overdose in a type 1 diabetic patient: Relation of serum insulin concentrations to the duration of hypoglycemia, *J Diabetes Complications*, 14(1): 60–62.

Sunderland N, Wong S, Lee CK. (2016). Fatal insulin overdoses: Case report and update on testing methodology, *J Forensic Sci*, 61(Suppl 1): S281–S284.

Thevis M, Thomas A, Schänzer W, Ostman P, Ojanperä I. (2012). Measuring insulin in human vitreous humour using LC-MS/MS, *Drug Test Anal*, 4(1): 53–56.

Isopropanol

Brand name: Rubbing alcohol
Classification: Solvent/disinfectant
λ: 3–4 h
V_d: 0.6 L/kg
Usual dosage: 60%–70% aqueous solution applied topically

Source	Nontoxic	Toxic	Lethal
Blood	8–390 mg/L	150–5600 mg/L	1000–4780 mg/L
Vitreous	8–500 mg/L		1300–2440 mg/L
Liver			53[a]–2660 mg/kg

[a] 30 h after ingestion.

Comments

- Metabolized to and from acetone
- Can be created antemortem and postmortem
- Often a component of embalming fluid in which acetone is absent
- Concentrations <1000 mg/L usually do NOT indicate exposure/intoxication
- Concentrations >1000 mg/L and isopropanol: Acetone ratio > 1 usually indicative of intoxication

Selected Sources

Alexander CB, McBay AJ, Hudson RP. (1982). Isopropanol and isopropanol deaths-ten years' experience, *J Forensic Sci*, 27(3): 541–548.
Bexar County Medical Examiner's Office data 1996–2015.
Gaulier JM, Lamballais F, Yazdani F, Lachâtre G. (2011). Isopropyl alcohol concentrations in postmortem tissues to document fatal intoxication, *J Anal Toxicol*, 35(4): 254–255.
Jenkins AJ, Merrick TC, Oblock JM. (2008). Evaluation of isopropanol concentrations in the presence of acetone in postmortem biological fluids, *J Anal Toxicol*, 32(8): 719–720.
Molina DK. (2010). A characterization of sources of isopropanol detected on postmortem toxicologic analysis, *J Forensic Sci*, 55(4): 998–1002.
Pappas AA, Ackerman BH, Olsen KM, Taylor EH. (1991). Isopropanol ingestion: A report of six episodes with isopropanol and acetone serum concentration time data, *J Tox Clin Tox*, 29(1): 11–21.

Lamotrigine

Brand name: Lamictal
Classification: Anticonvulsant
λ: 12–74 h
V_d: 0.9–1 L/kg
Usual dosage: 25–200 mg bid

Source	Therapeutic/Nontoxic	Toxic	Lethal
Blood	0.9–14 mg/L	16–78 mg/L	36[a]–85 mg/L
Vitreous	0.3–1.8 mg/L		
Liver	16–36 mg/kg		220 mg/kg
Kidney			110 mg/kg
Skeletal muscle			324 mg/kg

[a] 19 h post ingestion.

Comments

• Can cause hepatic necrosis

Selected Sources

Algahtani HA, Aldarmahi AA, Al-Rabia MW, Almalki WH, Bryan Young G. (2014). Generalized myoclonus and spasticity induced by lamotrigine toxicity: A case report and literature review. *Clin Neuropharmacol*, 37(2): 52–54.

Bexar County Medical Examiner's Office data 1996–2015.

Buckley NA, Whyte IM, Dawson AH. (1993). Self-poisoning with lamotrigine, *Lancet*, 342: 1552–1553.

Chavez P, Casso Dominguez A, Herzog E. (2015). Evolving electrocardiographic changes in lamotrigine overdose: A case report and literature review, *Cardiovasc Toxicol*, 15(4): 394–398.

Dinnerstein E, Jobst BC, Williamson PD. (2007). Lamotrigine intoxication provoking status epilepticus in an adult with localization-related epilepsy, *Arch Neurol*, 64: 1344–1346.

French LK, McKeown NJ, Hendrickson RG. (2011). Complete heart block and death following lamotrigine overdose, *Clin Toxicol*, 49(4): 330–333.

Levine B, Jufer RA, Smialek JE. (2000). Lamotrigine distribution in two postmortem cases, *J Anal Toxicol*, 24(7): 635–637.

O'Donnell J, Bateman DN. (2000). Lamotrigine overdose in an adult, *J Toxicol Clin Toxicol*, 38(6): 659–660.

Pricone MG, King CV, Drummer OH, Opeskin K, McIntyre IM. (2000). Postmortem investigation of lamotrigine concentrations, *J Forensic Sci*, 45(1): 11–15.

Schwartz MD, Geller RJ. (2007). Seizures and altered mental status after lamotrigine overdose, *Ther Drug Monit*, 29(6): 843–844.

Levetiracetam

Brand name: Keppra
Classification: Anticonvulsant
λ: 5–11 h
V_d: 0.5–0.7 L/kg
Usual dosage: 500–1500 mg bid

Source	Therapeutic/Nontoxic	Toxic	Lethal
Blood	3–70 mg/L	72–463 mg/L	190–230 mg/L[a]
Liver	14 mg/kg		
Kidney	1.8 mg/kg		
Skeletal muscle	76 mg/kg		

[a] Suicide with tape over mouth in presence of heart disease and benzoylecgonine.

Selected Sources

Barrueto F, Williams K, Howland MA, Hoffman RS, Nelson LS. (2002). A case of levetiracetam (Keppra) poisoning with clinical and toxicokinetic data, *J Tox Clin Tox*, 40(7): 881–884.

Bexar County Medical Examiner's Office data 1996–2015.

Bishop-Freeman SC, Kornegay NC, Winecker RE. (2012). Postmortem levetiracetam (Keppra®) data from North Carolina, *J Anal Toxicol*, 36(6): 422–428.

Levine B, Phipps RJ, Naso C, Fahie K, Fowler D. (2010). Tissue distribution of newer anticonvulsant drugs in postmortem cases, *J Anal Toxicol*, 34(8): 506–509.

Page CB, Mostafa A, Saiao A, Grice JE, Roberts MS, Isbister GK. (2016). Cardiovascular toxicity with levetiracetam overdose, *Clin Toxicol*, 54(2): 152–154.

Patsalos PN. (2004). Clinical pharmacokinetics of levetiracetam, *Clin Pharmacokinet*, 43(11): 707–724.

Medical Economics. (2007). *Physicians' Desk Reference*, (61st ed.), Thomson PDR, Montvale, NJ, pp. 3314–3320.

Levorphanol

Brand name: Levo-Dromoran
Classification: Opioid
λ: 11–16 h
V_d: 10–13 L/kg
Usual dosage: 1–3 mg/dose

Source	Therapeutic/Nontoxic	Toxic	Lethal
Blood	0.005–0.1 mg/L	0.1 mg/L	0.8–2.7 mg/L
Liver			5.4–11 mg/kg
Kidney			1–3.4 mg/kg
Brain			1.8 mg/kg

Comments

- Tolerance can develop and should be considered when interpreting drug concentrations

Selected Sources

Bednarczyk LR. (1979). A death due to levorphanol, *J Anal Toxicol*, 3: 217–219.
Dixon R, Crews T, Inturrisi C, Foley K. (1983). Levorphanol: pharmacokinetics and steady-state plasma concentrations in patients with pain, *Res Comm Chem Path Pharm*, 41(1): 3–17.
Turner JE, Richards RG. (1977). A fatal case involving levorphanol, *J Anal Toxicol*, 1: 103–104.

Lisdexamfetamine

Brand name: Vyvanse
Classification: Stimulant
λ: 0.4–0.6 h
V_d: Unknown
Usual dosage: 30–70 mg qd

Source	Therapeutic/Nontoxic	Toxic	Lethal
Blood	0.03–0.05 mg/L LDA 0.02–0.15 mg/L amphet	See amphetamine	

Comments

- Prodrug of d-amphetamine
- Rapidly converted to amphetamine in the gastrointestinal tract

Selected Sources

Krishnan SM, Stark JG. (2008). Multiple daily-dose pharmacokinetics of lisdexamfetamine dimesylate in healthy adult volunteers, *Curr Med Res Opin*, 24(1): 33–40.

Krishnan S, Zhang Y. (2008). Relative bioavailability of lisdexamfetamine 70-mg capsules in fasted and fed healthy adult volunteers and in solution: A single-dose, crossover pharmacokinetic study, *J Clin Pharm*, 48(3): 293–302.

Medical Economics. (2008). *Physicians' Desk Reference*, (62nd ed.), Thomson PDR, Montvale, NJ, pp. 3115–3118.

Protiti Sarker P, Baker G, Hwang R. (2010). Case notes: Pharmacokinetic and pharmacodynamic distribution of lisdexamfetamine (A prodrug of dextroamphetamine) in a postmortem sample, *ToxTalk*, 34(4): 9.

Lithium

Brand names: Lithate, Lithobid, and Eskalith
Classification: Mood stabilizer (antimanic)
λ: 20–50 h
V_d: 0.3–1 L/kg
Usual dosage: 600–1800 mg qd

Source	Therapeutic/Nontoxic	Toxic	Lethal
Blood	0.6–1.2 mEq/L	1.5–8.2 mEq/L	1.9–14 mEq/L
Liver			0.2–9.4 mEq/kg
Kidney			0.6–9.3 mEq/kg
Brain			0.4–6.5 mEq/kg
Skeletal muscle			0.4–2.2 mEq/kg
Cardiac muscle			0.4 mEq/kg

Comments

- To convert mEq/L to mg/L, multiply by 6.94; mEq/L = mmol/L for lithium

Selected Sources

Achong MR, Fernandez PG, McLeod PJ. (1975). Fatal self-poisoning with lithium carbonate, *Can Med Assoc J*, 112(7): 868–870.

Amdisen A, Gottfries CG, Jacobsson L, Winblad B. (1974). Grave lithium intoxication with fatal outcome, *Acta Psychiatrica Scandinavica*, 255S: 25–33.

Chapman AJ, Lewis G. (1972). Iatrogenic lithium poisoning: A case report with necropsy findings, *J Oklahoma State Med Assoc*, 65(12): 491–494.

Giusti GV, Chiarotti M. (1981). Two cases of death associated with the use of lithium carbonate, *Am J Forensic Med Path*, 2(1): 41–43.

Lum G. (2007). Lithium self-intoxication treated with hemodialysis, *Lab Med*, 38(11): 667–668.

Medical Economics. (2006). *Physicians' Desk Reference*, (60th ed.), Thomson PDR, Montvale, NJ, pp. 1670–1672.

Winek CL, Bricker JD, Fochtman FW. (1980). Lithium intoxication. A case study, *Forensic Sci Intl*, 15(3): 227–231.

Loperamide

Brand name: Imodium
Classification: Antidiarrheal and synthetic opioid
λ: 9–40 h
V_d: Unknown
Usual dosage: 2–4 mg/dose

Source	Therapeutic/Nontoxic	Toxic	Lethal
Blood	0.0002–0.07 mg/L	0.02–0.2 mg/L	0.08–2.6 mg/L
Liver	0.15–0.6 mg/kg		0.5–30 mg/kg
Kidney			8.5 mg/kg

Comments

- Abused for opiate effects
- Metabolized by CYP2C8 and CYP3A4 as well as CYP2B6 and CYP2D6
- May prolong QT interval

Selected References

Bishop-Freeman SC, Feaster MS, Beal J, Miller A, Hargrove RL, Brower JO, Winecker RE. (2016). Loperamide-related deaths in North Carolina, *J Anal Toxicol*, 40(8): 677–686.

Dierksen J, Gonsoulin M, Walterscheid JP. (2015). Poor man's methadone: A case report of loperamide toxicity, *Am J Forensic Med Pathol*, 36(4): 268–270.

Eggleston W, Marraffa JM, Stork CM, Mercurio-Zappala M, Su MK, Wightman RS, Cummings KR, Schier JG. (2016). Notes from the field: Cardiac dysrhythmias after loperamide abuse—New York, 2008–2016, *MMWR Morb Mortal Wkly Rep*, 65(45): 1276–1277.

Gray TR, Carr K. (2013). Fatal overdose with the anti-diarrheal medication loperamide. *Presented at the American Academy of Forensic Sciences Annual Meeting*, Washington, DC.

Sklerov J, Levine B, Moore KA, Allan C, Fowler D. (2005). Tissue distribution of loperamide and N-desmethylloperamide following a fatal overdose, *J Anal Toxicol*, 29(7): 750–754.

Loratadine

Brand names: Claritin and Tavist
Classification: Antihistamine
λ: 4–15 h
V_d: 119 L/kg
Usual dosage: 5–10 mg qd

Source	Therapeutic/Nontoxic	Toxic	Lethal
Blood	0.007–0.03 mg/L	0.3 mg/L[a]	No data available

[a] 3 y/o pediatric patient.

Comments

- Active metabolite: Desloratadine
- Metabolized by CYP 3A4 and 2D6
- May cause tachycardia and increased blood pressure; may be hepatotoxic

Selected Sources

Cobb DB, Watson WA, Fernández MC. (2001). High-dose loratadine exposure in a six-year-old child, *Vet Hum Tox*, 43(3): 163–164.

Gokel Y, Satar S, Sebe A. (2000). Loratadine toxicity, *Am J Emer Med*, 18(5): 639–640.

Manning BH, Tai W, Kearney TE. (2006). A prospective investigation of pediatric loratadine ingestions: Establishing a dose-response relationship, *Clin Tox*, 44(5): 767.

Schiano TD, Bellary SV, Cassidy MJ, Thomas RM, Black M. (1996). Subfulminant liver failure and severe hepatotoxicity caused by loratadine use, *Ann Int Med*, 125(9): 738–740.

Simons FER, Simons KJ. (1999). Clinical pharmacology of new histamine H receptor antagonists, *Clin Pharmacokinet*, 36(5): 329–352.

Ten Eick AP, Blumer JL, Reed MD. (2001). Safety of antihistamines in children, *Drug Safety*, 24(2): 119–147.

Lorazepam

Brand name: Ativan
Classification: Benzodiazepine
λ: 9–40 h
V_d: 1–1.5 L/kg
Usual dosage: 0.5–5 mg bid/tid

Source	Therapeutic/Nontoxic	Toxic	Lethal
Blood	0.01–0.2 mg/L	0.3–0.6 mg/L	See below[a]
Liver	0.1 mg/kg		
Skeletal muscle	0.05–0.2 mg/kg		

[a] All fatalities are mixed with other drugs; no pure fatalities reported.

Comments

- Tolerance can develop and should be considered when interpreting drug concentrations

Selected Sources

Allen MD, Greenblatt DJ, LaCasse Y, Shader RI. (1980). Pharmacokinetic study of lorazepam overdosage, Am J Psychiatry, 137(11): 1414–1415.

Bexar County Medical Examiner's Office data 1996–2015.

Filter ER, Gorczynski L, Fernandes JR. (2007). Fatal intoxication with a selective serotonin reuptake inhibitor, lorazepam, and codeine, Am J Forensic Med Path, 28(4): 361–363.

Kyriakopoulos AA, Greenblatt DJ, Shader RI. (1978). Clinical pharmacokinetics of lorazepam: A review, J Clin Psychiatry, 39(10 Pt 2): 16–23.

Loxapine

Brand names: Loxitane and Loxapac
Classification: Antipsychotic
λ: 1–14 h
V_d: Unknown
Usual dosage: 10–50 mg bid

Source	Therapeutic/Nontoxic	Toxic	Lethal
Blood	0.01–0.2 mg/L	0.2–0.7 mg/L	1.2–9.5 mg/L
Vitreous			1.5 mg/L
Liver	0.7 mg/kg		12–150 mg/kg
Brain	0.3 mg/kg		4.5 mg/kg

Comments

- Active metabolites: Amoxapine and 8-hydroxyloxapine
- Can cause seizures

Selected Sources

Bexar County Medical Examiner's Office data 1996–2015.
Cooper TB, Bost R, Sunshine I. (1981). Postmortem blood and tissue levels of loxapine and its metabolites, *J Anal Toxicol*, 5(2): 99–100.
Lutz T, Jindal SP, Cooper TB. (1982). GLC/MS assay for loxapine in human biofluids and tissues with deuterium labeled analog as an internal standard, *J Anal Toxicol*, 6(6): 301–304.
Mazzola CD, Miron S, Jenkins AJ. (2000). Loxapine intoxication: Case report and literature review, *J Anal Toxicol*, 24(7): 638–641.
Reynolds PC, Som CW, Hermann PW. (1979). Loxapine fatalities, *Clin Tox*, 14(2): 181–185.
Simpson GM, Cooper TB, Lee JH, Young MA. (1978). Clinical and plasma level characteristics of intramuscular and oral loxapine, *Psychopharmacology*, 56(2): 225–232.
Vasiliades J, Sahawneh TM, Owens C. (1979). Determination of therapeutic and toxic concentrations of doxepin and loxapine using gas-liquid chromatography with a nitrogen-sensitive detector, and gas chromatography-mass spectrometry of loxapine, *J Chromatography A*, 164(4): 457–470.

Lurasidone

Brand name: Latuda
Classification: Atypical antipsychotic
λ: 18–37 h
V_d: 80–90 L/kg
Usual dosage: 20–160 mg/d

Source	Therapeutic/Nontoxic	Toxic	Lethal
Blood	0.05–0.2 mg/L	No data available	

Comments

- May cause neuroleptic malignant syndrome
- Metabolized by CYP 3A4
- Active metabolite: ID-14283

Selected Sources

Bexar County Medical Examiner's Office data 1996–2016.
Katteboina MY, Pilli NR, Mullangi R, Seelam RR, Satla SR. (2016). LC-MS/MS assay for the determination of lurasidone and its active metabolite, ID-14283 in human plasma and its application to a clinical pharmacokinetic study, *Biomed Chromatogr*, 30(7): 1065–1074.
Latuda package insert, Sunovion Pharmaceuticals, 2017.
Molnar GP, Grimsich LC, Catalano G, Catalano MC. (2014). Acute lurasidone overdose, *J Clin Psychopharmacol*, 34(6): 768–770.
Preskorn S, Ereshefsky L, Chiu YY, Poola N, Loebel A. (2013). Effect of food on the pharmacokinetics of lurasidone: Results of two randomized, open-label, crossover studies, *Hum Psychopharmacol*, 28(5): 495–505.

Lysergic Acid Diethylamide

Brand name: Not applicable
Street names: LSD, Acid; w/ heroin: Frisco Special and Frisco Speedball
Classification: Hallucinogen
λ: 1–5 h
V_d: 0.2–1 L/kg
Usual dosage: 100–500 mg/dose

Source	Nontoxic	Toxic	Lethal
Blood	0.001–0.007 mg/L	0.001–0.03 mg/L	0.005–0.01 mg/L

Comments

- Fatalities are usually due to the injuries sustained while intoxicated rather than due to the drug itself

Selected Sources

Dolder PC, Schmid Y, Steuer AE, Kraemer T, Rentsch KM, Hammann F, Liechti ME. (2017). Pharmacokinetics and pharmacodynamics of lysergic acid diethylamide in healthy subjects, *Clin Paharmacokinet*, 56(10): 1219–1230.

Fysh RR, Oon MC, Robinson KN, Smith RN, White PC, Whitehouse MJ. (1985). A fatal poisoning with LSD, *Forensic Sci Intl*, 28(2): 109–113.

Karch SB (Ed). (1998). *Drug Abuse Handbook*. CRC Press, Boca Raton, FL, pp. 188–189.

Klock JC, Boerner U, Becker CE. (1975). Coma, hyperthermia, and bleeding associated with massive LSD overdose, a report of eight cases, *Clin Tox*, 8(2): 191–203.

Passie T, Halpern JH, Stichtenoth DO, Emrich HM, Hintzen A. (2008). The pharmacology of lysergic acid diethylamide: A review, *CNS Neurosci Ther*, 14(4): 295–314.

Smith RN, Robinson K. (1985). Body fluid levels of lysergide (LSD), *Forensic Sci Intl*, 28(3–4): 229–237.

Meclizine

Brand names: Antivert and Vertin-32
Classification: Antihistamine
λ: 5–6 h
V_d: Unknown
Usual dosage: 25–50 mg qd

Source	Therapeutic/Nontoxic	Toxic	Lethal
Blood	0.005–2.2 mg/L	No data available	

Selected Sources

Bexar County Medical Examiner's Office data 1996–2015.
Fouda HG, Falkner FC, Hobbs DC, Luther EW. (1978). Selected ion monitoring assay for meclizine in human plasma, *Biomed Mass Spectrometry*, 5(8): 491–494.

Melperone

Brand names: Buronil, Burnil, and Eunerpan
Classification: Antipsychotic
λ: 2–6 h
V_d: 7–10 L/kg
Usual dosage: 100–300 mg qd

Source	Therapeutic/Nontoxic	Toxic	Lethal
Blood	0.01–0.4 mg/L	1.8 mg/L	1–23 mg/L

Selected Sources

Borgström L, Larsson H, Molander L. (1982). Pharmacokinetics of parenteral and oral melperone in man, *Eur J Clin Pharm*, 23(2): 173–176.

Druid H, Holmgren P. (1997). A compilation of fatal and control concentrations of drugs in postmortem femoral blood, *J Forensic Sci*, 42(1): 79–87.

Kratzsch C, Peters FT, Kraemer T, Weber AA, Maurer HH. (2003). Screening, library-assisted identification and validated quantification of fifteen neuroleptics and three of their metabolites in plasma by liquid chromatography/mass spectrometry with atmospheric pressure chemical ionization, *J Mass Spectrum*, 38(3): 283–295.

Stein S, Schmoldt A, Schulz M. (2000). Fatal intoxication with melperone, *Forensic Sci Intl*, 113(1–3): 409–413.

Memantine

Brand name: Namenda
Classification: Anti-Alzheimer's agent
λ: 60–100 h
V_d: 9–11 L/kg
Usual dosage: 5–20 mg/d

Source	Therapeutic/Nontoxic	Toxic	Lethal
Blood	0.03–4 mg/L	12 mg/L	No data available
Vitreous	0.39 mg/L		
Liver	3–25.5 mg/kg		
Skeletal muscle	1.2 mg/kg		

Selected Sources

Bexar County Medical Examiner's Office data 2004–2015.

Bynum N, Poklis J, Garside D, Winecker R. (2007). Postmortem memantine concentrations, *J Anal Toxicol*, 31(4): 233–236.

Cekmen N, Bedel P, Erdemli O. (2011). A memantin HCL intoxication responsive to plasmapheresis therapy, *Bratisl Lek Listy*, 112(9): 527–529.

Moritoyo T, Hasunuma T, Harada K et al. (2012). Effect of renal impairment on the pharmacokinetics of memantine. *J Pharmacol Sci*, 119(4): 324–329.

Nagasawa S, Yajima D, Torimitsu S, Chiba F, Iwase H. (2015). Postmortem memantine concentration in a non-intoxication case, and the possibility of postmortem redistribution: A case report, *Forensic Sci Int*, 257: e12–e15.

Meperidine

Brand names: Demerol and Pethidine
Classification: Opioid
λ: 3–8 h
V_d: 3–6 L/kg
Usual dosage: 50–150 mg q 3–4 h

Source	Therapeutic/Nontoxic	Toxic	Lethal
Blood	0.2–2 mg/L	0.5–6.5 mg/L	6–21 mg/L
Liver	0.8–5 mg/kg		2–30 mg/kg
Brain			9.5–17 mg/kg
Skeletal muscle			19 mg/kg

Comments

- Active metabolite: Normeperidine
- Tolerance can develop and should be considered when interpreting drug concentrations
- Metabolized by CYP 2B6

Selected Sources

Armstrong PJ, Bersten A. (1986). Normeperidine toxicity, *Anesthesia Analgesia*, 65(5): 536–538.

Bexar County Medical Examiner's Office data 1996–2015.

Daldrup T. (2004). A forensic toxicological dilemma: The interpretation of post-mortem concentrations of central acting analgesics, *Forensic Sci Intl*, 142(2–3): 157–160.

Geller RJ. (1993). Meperidine in patient-controlled analgesia: A near-fatal mishap, *Anesthesia Analgesia*, 76(3): 655–657.

Holmberg L, Odar-Cederlöf I, Boréus LO, Heyner L, Ehrnebo M. (1982). Comparative disposition of pethidine and norpethidine in old and young patients, *Eur J Clin Pharm*, 22(2): 175–179.

Karunatilake H, Buckley NA. (2007). Severe neurotoxicity following oral meperi-dine (pethidine) overdose, *Clin Tox*, 45(2): 200–201.

Siek TJ. (1978). The analysis of meperidine and normeperidine in biological speci-mens, *J Forensic Sci*, 23(1): 6–13.

Meprobamate

Brand name: Miltown
Classification: Sedative/anxiolytic
λ: 6–16 h
V_d: 0.7 L/kg
Usual dosage: 200–600 mg tid/qid

Source	Therapeutic/Nontoxic	Toxic	Lethal
Blood	7–25 mg/L	30–208 mg/L	73–346 mg/L
Vitreous	8–20 mg/L		
Liver			58–600 mg/kg
Kidney			285–550 mg/kg
Brain			118–140 mg/kg
Skeletal muscle	4–20 mg/kg		93 mg/kg

Comments

- Metabolite of carisoprodol
- Tolerance can develop and should be considered when interpreting drug concentrations

Selected Sources

Bailey DN, Shaw RF. (1983). Interpretation of blood glutethimide, meprobamate, and methyprylon concentrations in nonfatal and fatal intoxications involving a single drug, *J Tox Clin Tox*, 20(2): 133–145.

Bévalot F, Gustin MP, Cartiser N, Le Meur C, Malicier D, Fanton L. (2011). Interpretation of drug concentrations in an alternative matrix: The case of meprobamate in vitreous humor, *Int J Legal Med*, 125(3): 463–468.

Bexar County Medical Examiner's Office data 1996–2015.

Felby S. (1970). Concentrations of meprobamate in the blood and liver following fatal meprobamate poisoning, *Acta Pharmacologica et Toxicologica*, 28(5): 334–337.

Gaillard Y, Billault F, Pépin G. (1997). Meprobamate overdosage: A continuing problem. Sensitive GC-MS quantitation after solid phase extraction in 19 fatal cases, *Forensic Sci Intl*, 86(3): 173–180.

Jenis EH, Payne RJ, Goldbaum LR. (1969). Acute meprobamate poisoning. A fatal case following a lucid interval, *JAMA*, 207(2): 361–362.

Kintz P, Tracqui A, Mangin P, Lugnier AA. (1988). Fatal meprobamate self-poisoning, *Am J For Med Path*, 9(2): 139–140.

Maddock RK, Bloomer HA. (1967). Meprobamate overdosage. Evaluation of its severity and methods of treatment, *JAMA*, 201(13): 999–1003.

Mescaline

Brand name: Not applicable
Alternate names: Mescalito and peyote
Classification: Psychodelic
λ: 6 h
V_d: Unknown
Usual dosage: 100–500 mg/dose

Source	Intoxicated	Lethal
Blood	0.48–15 mg/L	See comments
Vitreous	2.4 mg/L	
Liver	8–71 mg/kg	
Brain	2.2 mg/kg	

Comments

- Fatalities usually secondary to trauma while intoxicated
- From *Lophophora williamsii* (cactus)

Selected Sources

Henry JL, Epley J, Rohrig TP. (2003). The analysis and distribution of mescaline in postmortem tissues, *J Anal Toxicol*, 27(6): 381–382.
Nolte KB, Zumwalt RE. (1999). Fatal peyote ingestion associated with mallory-weiss lacerations, *Western J Med*, 170(6): 328.

Metaxalone

Brand name: Skelaxin
Classification: Muscle relaxant
λ: 1–15 h
V_d: Unknown
Usual dosage: 800 mg tid/qid

Source	Therapeutic/Nontoxic	Toxic	Lethal
Blood	0.7–9 mg/L	20 mg/L	14–63 mg/L
Vitreous			3–12 mg/L
Liver	9–14 mg/kg		45–195 mg/kg
Brain			74–163 mg/kg

Selected Sources

Bexar County Medical Examiner's Office data 1996–2015.

Bishop-Freeman SC, Miller A, Hensel EM, Winecker RE. (2015). Postmortem metaxalone (Skelaxin®) data from North Carolina, *J Anal Toxicol*, 39(8): 629–636.

Curtis B, Jenkins C, Wiens AL. (2015). A rare fatality attributed solely to metaxalone, *J Anal Toxicol*, 39(4): 321–323.

Gruszecki AC, Kloda S, Simmons GT, Daly TM, Hardy RW, Robinson CA. (2003). Polydrug fatality involving metaxalone, *J Forensic Sci*, 48(2): 432–434.

Moore KA, Levine B, Fowler D. (2005). A fatality involving metaxalone, *Forensic Sci Intl*, 149(2–3): 249–251.

Medical Economics. (2006). *Physicians' Desk Reference*, (60th ed.) Thomson PDR, Montvale, NJ, pp. 1685–1686.

Poklis JL, Ropero-Miller JD, Garside D, Winecker RE. (2004). Metaxalone (Skelaxin)-related death, *J Anal Toxicol*, 28(6): 537–541.

Stephenson J. (2009). Case Notes #1: Driving under the influence of a possibly lethal level of metaxalone, *ToxTalk*, 33(3): 8.

Methadone

Brand names: Dolophine and Methadose
Street name: Frizzies
Classification: Opioid
λ: 8–59 h
V_d: 3–5 L/kg
Usual dosage: 30–120 mg qd

Source	Therapeutic/Nontoxic	Toxic	Lethal
Blood	0.01–1.8 mg/L	0.2–1 mg/L	0.2–6.1 mg/L
Vitreous			0.03–0.08 mg/L
Liver	0.3–8.4 mg/kg		0.8–50 mg/kg
Kidney			1–8 mg/kg
Brain	0.1–0.5 mg/kg		0.4–3.7 mg/kg
Skeletal muscle	0.4–1.3 mg/kg		0.5–1.7 mg/kg

Comments

- Tolerance can develop and should be considered when interpreting drug concentrations
- Metabolized by CYP 3A4, 2B6, 1A2, and 2D6
- Prolongs QT interval, especially dangerous at initiation of treatment

Selected Sources

Bastos ML, Galante L. (1976). Toxicological findings in victims of traumatic deaths, *J Forensic Sci*, 21(1): 176–186.

Bexar County Medical Examiner's Office data 1996–2015.

Li L, Levine B, Smialek JE. (2000). Fatal methadone poisoning in children: Maryland 1992–1996, *Subst Use Misuse*, 35(9): 1141–1148.

Okic M, Cnossen L, Crifasi JA, Long C, Mitchell EK. (2013). Opioid overdose mortality in Kansas, 2001–2011: Toxicologic evaluation of intent, *J Anal Toxicol*, 37(9): 629–635.

Robinson AE, William FM. (1971). The distribution of methadone in man, *J Pharm Pharmacol*, 23: 353–358.

Wolf BC, Lavezzi WA, Sullivan LM, Flannagan LM. (2004). Methadone-related deaths in palm beach county, *J Forensic Sci*, 49(2): 375–378.

Ziminski KR, Wemyss CT, Bidanset JH, Manning TJ, Lukash L. (1984). Comparative study of postmortem barbiturates, methadone, and morphine in vitreous humor, blood, and tissue, *J Forensic Sci*, 29(3): 903–909.

Methamphetamine

Brand names: Desoxyn (d-isomer); Vicks inhaler (l-isomer)
Street names: Chalk, Crystal, Ice, Meth, Speed, and Crank
Classification: Stimulant
λ: 6–15 h
V_d: 3–7 L/kg
Usual dosage: 2–5 mg tid/qid

Source	Therapeutic/Nontoxic	Toxic	Lethal
Blood	0.02–7.8 mg/L	0.15–9.5 mg/L	0.1–69 mg/L
Liver			0.2–206 mg/kg
Kidney			0.2–87 mg/kg
Brain			0.2–144 mg/kg
Skeletal muscle	0.2–2.8 mg/kg		0.5–48 mg/kg

Comments

- Most laboratories do not differentiate between l- and d-isomers
  - D-methamphetamine illicit; also metabolite of benzphetamine and famprofazone
  - L-methaphetamine; metabolite of selegiline and famprofazone
- Active metabolite: Amphetamine
- Deaths are due to cardiovascular and CNS effects

Selected Sources

Bexar County Medical Examiner's Office data 1996–2015.
Cravey RH, Jain NC. (1973). Testing for amphetamines: Medico-legal hazards, *Trauma*, 15(1): 49–94.
de la Torre R, Farré M, Navarro M, Pacifici R, Zuccaro P, Pichini S. (2004). Clinical pharmacokinetics of amfetamine and related substances: Monitoring in conventional and non-conventional matrices, *Clin Pharmacokinetics*, 43(3): 157–185.
Fukunaga T, Mizoi Y, Adachi J, Tatsuno Y, Fujiwara S, Ueno Y. (1987). Methamphetamine concentrations in blood, urine, and organs of fatal cases after abuse, *Nihon Hoigaku Zasshi*, 41(4): 328–334.
Inoue H, Ikeda N, Kudo K, Ishida T, Terada M, Matoba R. (2006). Methamphetamine-related sudden death with a concentration which was of a "Toxic Level", *Legal Med*, 8(3): 150–155.
Logan BK, Fligner CL, Haddix T. (1998). Cause and manner of death in fatalities involving methamphetamine, *J Forensic Sci*, 43(1): 28–34.

Methanol

Brand name: Wood alcohol
Alternate name: Methyl alcohol
Classification: Solvent
λ: 2–24 h
V_d: 0.4–0.7 L/kg
Usual dosage: Not applicable

Source	Nontoxic	Toxic	Lethal
Blood	1.5–30 mg/L	200–1300 mg/L	230–7400 mg/L
Vitreous			120–3960 mg/L
Liver			56–4490 mg/kg
Kidney			67–5130 mg/kg
Brain			450–1811 mg/kg
Skeletal muscle			1120 mg/kg
Cardiac muscle			3450 mg/kg

Comments

- The presence of methanol and formaldehyde indicates embalming solution
- Formaldehyde is not part of methanol metabolism

Selected Sources

Andresen H, Schmoldt H, Matschke J, Flachskampf FA, Turk EE. (2008). Fatal methanol intoxication with different survival times—Morphological findings and postmortem methanol distribution, *Forensic Sci Int*, 179(2–3): 206–210.
Bexar County Medical Examiner's Office data 1996–2015.
Chen NBW, Donoghue ER, Schaffer MI. (1985). Methanol intoxication: Distribution in postmortem tissues and fluids including vitreous humor, *J Forensic Sci*, 30(1): 213–216.
Pla A, Hernandez AF, Gil F, Garcia-Alonso M, Villanueva E. (1991). A fatal case of oral ingestion of methanol. Distribution in postmortem tissues and fluids including pericardial fluid and vitreous humor, *Forensic Sci Int*, 49(2): 193–196.
Tonkabony SEH. (1975). Post-mortem blood concentration of methanol in 17 cases of fatal poisoning from contraband vodka, *Forensic Sci*, 6(1–2): 1–3.

Methocarbamol

Brand name: Robaxin
Classification: Muscle relaxant
λ: 1–2 h
V_d: Unknown
Usual dosage: 1500 mg qid

Source	Therapeutic/Nontoxic	Toxic	Lethal[a]
Blood	16–40 mg/L	250 mg/L	257–525[a] mg/L
Liver			459 mg/kg
Kidney			83 mg/kg

[a] Co-intoxiant: ethanol, 0.13 g/dL.

Selected Sources

Ferslew KE, Hagardorn AN, McCormick WF. (1990). A fatal interaction of metho-carbamol and ethanol in an accidental poisoning, *J Forensic Sci*, 35(2): 477–482.

Kemal M, Imami R, Poklis A. (1982). A fatal methocarbamol intoxication, *J Forensic Sci*, 27(1): 217–222.

Schulz M, Schmoldt A. (2003). Therapeutic and toxic blood concentrations of more than 800 drugs and other xenobiotics, *Pharmazie*, 58(7): 447–474.

Sica DA, Comstock TJ, Davis J, Manning L, Powell R, Melikian A. (1990). Pharmacokinetics and protein binding of methocarbamol in renal insufficiency and normals, *Eur J Clin Pharm*, 39(2): 193–194.

Methylenedioxymethamphetamine

Brand name: Not applicable
Street names: MDMA, XTC, Ecstasy, and Adam
Classification: Hallucinogenic stimulant
λ: 6–9 h
V_d: 5.5–8.5 L/kg
Usual dosage: 50–150 mg/dose

Source	Nontoxic	Toxic	Lethal
Blood	0.1–2.4 mg/L	0.3–1.8 mg/L	0.5–54 mg/L
Vitreous			1.9–3.4 mg/L
Liver			5.1–34 mg/kg
Kidney			12–14 mg/kg
Brain			8.4–17 mg/kg
Skeletal muscle			4.5 mg/kg
Cardiac muscle			14 mg/kg

Comments

- Active metabolite: MDA (methylenedioxyamphetamine; λ 6–10 h)
- Metabolized by CYP 2D6

Selected Sources

Bexar County Medical Examiner's Office data 1996–2015.

de Letter EA, Clauwaert KM, Lambert WE, van Bocxlaer JF, de Leenheer AP, Piette MHA. (2002). Distribution study of 3,4-methylenedioxymethamphetamine and 3,4-methylenedioxyamphetamine in a fatal overdose, *J Anal Toxicol*, 26(2): 113–118.

Fernando T, Gilbert JD, Carroll CM, Byard RW. (2012). Ecstasy and suicide, *J Forensic Sci*, 57(4): 1137–1139.

García-Repetto R, Moreno E, Soriano T, Jurado C, Giménez MP, Menéndez M. (2003). Tissue concentrations of MDMA and its metabolite MDA in three fatal cases of overdose, *Forensic Sci Intl*, 135(2): 110–114.

Greene SL, Dargan PI, O'connor N, Jones AL, Kerins M. (2003). Multiple toxicity from 3,4-Methylenedioxymethamphetamine ("Ecstasy"), *Am J Emer Med*, 21(2): 121–124.

Milroy CM. (2011). "Ecstasy" associated deaths: What is a fatal concentration? Analysis of a case series, *Forensic Sci Med Pathol*, 7(3): 248–252.

Rohrig TP, Prouty RW. (1992). Tissue distribution of Methylenedioxymethamphetamine, *J Anal Toxicol*, 16(1): 52–53.

Methylphenidate

Brand names: Ritalin, Methylin, and Concerta
Street names: Uppers and West Coast
Classification: Stimulant
λ: 2–4 h
V_d: 11–33 L/kg
Usual dosage: 5–20 mg bid/tid

Source	Therapeutic/Nontoxic	Toxic	Lethal
Blood	0.01–0.2 mg/L	0.1–18 mg/L	1–3 mg/L
Vitreous			0.8 mg/L
Liver			0.3–3.6 mg/kg
Kidney			3.0 mg/kg

Selected Sources

Bexar County Medical Examiner's Office data 1996–2015.

Cantrell FL, Ogera P, Mallett P, McIntyre IM. (2014). Fatal oral methylphenidate intoxication with postmortem concentrations, *J Forensic Sci*, 59(3): 847–849.

de la Torre R, Farré M, Navarro M, Pacifici R, Zuccaro P, Pichini S. (2004). Clinical pharmacokinetics of amfetamine and related substances: Monitoring in conventional and non-conventional matrices, *Clin Pharmacokinetics*, 43(3): 157–185.

Klampfl, KK. (2010). Case report: Intoxication with high dose of long-acting meth-ylphenidate (Concerta®) in a suicidal 14-year-old girl. *Atten Def Hype Dis*, 2(4): 221–224.

Levine B, Caplan YH, Kauffman G. (1986). Fatality resulting from methylphenidate overdose, *J Anal Toxicol*, 10(5): 209–210.

Markowitz JS, Logan BK, Diamond F, Patrick KS. (1999). Detection of the novel metabolite ethylphenidate after methylphenidate overdose with alcohol coingestion, *J Clin Psychopharmacol*, 19(4): 362–366.

Schubert B. (1970). Detection and identification of methylphenidate in human urine and blood samples, *Acta Chemica Scandinavica*, 24(2): 433–438.

Metoclopramide

Brand name: Reglan
Classification: Gastrointestinal motility agent; dopaminergic antagonist
λ: 3–9 h
V_d: 2–5 L/kg
Usual dosage: 5–15 mg q 6 h

Source	Therapeutic/Nontoxic	Toxic	Lethal
Blood	0.03–3 mg/L	No data available	4.4[a]–46[b] mg/L
Liver	0.8 mg/kg		

[a] Co-intoxicant: Diltiazem, 8.5 mg/L.
[b] Co-intoxicants: Propranolol, 60 mg/L; doxepin, 72 mg/L.

Comments

- Associated with dystonias and neuroleptic malignant syndrome

Selected Sources

Batts KF, Munter DW. (1998). Metoclopramide toxicity in an infant, *Pediatr Emerg Care*, 14(1): 39–41.

Beno JM, Nemeth DR. (1991). Diltiazem and metoclopramide overdose, *J Anal Toxicol*, 15(5): 285–287.

Bexar County Medical Examiner's Office data 1996–2015.

Friedman LS, Weinrauch LA, D'Elia JA. (1987). Metoclopramide-induced neuroleptic malignant syndrome, *Arch Intern Med*, 147(8): 1495–1497.

Saller R, Hellenbrecht D, Briemann L, Hellstern A, Hess H, Mitrou P, Hodgson M, Achtert G, Brockmann P, Hausleiter HJ. (1985). Metoclopramide kinetics at high-dose infusion rates for prevention of cisplatin-induced emesis, *Clin Pharmacol Ther*, 37(1): 43–47.

Metoprolol

Brand names: Toprol and Lopressor
Classification: β-blocker
λ: 3–9 h
V_d: 2.5–6 L/kg
Usual dosage: 25–400 mg qd

Source	Therapeutic/Nontoxic	Toxic	Lethal
Blood	0.07–2.6 mg/L	7.8–18 mg/L	3.5–75 mg/L
Vitreous			3.3–42 mg/L
Liver	0.01–1.6 mg/kg		6.3–230 mg/kg
Kidney	0.01–0.5 mg/kg		7.1 mg/kg
Brain	0.04–0.2 mg/kg		
Skeletal muscle	0.2–2.3 mg/kg		

Comments

- Metabolized by CYP 2D6

Selected Sources

Bexar County Medical Examiner's Office data 1996–2015.
Moller BH. (1976). Letter: Massive intoxication with metoprolol, *Br Med J*, 1(6003): 222.
Oertel R, Pietsch J, Arenz N, Zeitz SG, Goltz L, Kirch W. (2011). Distribution of metoprolol, tramadol, and midazolam in human autopsy material, *J Chromatogr A*, 1218(30): 4988–4994.
Page C, Hacket LP, Isbister GK. (2009). The use of high-dose insulin-glucose euglycemia in beta-blocker overdose: A case report, *J Med Toxicol*, 5(3): 139–143.
Quarterman CP, Kendall MJ, Jack DB. (1981). The effect of age on the pharmacokinetics of metoprolol and its metabolites, *Br J Clin Pharm*, 11(3): 287–294.
Riker CD, Wright RK, Matusiak W, de Tuscan BE. (1987). Massive metoprolol ingestion associated with a fatality—A case report, *J Forensic Sci*, 32(5): 1447–1452.
Shore ET, Cepin D, Davidson MJ. (1981). Metoprolol overdose, *Ann Emer Med*, 10(10): 524–527.
Sire S. (1976). Metoprolol intoxication, *Lancet*, 2(7995): 1137.
Stajić M, Granger RH, Beyer JC. (1984). Fatal metoprolol overdose, *J Anal Toxicol*, 8(5): 228–230.
Wallin CJ, Hulting J. (1983). Massive metoprolol poisoning treated with prenalterol, *Acta Med Scand*, 214(3): 253–255.

Mexiletine

Brand name: Mexitil
Classification: Antiarrhythmic
λ: 8–16 h
V_d: 5–7 L/kg
Usual dosage: 100–300 tid

Source	Therapeutic/Nontoxic	Toxic	Lethal
Blood	0.4–5.7 mg/L	2–20 mg/L	10–45 mg/L
Vitreous			9–17 mg/L
Liver			55–433 mg/kg
Kidney			170 mg/kg
Brain			84 mg/kg

Comments

- Metabolized by CYP2D6 and CYP1A2

Selected Sources

Bexar County Medical Examiner's Office data 1996–2015.

Bradbrook ID, Feldschreiber P, Morrison PJ, Rogers HJ, Spector RG. (1981). Plasma mexiletine concentrations following combined oral and intramuscular administration. *Eur J Clin Pharmacol*, 19(4): 301–304.

Hruby K, Missliwetz J. (1985). Poisoning with oral antiarrhythmic drugs. *Int J Clin Pharmacol Ther Toxicol*, 23(5): 253–257.

Kempton J, Manoukian A, Levine B, Smialek J. (1994). A mexiletine intoxication, *J Anal Toxicol*, 18(6): 346–347.

Nelson LS, Hoffman RS. (1994). Mexiletine overdose producing status epilepticus without cardiovascular abnormalities, *J Toxicol Clin Toxicol*, 32(6): 731–736.

Nora MO, Chandrasekaran K, Hammill SC, Reeder GS. (1989). Prolongation of ventricular depolarization. ECG manifestation of mexiletine toxicity, *Chest*, 95(4): 925–928.

Rohrig TP, Harty LE. (1994). Postmortem distribution of mexiletine in a fatal overdose, *J Anal Toxicol*, 18(6): 354–356.

Midazolam

Brand name: Versed
Classification: Benzodiazepine
λ: 1–4 h
V_d: 1–6 L/kg
Usual dosage: 1–5 mg/dose

Source	Therapeutic/Nontoxic	Toxic	Lethal
Blood	0.03–1.4 mg/L	0.2–2 mg/L	2.4–62 mg/L
Liver	0.02–1.7 mg/kg		
Kidney	0.01–1.1 mg/kg		
Brain	0.1–4.4 mg/kg		
Skeletal muscle	0.3 mg/kg		

Comments

- Metabolized by CYP 3A

Selected Sources

Bexar County Medical Examiner's Office data 1996–2015.

Blumer JL. (1998). Clinical pharmacology of midazolam in infants and children, *Clin Pharmacokinetics*, 35(1): 37–47.

Druid H, Holmgren P. (1997). A compilation of fatal and control concentrations of drugs in postmortem femoral blood, *J Forensic Sci*, 42(1): 79–87.

Malinovsky JM, Populaire C, Cozian A, Lepage JY, Lejus C, Pinaud M. (1995). Premedication with midazolam in children. Effect of intranasal, rectal and oral routes on plasma midazolam concentrations, *Anaesthesia*, 50(4): 351–354.

Michalodimitrakis M, Christodoulou P, Tsatsakis AM, Askoxilakis I, Stiakakis I, Mouzas I. (1999). Death related to midazolam overdose during endoscopic retrograde cholangiopancreatography, *Am J ForensicMed Path*, 20(1): 93–97.

Oertel R, Pietsch J, Arenz N, Zeitz SG, Goltz L, Kirch W. (2011). Distribution of metoprolol, tramadol, and midazolam in human autopsy material, *J Chromatogr A*, 1218(30): 4988–4994.

Milnacipran

Brand name: Ixel
Classification: Antidepressant (SNRI)
λ: 7–8 h
V_d: 3–8 L/kg
Usual dosage: 50–100 mg qd

Source	Therapeutic/Nontoxic	Toxic	Lethal
Blood	0.1–0.4 mg/L	3–8 mg/L	20–22 mg/L

Selected Sources

Fanton L, Bevalot F, Grait H, Le Meur C, Gaillard Y, Malicier D. (2008). Fatal intoxication with milnacipran, *J Forensic Legal Med*, 15: 388–390.

Levine M, Truitt CA, O'Connor AD. (2011). Cardiotoxicity and serotonin syndrome complicating a milnacipran overdose, *J Med Toxicol*, 7(4): 312–316.

Puozzo C, Panconi E, Deprez D. (2002). Pharmacology and pharmacokinetics of milnacipran, *Intl Clin Psychopharmacology*, 17(1): S25–S35.

Rop PP, Sournac MH, Burle J, Fornaris M, Coiffait PE. (2002). Blood concentration of milnacipran in a case of a fatal automobile accident, *J Anal Toxicol*, 26(2): 123–126.

Mirtazapine

Brand name: Remeron
Classification: Antidepressant (tetracyclic)
λ: 12–20 h
V_d: 9–15 L/kg
Usual dosage: 15–45 mg qd

Source	Therapeutic/Nontoxic	Toxic	Lethal
Blood	0.02–0.3 mg/L	0.2–2.3 mg/L	2.6–9.3 mg/L
Vitreous	0.01–0.04 mg/L		
Liver	0.2–0.5 mg/kg		1.7–15 mg/kg
Kidney			1.8 mg/kg
Brain			0.6 mg/kg
Skeletal muscle	0.3 mg/kg		0.3 mg/kg

Comments

- Metabolized by CYP 1A2 and 2D6

Selected Sources

Bexar County Medical Examiner's Office data 2003–2015.
Gerritsen AW. (1997). Safety in overdose of mirtazapine: A case report, *J Clin Psych*, 58(6): 271.
Holzbach R, Jahn H, Pajonk FG, Mähne C. (1998). Suicide attempts with mirtazapine overdose without complications, *Biol Psychiatry*, 44(9): 925–926.
Kirkton C, McIntyre IM. (2006). Therapeutic and toxic concentrations of mirtazapine, *J Anal Toxicol*, 30(9): 687–691.
Nikolaou P, Dona A, Papoutsis I, Spiliopoulou C, Maravelias C. (2009). Death due to mirtazapine overdose, *Clin Toxicol*, 47: 453.
Retz W, Maier S, Maris F, Rösler M. (1998). Non-fatal mirtazapine overdose, *Intl Clin Psychopharmacology*, 13(6): 277–279.
Timmer CJ, Sitsen JM, Delbressine LP. (2000). Clinical pharmacokinetics of mirtazapine, *Clin Pharmacokinetics*, 38(6): 461–474.
Vignali C, Groppi A, Brandolini F, Avato FM, Talarico A, Gaudio RM, Morini L. (2017). Mirtazapine fatal poisoning, *Forensic Sci Intl*, 276: e8–e12.
Wenzel S, Aderjan R, Mattern R, Pedal I, Skopp G. (2006). Tissue distribution of mirtazapine and desmethylmirtazapine in a case of mirtazapine poisoning, *Forensic Sci Intl*, 156(2–3): 229–236.

Mitragynine

Brand names: Kratom and Biak-Biak
Classification: Alkaloid
λ: 23 h
V_d: 38 L/kg
Usual dosage: 5–45 mg per dose

Source	Therapeutic/Nontoxic	Toxic	Lethal
Blood	0.02–0.5 mg/L		0.2–1.1 mg/L
Vitreous			0.05–0.15 mg/L
Liver			0.1–0.4 mg/kg
Kidney			0.2 mg/kg[a]
Spleen			0.2 mg/kg[a]
Lung			0.01 mg/kg[a]

[a] Co-intoxicants present.

Comments

- From *Mitragyna speciosa*; leaves often chewed, smoked or brewed into a tea; also sold in capsule and liquid form
- Low to moderate doses can cause mild stimulant effects; higher doses produce opioid-like effects

Selected Sources

Bexar County Medical Examiner's Office data 2003–2015.

Holler JM, Vorce SP, McDonough-Bender PC, Magluilo J, Solomon CJ, Levine B. (2011). A drug toxicity death involving propylhexadrine and mitragynine, *J Anal Toxicol*, 35: 54–59.

Karinen R, Fosen JT, Rogde S, Vindenes V. (2014). An accidental poisoning with mitragynine, *Forensic Sci Intl*, 24: e29–e32.

Kronstrand R, Roman M, Thelander G, Eriksson A. (2011). Unintentional fatal intoxications with mitragynine and o-desmethyltramadol from herbal blend krypton, *J Anal Toxicol*, 35: 242–247.

McIntyre IM, Trochta A, Stolberg S, Campman SC. (2015). Mitragynine "Kratom" related fatality: A case report with postmortem concentrations, *J Anal Toxicol*, 39: 152–153.

Nelson JL, Lapoint J, Hodgman MJ, Aldous KM. (2010). Seizure and coma following kratom (Mitragynia specios korth) exposure, *J Med Toxicol*, 6: 424–426.

Trakulsrichai S, Sathirakul K, Auparakkitanon S, Krongvorakul J, Sueajai J, Noumjad N, Sukasem C, Wananukul W. (2015). Pharmacokinetics of mitragynine in man, *Drug Des Devel Ther*, 9: 2421–2429.

Mizolastine

Brand names: Mizollen and Mistamine
Classification: Antihistamine
λ: 6–17 h
V_d: 1–1.5 L/kg
Usual dosage: 10 mg qd

Source	Therapeutic/Nontoxic	Toxic	Lethal
Blood	0.05–2.5 mg/L	No data available	

Selected Sources

Lebrun-Vignes B, Diquet B, Chosidow O. (2001). Clinical pharmacokinetics of mizolastine, *Clin Pharmacokinetics*, 40(7): 501–507.

Rosenzweig P, Thebault JJ, Caplain H, Dubruc C, Bianchetti G, Fuseau E. (1992). Pharmacodynamics and pharmacokinetics of mizolastine (SL 85.0324), a new nonsedative H1 antihistamine, *Ann Allergy*, 69(2): 135–139.

Simons FER, Simons KJ. (1999). Clinical pharmacology of new histamine H receptor antagonists, *Clin Pharmacokinetics*, 36(5): 329–352.

Moclobemide

Brand names: Aurorix and Manerix
Classification: Antidepressant (MAOI)
λ: 1–4 h
V_d: 0.8–1 L/kg
Usual dosage: 100–200 mg bid/tid

Source	Therapeutic/Nontoxic	Toxic	Lethal
Blood	0.2–2 mg/L	3–61 mg/L	15–498 mg/L
Liver			45–432 mg/kg
Kidney			57 mg/kg
Cardiac muscle			21 mg/kg

Comments

- Not available in the United States
- Metabolized by CYP 2C18, CYP 2D6, and CYP 1A2

Selected Sources

Bleumink GS, van Vliet AC, van der Tholen A, Stricker BH. (2003). Fatal combination of moclobemide overdose and whisky, *Neth J Med*, 61(3): 88–90.

Caccia S. (1998). Metabolism of the newer antidepressants. An overview of the pharmacological and pharmacokinetic implications, *Clin Pharmacokinetics*, 34(4): 281–302.

Camaris C, Little D. (1997). A fatality due to moclobemide, *J Forensic Sci*, 42(5): 954–955.

Gaillard Y, Pépin G. (1997). Moclobemide fatalities: Report of two cases and analytical determinations by GC-MS and HPLC-PDA after solid-phase extraction, *Forensic Sci Intl*, 87(3): 239–248.

Giroud C, Horisberger B, Eap C, Augsburger M, Ménétrey A, Baumann P. (2004). Death following acute poisoning by moclobemide, *Forensic Sci Intl*, 140(1): 101–107.

Iwersen S, Schmoldt A. (1996). Three suicide attempts with moclobemide, *J Tox Clin Toxicol*, 34(2): 223–225.

Raaflaub J, Haefelfinger P, Trautmann KH. (1984). Single-dose pharmacokinetics of the MAO-inhibitor moclobemide in man, *Drug Res/Arzneimittel-Forschung*, 34(1): 80–82.

Rogde S, Hilberg T, Teige B. (1999). Fatal combined intoxication with New Antidepressants. Human cases and an experimental study of postmortem moclobemide redistribution, *Forensic Sci Intl*, 100(1–2): 109–116.

Modafinil

Brand name: Provigil
Classification: Stimulant
λ: 10–17 h
V_d: 0.8 L/kg
Usual dosage: 200–400 mg qd

Source	Therapeutic/Nontoxic	Toxic	Lethal
Blood	3–17 mg/L	13[a]–18[b] mg/L	No data available

[a] 18 h after intial presentation.
[b] Co-intoxicant: escitolopram.

Comments

- Armodafinil (Nuvigil) is R-enantiomer of modafinil; most laboratories cannot differentiate between the two

Selected Sources

Gresham C, Wallace KL. (2008). Challenges in detection and confirmation of modafinil use, *Clin Toxicol*, 46: 642.

Hellriegel ET, Arora S, Nelson M, Robertson P. (2002). Steady-state pharmacokinetics and tolerability of modafinil administered alone or in combination with dextroamphetamine in healthy volunteers, *J Clin Pharm*, 42(4): 450–460.

Johnson-Arbor K, Christ M. (2008). Prolonged delirium in a pediatric patient after modafinil and escitalopram ingestion, *Clin Toxicol*, 46: 623.

Robertson P, Hellriegel ET. (2003). Clinical pharmacokinetic profile of modafinil, *Clin Pharmacokinetics*, 42(2): 123–137.

Molindone

Brand name: Moban
Classification: Antipsychotic
λ: 2 h
V_d: 3–6 L/kg
Usual dosage: 5–50 mg tid/qid

Source	Therapeutic/Nontoxic	Toxic	Lethal
Blood	0.005–0.4 mg/L	0.15 mg/L	6–19 mg/L
Liver			26–69 mg/kg

Selected Sources

Bexar County Medical Examiner's Office data 1996–2015.

Flammia DD, Bateman HR, Saady JJ, Christensen ED. (2004). Tissue distribution of molidone in a multidrug overdose, *J Anal Toxicol*, 28(6): 533–536.

Johnson SB, Alvarez WA, Freinhar JP. (1986). A case of massive rhabdomyolysis following molindone administration, *J Clin Psychiatry*, 47(12): 607–608.

Zetin M, Cramer M, Garber D, Plon L, Paulshock M, Hoffman HE. (1985). Bioavailability of oral and intramuscular molindone hydrochloride in schizophrenic patients, *Clin Therapeutics*, 7(2): 169–175.

Morphine

Brand names: MS Contin, Roxanol, Kadian, Avinza, and Oramorph
Street names: Dreamer, Hows, M, and Miss Emma
Classification: Opiate
λ: 1.3–6.7 h
V_d: 2–5 L/kg
Usual dosage: 5–30 mg q 4–8 h

Source	Therapeutic/Nontoxic	Toxic	Lethal
Blood	0.001–0.6 mg/L	0.3–2.5 mg/L	0.2–7.2 mg/L
Vitreous			0.03–0.8 mg/L
Liver			0.05–18 mg/kg
Kidney			0.05–7 mg/kg
Brain			0.05–1 mg/kg
Skeletal muscle			0.1–2 mg/kg

Comments

- Tolerance can develop and should be considered when interpreting drug concentrations
- Metabolite of heroin
- Active metabolites: Morphine-6-glucuronide and normorphine
- Above concentrations are not differentiated between free or total morphine as not all references specified what was measured

Selected Sources

Chan SC, Chan EM, Kaliciak HA. (1986). Distribution of morphine in body fluids and tissues in fatal overdose, *J Forensic Sci*, 31(4): 1487–1491.

Felby S, Christensen H, Lund A. (1974). Morphine concentrations in blood and organs in cases of fatal poisoning, *Forensic Sci*, 3(1): 77–81.

Stanski DR, Greenblatt DJ, Lappas DG, Koch-Weser J, Lowenstein E. (1976). Kinetics of high-dose intravenous morphine in cardiac surgery patients, *Clin Pharm Therapeutics*, 19(6): 752–756.

Wallace JE, Blum K, Singh JM. (1974). Determination of drugs in biological specimens—A review, *J Tox Clin Toxicol*, 7(5): 477–495.

Ziminski KR, Wemyss CT, Bidanset JH, Manning TJ, Lukash L. (1984). Comparative study of postmortem barbiturates, methadone, and morphine in vitreous humor, blood, and tissue, *J Forensic Sci*, 29(3): 903–909.

Naloxone

Brand name: Narcan
Classification: Opioid antagonist
λ: 30–80 min
V_d: 0.8–3 L/kg
Usual dosage: 0.4–2 mg/dose

Source	Therapeutic/Nontoxic	Toxic	Lethal
Blood	0.004–0.1 mg/L	No data available	

Comments

- Used to treat opiate and opioid overdoses

Selected Sources

Bexar County Medical Examiner's Office data 1996–2015.
Ngai SH, Berkowitz BA, Yang JC, Hempstead J, Spector S. (1976). Pharmacokinetics of naloxone in rats and in man: Basis for its potency and short duration of action, *Anesthesiology*, 44(5): 398–401.
Reid RW, Deakin A, Leehey DJ. (1993). Measurement of naloxone in plasma using high-performance liquid chromatography with electrochemical detection, *J Chromatography A*, 614(1): 117–122.

Naltrexone

Brand names: Depade and Revia
Classification: Opioid antagonist
λ: 1–10 h
V_d: 14–16 L/kg
Usual dosage: 25–50 mg qd

Source	Therapeutic/Nontoxic	Toxic	Lethal
Blood	0.002–0.05 mg/L	No data available	

Selected Sources

Verebey K, Mulé SJ. (1979). Naltrexone, 6 beta-naltrexol and 2-hydroxy-3-methoxy-6 beta-naltrexol plasma levels in schizophrenic patients after large oral doses of naltrexone, *NIDA Res Monograph*, 27: 296–301.

Verebey K, Volavka J, Mulé SJ, Resnick RB. (1976). Naltrexone: Disposition, metabolism, and effects after acute and chronic dosing, *Clin Pharm Therapeutics*, 20(3): 315–328.

Naproxen

Brand names: Naprosyn, Aleve, and Anaprox
Classification: NSAID
λ: 10–18 h
V_d: 0.1–0.2 L/kg
Usual dosage: 250–500 mg bid/tid

Source	Therapeutic/Nontoxic	Toxic	Lethal
Blood	20–125 mg/L	414–1580 mg/L	760–1040 mg/L
Liver			520 mg/kg

Comments

- Metabolized by CYP 1A2 and 2C9

Selected Sources

Anttila M, Haataja M, Kasanen A. (1980). Pharmacokinetics of naproxen in subjects with normal and impaired renal function, *Eur J Clin Pharm*, 18(3): 263–268.
Bexar County Medical Examiner's Office data 1996–2015.
Fredell EW, Strand LJ. (1977). Naproxen overdose, *JAMA*, 238(9): 938.
Mullen WM, Meier KM, Hagar SM, Olson KR. (2003). Severe naproxen overdose with elevated serum levels, *J Tox Clin Toxicol*, 41(5): 655.
Medical Economics. (2006). *Physicians' Desk Reference*, (60th ed.) Thomson PDR, Montvale, NJ, p. 2769.
van den Ouweland FA, Franssen MJ, van de Putte LB, Tan Y, van Ginneken CA, Gribnau FW. (1987). Naproxen pharmacokinetics in patients with rheumatoid arthritis during active polyarticular inflammation, *Br J Clin Pharm*, 23(2): 189–193.

Nefazodone

Brand name: Serzone
Classification: Antidepressant
λ: 2–4 h
V_d: 0.2–0.9 L/kg
Usual dosage: 100–300 mg bid

Source	Therapeutic/Nontoxic	Toxic	Lethal
Blood	0.2–3.9 mg/L	5.5–7.5 mg/L	No data available

Comments

- Active metabolites: Hydroxynefazodone, triazolodione, and meta-chlorophenylpiperazine
- Metabolized by CYP 3A

Selected Sources

Barbhaiya RH, Buch AB, Greene DS. (1996). A study of the effect of age and gender on the pharmacokinetics of nefazodone after single and multiple doses, *J Clin Psychopharmacology*, 16(1): 19–25.

Gaffney PN, Schuckman HA, Beeson MS. (1998). Nefazodone overdose, *Ann Pharmacotherapy*, 32(11): 1249–1250.

Isbister GK, Hackett LP. (2003). Nefazodone poisoning: Toxicokinetics and toxicodynamics using continuous data collection, *J Toxicol Clin Toxicol*, 41(2): 167–173.

Nicotine

Brand names: Nicorette, Nicotrol, Nicoderm, Habitrol, and Prostep
Classification: Alkaloid
λ: 24–84 min
V_d: 1–3 L/kg
Usual dosage: 0.2–4 mg/dose

Source	Therapeutic/Nontoxic	Toxic	Lethal
Blood	0.003–0.2 mg/L	0.05–1 mg/L	3.7–5800 mg/L
Liver	0.01–0.3 mg/kg		4–2270 mg/kg
Kidney	0.007–0.2 mg/kg		10–1128 mg/kg
Brain	0.001–0.09 mg/kg		8–1910 mg/kg
Skeletal muscle	0.003–0.05 mg/kg		12 mg/kg

Comments

- Metabolized by CYP 2A6
- 1 cigarette = 0.1–2 mg nicotine; e-cigarette = 6–18 mg nicotine
- Concentrations in nonsmokers 0–0.006 mg/L; with passive inhalation, 0.001–0.003 mg/L; and in adult smokers, 0.01–0.05 mg/L

Selected Sources

Bartschat S, Mercer-Chalmers-Bender K, Beike J, Rothschild MA, Jübner M. (2015). Not only smoking is deadly: Fatal ingestion of e-juice-a case report, *Int J Legal Med*, 129(3): 481–486.

Davies P, Levy S, Pahari A, Martinez D. (2001). Acute nicotine poisoning associated with a traditional remedy for eczema, *Arc Disease in Childhood*, 85(6): 500–502.

Grusz-Harday E. (1967). Fatal nicotine poisoning. *Archiv für Toxikologie*, 23(1): 35–41.

Krauland W, Schneider V, Klug E. (1973). Fatal nicotine poisoning due to miscalculated nicotine test, *Zeitschrift für Rechtsmedizin*, 72(4): 269–277.

Lavoie FW, Harris TM. (1991). Fatal nicotine ingestion, *J Emer Med*, 9(3): 133–136.

Sanchez P, Ducassé JL, Lapeyre-Mestre M, Martinet O, Rougé P, Jorda MF. (1996). Nicotine poisoning as a cause of cardiac arrest?, *J Tox Clin Toxicol*, 34(4): 475–476.

Schipper EM, de Graaff LC, Koch BC, Brkic Z, Wilms EB, Alsma J, Schuit SC. (2014). A new challenge: Suicide attempt using nicotine fillings for electronic cigarettes, *Br J Clin Pharmacol*, 78(6): 1469–1471.

Urakawa N, Nagata T, Kudo K, Kimura K, Imamura T. (1994). Simultaneous determination of nicotine and cotinine in various human tissues using capillary gas chromatography/mass, *Intl J Legal Med*, 106(5): 232–236.

Woolf A, Burkhart K, Caraccio T, Litovitz T. (1996). Self-poisoning among adults using multiple transdermal nicotine patches, *J Tox Clin Toxicol*, 34(6): 691–698.

Nifedipine

Brand names: Adalat, Nifediac, and Afeditab
Classification: Calcium channel blocker
λ: 2–8 h
V_d: 1–1.5 L/kg
Usual dosage: 30–120 mg qd

Source	Therapeutic/Nontoxic	Toxic	Lethal
Blood	0.02–0.1 mg/L	0.1–0.6 mg/L	0.2–0.5 mg/L
Liver			1.1 mg/kg

Comments

- Metabolized by CYP 3A

Selected Sources

Bexar County Medical Examiner's Office data 1996–2015.

Debbas NM, Jackson SH, Shah K, Abrams SM, Johnston A, Turner P. (1986). The bioavailability and pharmacokinetics of slow release nifedipine during chronic dosing in volunteers, *Br J Clin Pharm*, 21(4): 385–388.

Ferner RE, Monkman S, Riley J, Cholerton S, Idle JR, Bateman DN. (1990). Pharmacokinetics and toxic effects of nifedipine in massive overdose, *Hum Exper Tox*, 9(5): 309–311.

Kleinbloesem CH, van Brummelen P, Faber H, Breimer DD. (1987). Pharmacokinetics and hemodynamic effects of long-term nifedipine treatment in hypertensive patients, *J Cardiovascular Pharm*, 9(2): 202–208.

Kleinbloesem CH, van Brummelen P, van de Linde JA, Voogd PJ, Breimer DD. (1984). Nifedipine: Kinetics and dynamics in healthy subjects, *Clin Pharm Ther*, 35(6): 742–749.

Purdue BN, Fernando GCA, Busuttil A. (1991). Two deaths from intravenous nifedipine abuse, *Int J Leg Med*, 104: 289.

Schiffl H, Ziupa J, Schollmeyer P. (1984). Clinical features and management of nifedipine overdosage in a patient with renal insufficiency, *J Tox Clin Tox*, 22(4): 387–395.

Nitrazepam

Brand name: Mogadon
Classification: Benzodiazepine
λ: 17–48 h
V_d: 2–5 L/kg
Usual dosage: 2.5–10 mg qd

Source	Therapeutic/Nontoxic	Toxic	Lethal
Blood	0.01–0.5 mg/L	0.2 mg/L	0.4–9 mg/L
Liver			0.7–4 mg/kg
Kidney			0.7 mg/kg
Brain			2–6 mg/kg
Skeletal muscle			2.1 mg/kg

Comments

- Tolerance can develop and should be considered when interpreting drug concentrations

Selected Sources

Brødsgaard I, Hansen AC, Vesterby A. (1995). Two cases of lethal nitrazepam poisoning, *Am J Forensic Med Path*, 16(2): 151–153.

Druid H, Holmgren P. (1997). A compilation of fatal and control concentrations of drugs in postmortem femoral blood, *J Forensic Sci*, 42(1): 79–87.

Drummer OH, Ranson DL. (1996). Sudden death and benzodiazepines, *Am J Forensic Med Path*, 17(4): 336–342.

Giusti GV, Chiarotti M. (1979). Lethal nitrazepam intoxications, report of two cases, *Zeitschrift für Rechtsmedizin*, 84(1): 75–78.

Jönsson AK, Söderberg C, Espnes KA, Ahlner J, Eriksson A, Reis M, Druid H. (2014). Sedative and hypnotic drugs—Fatal and non-fatal reference blood concentrations, *Forensic Sci Int*, 236: 138–145.

Kangas L, Iisalo E, Kanto J, Lehtinen V, Pynnönen S, Ruikka I. (1979). Human pharmacokinetics of nitrazepam: Effect of age and diseases, *Eur J Clin Pharm*, 15(3): 163–170.

Loveland MR. (1974). Fatal nitrazepam poisoning, *Bull Intl Assoc Forensic Toxic*, 10(1): 16–17.

Oliver JS, Smith H. (1974). Determination of nitrazepam in poisoning cases, *Forensic Sci*, 4(2): 183–186.

Nortriptyline

Brand names: Pamelor and Aventyl
Classification: Antidepressant (TCA)
λ: 15–90 h
V_d: 20–57 L/kg
Usual dosage: 20–50 mg bid/tid

Source	Therapeutic/Nontoxic	Toxic	Lethal
Blood	0.01–0.4 mg/L	0.5–2.3 mg/L	0.8–86 mg/L
Vitreous			1.4 mg/L
Liver			11–664 mg/kg
Kidney			9–904 mg/kg
Brain			97–202 mg/kg
Skeletal muscle	0.2–1 mg/kg		2.5–4 mg/kg

Comments

- Metabolite of amitriptyline
- Metabolized by CYP 2D6
- May prolong QT interval

Selected Sources

Bexar County Medical Examiner's Office data 1996–2015.
Bonnichsen R, Maehly AC, Sköld G. (1970). A report on autopsy cases involving amitriptyline and nortriptyline, *Z Rechtsmed*, 67: 190.
Franssen EJ, Kunst PW, Bet PM, Strack van Schijndel RJ, van Loenen AC, Wilhelm AJ. (2003). Toxicokinetics of nortriptyline and amitriptyline: Two case reports, *Ther Drug Monit*, 25(2): 248–251.
Furlanut M, Benetello P, Spina E. (1993). Pharmacokinetic optimisation of tricyclic antidepressant therapy, *Clin Pharmacokinetics*, 24(4): 301–318.
Iversen BM, Willassen YW, Bakke OM. (1978). Charcoal haemoperfusion in nortriptyline poisoning, *Lancet*, 1(8060): 388–389.
Robinson AE, Coffer AI, McDowall RD. (1974). Toxicology of some autopsy cases involving tricyclic antidepressant drugs, *Zeitschrift für Rechtsmedizin*, 74(4): 261–266.
Rohrig TP, Prouty RW. (1989). A nortriptyline death with unusually high tissue concentrations, *J Anal Toxicol*, 13(5): 303–304.
Rudorfer MV, Robins E. (1981). Fatal nortriptyline overdose, plasma levels, and in vivo methylation of tricyclic antidepressants, *Am J Psychiatry*, 138(7): 982–983.

Olanzapine

Brand name: Zyprexa
Classification: Antipsychotic
λ: 21–54 h
V_d: 10–26 L/kg
Usual dosage: 5–20 mg qd

Source	Therapeutic/Nontoxic	Toxic	Lethal
Blood	0.009–0.5 mg/L	0.05–1 mg/L	1–21 mg/L
Vitreous	0.4–1 mg/L		1–2 mg/L
Liver	0.4–9 mg/kg		6–52 mg/kg
Kidney			2–6.5 mg/kg
Brain			0.2–2 mg/kg

Comments

- Metabolized by CYP 1A2

Selected Sources

Bexar County Medical Examiner's Office data 1996–2015.

Cohen LG, Fatalo A, Thompson BT, Di Centes Bergeron G, Flood JG, Poupolo PR. (1999). Olanzapine overdose with serum concentrations, *Ann Emer Med*, 34(2): 275–278.

Elian AA. (1998). Fatal overdose of olanzepine, *Forensic Sci Intl*, 91(3): 231–235.

Gerber JE, Cawthon B. (2000). Overdose and death with olanzapine: Two case reports, *Am J Forensic Med Path*, 21(3): 249–251.

Kratzsch C, Peters FT, Kraemer T, Weber AA, Maurer HH. (2003). Screening, library-assisted identification and validated quantification of fifteen neuro-leptics and three of their metabolites in plasma by liquid chromatography/mass spectrometry with atmospheric pressure chemical ionization, *J Mass Spectrum*, 38(3): 283–295.

O'Malley GF, Seifert S, Heard K, Daly F, Dart RC. (1999). Olanzapine overdose mimicking opioid intoxication, *Ann Emer Med*, 34(2): 279–281.

Stephens BG, Coleman DE, Baselt RC. (1998). Olanzapine-related fatality, *J Forensic Sci*, 43(6): 1252–1253.

Vance C, McIntyre IM. (2009). Postmortem tissue concentrations of olanzapine, *J Anal Toxicol*, 33(1): 15–26.

Oleandrin

Brand name: Anvirzel (oleandrin extract)
Classification: Cardiac glycoside
λ: Unknown
V_d: Unknown
Usual dosage: 15 mg qd

Source	Therapeutic/Nontoxic	Toxic	Lethal
Blood	0.001–0.007 mg/L	0.001–0.03 mg/L	0.01–12 mg/L
Liver			30 mg/kg
Kidney			39 mg/kg
Brain			10 mg/kg
Cardiac muscle			1–23 mg/kg

Comments

- From *Nerium oleander*
- Cross reacts with digoxin RIA

Selected Sources

Ansford AJ, Morris H. (1981). Fatal oleander poisoning, *Med J Aust*, 1(7): 360–361.

Arao T, Fuke C, Takaesu H, Nakamoto M, Morinaga Y, Miyazaki T. (2002). Simultaneous determination of cardenolides by sonic spray ionization liquid chromatography-ion trap mass spectrometry—A fatal case of oleander poisoning, *J Anal Toxicol*, 26(4): 222–227.

Bavunoğlu I, Balta M, Türkmen Z. (2016). Oleander poisoning as an example of self-medication attempt, *Balkan Med J*, 33(5): 559–562.

Blum LM, Rieders F. (1987). Oleandrin distribution in a fatality from rectal and oral Nerium oleander extract administration, *J Anal Toxicol*, 11(5): 219–221.

Dasgupta A, Datta P. (2004). Rapid detection of oleander poisoning using digoxin immunoassays: Comparison of five assays, *Ther Drug Monit*, 26(6): 658–663.

Gechtman C, Guidugli F, Marocchi A, Masarin A, Zoppi F. (2006). Unexpectedly dangerous escargot stew: Oleandrin poisoning through the alimentary chain, *J Anal Toxicol*, 30(9): 683–686.

Pietsch J, Oertel R, Trautmann S, Schulz K, Kopp B, Dressler J. (2005). A non-fatal oleander poisoning, *Intl J Legal Med*, 119(4): 236–240.

Tracqui A, Kintz P, Branche F Ludes, B. (1997). Confirmation of oleander poisoning by HPLC/MS. *Int J Leg Med*, 111(1): 32–34.

Wang X, Plomley JB, Newman RA, Cisneros A. (2000). LC/MS/MS analyses of an oleander extract for cancer treatment, *Anal Chem*, 72(15): 3547–3552.

Ondansetron

Brand name: Zofran
Classification: Antiemetic
λ: 2–6 h
V_d: 1–3 L/kg
Usual dosage: 8 mg q 8 h

Source	Therapeutic/Nontoxic	Toxic	Lethal
Blood	0.03–0.14 mg/L	No data available	

Comments

- Metabolized by CYP 1A2, 2D6, 3A
- May prolong QT interval

Selected Sources

Colthup PV, Felgate CC, Palmer JL, Scully NL. (1991). Determination of ondansetron in plasma and its pharmacokinetics in the young and elderly, *J Pharmaceutical Sci*, 80(9): 868–871.

Colthup PV, Palmer JL. (1989). The determination in plasma and pharmacokinetics of ondansetron, *Eur J Cancer Clin Oncol*, 25(Suppl 1): S71–S74.

Hsyu PH, Pritchard JF, Bozigian HP, Lloyd TL, Griffin RH, Shamburek R. (1994). Comparison of the pharmacokinetics of an ondansetron solution (8 mg) when administered intravenously, orally, to the colon, and to the rectum, *Pharmaceutical Res*, 11(1): 156–159.

Orphenadrine

Brand names: Norflex and Norgesic (w/acetaminophen and caffeine)
Classification: Anti-Parkinson/muscle relaxant
λ: 13–20 h
V_d: 4–8 L/kg
Usual dosage: 25–100 mg bid

Source	Therapeutic/Nontoxic	Toxic	Lethal
Blood	0.1–0.85 mg/L	2–3.6 mg/L	5–368 mg/L
Liver			7–410 mg/kg
Kidney			10–105 mg/kg
Brain			3–20 mg/kg

Selected Sources

Blomquist M, Bonnichsen R, Schubert B. (1971). Lethal orphenadrine intoxications. A report of five cases, *Z Rechtsmed* 68: 111.

Bozza-Marrubini M, Frigerio A, Ghezzi R, Parelli L, Restelli L, Selenati A. (1977). Two cases of severe orphenadrine poisoning with atypical features, *Acta Pharmacologica et Toxicologica*, 41(Supp 2): 137–152.

De Mercurio D, Chiarotti M, Giusti GV. (1979). Lethal orphenadrine intoxication: Report of a case, *Z Rechtsmed*, 82: 349.

Furlanut M, Bettio D, Bertin I, Colombo G, Benetello P. (1985). Orphenadrine serum levels in a poisoned patient, *Hum Tox*, 4(3): 331–333.

Labout JJ, Thijssen CT, Keijser GG, Hespe W. (1982). Difference between single and multiple dose pharmacokinetics of orphenadrine hydrochloride in man, *Eur J Clin Pharm*, 21(4): 343–350.

Paterson SC. (1985). Drug levels found in cases of fatal self-poisoning, *Forensic Sci Intl*, 27(2): 129–133.

Robinson AE, Holder AT, McDowall RD, Powell R, Sattar H. (1977). Forensic toxicology of some orphenadrine-related deaths, *Forensic Sci*, 9(1): 53–62.

Van Herreweghe I, Mertens K, Maes V, Ramet J. (1999). Orphenadrine poisoning in a child: Clinical and analytical data, *Intensive Care Med*, 25(10): 1134–1136.

Wilkinson LF, Thomson BM, Pannell LK. (1983). A report on the analysis of orphenadrine in post mortem specimens, *J Anal Toxicol*, 7(2): 72–75.

Oxazepam

Brand name: Serax
Classification: Benzodiazepine
λ: 5–15 h
V_d: 0.6–2 L/kg
Usual dosage: 15–30 mg tid/qid

Source	Therapeutic/Nontoxic	Toxic	Lethal
Blood	0.1–1.6 mg/L	0.5[a]–4 mg/L	2–6.3 mg/L
Brain	0.002–1.5 mg/kg		

[a] Child.

Comments

- Metabolite of temazepam and nordiazepam
- Tolerance can develop and should be considered when interpreting drug concentrations

Selected Sources

Druid H, Holmgren P. (1997). A compilation of fatal and control concentrations of drugs in postmortem femoral blood, *J Forensic Sci*, 42(1): 79–87.

Greenblatt DJ. (1981). Clinical pharmacokinetics of oxazepam and lorazepam, *Clin Pharmacokinetics*, 6(2): 89–105.

Jönsson AK, Söderberg C, Espnes KA, Ahlner J, Eriksson A, Reis M, Druid H. (2014). Sedative and hypnotic drugs—Fatal and non-fatal reference blood concentrations, *Forensic Sci Int*, 236: 138–145.

Knowles JA, Ruelius HW. (1972). Absorption and excretion of 7-chloro-1,3-dihydro-3-hydroxy-5-phenyl-2H-1,4-benzodiazepin-2-one (oxazepam) in humans. Determination of the drug by gas-liquid chromatography with electron capture detection, *Drug Res/Arzneimittel-Forschung*, 22(4): 687–692.

Moshkowitz M, Pines A, Finkelstein A, Hershkowitz R, Levo Y. (1990). Skin blisters as a manifestation of oxazepam toxicity, *J Tox Clin Tox*, 28(3): 383–386.

Shimkin PM, Shaivitz SA. (1966). Oxazepam poisoning in a child, *JAMA*, 196(7): 662–663.

Oxcarbazepine

Brand name: Trileptal
Classification: Anticonvulsant
λ: 1–5 h
V_d: 3–12 L/kg
Usual dosage: 300–1200 mg bid

Source	Therapeutic/Nontoxic	Toxic	Lethal
Blood	0.01–5 mg/L OX	8–12 mg/L OX	16–99 mg/L OX
	8–52 mg/L 10-OHC	32–65 mg/L 10-OHC	3–199 mg/L 10-OHC
Liver	7–29 mg/kg		19–219 mg/kg OX
			4–428 mg/kg OHC
Kidney	11–43 mg/kg		4–41 mg/kg OX
			1–74 mg/kg OHC
Skeletal muscle			1.8 mg/kg OX
			40 mg/kg OHC

OX = oxcarbazepine; 10-OHC = 10-hydroxycarbazepine.

Comments

- Active metabolite: 10-hydroxycarbazepine (λ 7–20 h; V_d 0.75 L/kg)
- Tolerance can develop and should be considered when interpreting drug concentrations

Selected Sources

Bexar County Medical Examiner's Office data 1996–2015.
Jolliff HA, Fehrenbacher N, Dart RC. (2001). Bradycardia, hypotension and tinnitus after accidental oxcarbazepine overdose, *J Tox Clin Tox*, 39(3): 316–317.
Klys M, Bystrowska B, Bujak-Gizycka B. (2003). Postmortem toxicology of carbamazepine, *J Anal Toxicol*, 27(4): 243–248.
Levine B, Phipps RJ, Naso C, Fahie K, Fowler D. (2010). Tissue distribution of newer anticonvulsant drugs in postmortem cases, *J Anal Toxicol*, 34(8): 506–509.
Linnet K, Steentoft A, Simonsen KW, Sabers A, Hansen SH. (2008). An oxcarbazepine-related fatality with an overview of 26 oxcarbazepine postmortem cases, *Forensic Sci Int*, 177(2–3): 248–251.
van Opstal JM, Janknegt R, Cilissen J, L'Ortije WHM, Nel JE, De Heer F. (2004). Severe overdosage with the antiepileptic drug oxcarbazepine, *Br J Clin Pharm*, 58(3): 329–331.

Oxycodone

Brand names: Roxicodone and Oxycontin; Percocet, Endocet, and
Roxicet (w/acetaminophen); Percodan (w/ ASA)
Classification: Opioid
λ: 3–8 h
V_d: 2–4 L/kg
Usual dosage: 5–30 mg q 4–6 h

Source	Therapeutic/Nontoxic	Toxic	Lethal
Blood	0.04–0.9 mg/L	0.2–2.4 mg/L	0.1–53 mg/L
Vitreous	0.03–0.4 mg/L		0.25–1 mg/L
Liver	0.06–2.3 mg/kg		0.2–6.6 mg/kg
Brain	0.06–1.9 mg/kg		1–2 mg/kg
Skeletal muscle	0.1–0.6 mg/kg		

Comments

- Active metabolite: Oxymorphone
- Tolerance can develop and should be considered when interpreting
  drug concentrations
- May prolong QT interval at high doses

Selected Sources

Anderson DT, Fritz KL, Muto JJ. (2002). Oxycontin: The concept of a "ghost pill"
and the postmortem tissue distribution of oxycodone in 36 cases, *J Anal
Toxicol*, 26(7): 448–459.
Bexar County Medical Examiner's Office data 1996–2015.
Darke S, Duflou J, Torok M. (2011). Toxicology and characteristics of fatal oxyco-
done toxicity cases in New South Wales, Australia 1999–2008, *J Forensic Sci*,
56(3): 690–693.
Okic M, Cnossen L, Crifasi JA, Long C, Mitchell EK. (2013). Opioid overdose mor-
tality in kansas, 2001–2011: Toxicologic evaluation of intent, *J Anal Toxicol*,
37(9): 629–635.
Schneir AB, Vadeboncoeur TF, Offerman SR, Barry JD, Ly BT, Williams SR. (2002).
Massive OxyContin ingestion refractory to naloxone therapy, *Ann Emer Med*,
40(4): 425–428.
Spiller HA. (2003). Postmortem oxycodone and hydrocodone blood concentrations,
J Forensic Sci, 48(2): 429–431.

Oxymorphone

Brand names: Opana and Numorphan
Classification: Opioid
λ: 7–11 h
V_d: 2–4 L/kg
Usual dosage: 5–20 mg q 4–6 h

Source	Therapeutic/Nontoxic	Toxic	Lethal
Blood	0.0003–0.01 mg/L	No data available	0.03–0.8 mg/L
Vitreous			0.05 mg/L
Liver			0.1–2 mg/kg

Comments

- Metabolite of oxycodone
- Tolerance can develop and should be considered when interpreting drug concentrations

Selected Sources

Adams MP, Ahdieh H. (2005). Single- and multiple-dose pharmacokinetic and dose-proportionality study of oxymorphone immediate-release tablets, *Drugs in R D*, 6(2): 91–99.

Bexar County Medical Examiner's Office data 2003–2015.

Crum ED, Bailey KM, Richards-Waugh LL, Clay DJ, Gebhardt MA, Kraner JC. (2013). Validation of blood and liver oxymorphone analysis using LC-MS-MS: Concentrations in 30 fatal overdoses, *J Anal Toxicol*, 37(8): 512–516.

Garside D, Hargrove RL, Winecker RE. (2009). Concentration of oxymorphone in postmortem fluids and tissue, *J Anal Toxicol*, 33(3): 121–128.

Guay DRP. (2007). Use of oral oxymorphone in the elderly, *Consult Pharm*, 22(5): 417–430.

Papaverine

Brand name: Para-Time
Classification: Vasodilator
λ: 1–1.5 h
V_d: 0.5–1.5 L/kg
Usual dosage: 150–300 mg bid

Source	Therapeutic/Nontoxic	Postmortem Procurement	Toxic	Lethal
Blood	0.2–4 mg/L	0.04–42 mg/L	No data available	

Comments

- Often used postmortem to dilate veins for procurement procedures
- Overdose may result in hepatotoxicity or lactic acidosis
- Can be found as a component in heroin

Selected Sources

Bexar County Medical Examiner's Office data 1996–2015.
Guttman DE, Kostenbauder HB, Wilkinson GR, Dubé PH. (1974). GLC determination of papaverine in biological fluids, *J Pharm Sci*, 63(10): 1625–1626.
Lee BY, Sakamoto H, Trainor F, Brody G, Cho YW. (1978). Comparison of soft gelatin capsule versus sustained release formulation of papaverine HCl: Vasodilation and plasma levels, *Int J Clin Pharmacol Biopharmacy*, 16(1): 32–39.
Ronnov-Jessen V, Tjernlund A. (1969). Hepatotoxicity due to treatment with papaverine. Report of four cases, *NEJM*, 281(24): 1333–1335.
Vaziri ND, Stokes J, Treadwell TR. (1981). Lactic acidosis, a complication of papaverine overdose, *Clin Tox*, 18(4): 417–423.

Paroxetine

Brand names: Paxil and Pexeva
Classification: Antidepressant (SSRI)
λ: 7–65 h
V_d: 3–28 L/kg
Usual dosage: 20–40 mg qd

Source	Therapeutic/Nontoxic	Toxic	Lethal
Blood	0.002–0.9 mg/L	0.35–1.8 mg/L	1–16 mg/L
Vitreous	0.003–0.03 mg/L		
Liver	0.1–5.2 mg/kg		110–113 mg/kg
Lung	0.3–10 mg/kg		
Kidney	0.02–1.6 mg/kg		
Spleen	0.06–2.6 mg/kg		
Skeletal muscle	0.001–0.1 mg/kg		
Brain	0.1–2.2 mg/kg		
Cardiac muscle	0.03–0.6 mg/kg		

Comments

• Prolongs QT interval

Selected Sources

Bexar County Medical Examiner's Office data 1996–2015.

DeVane CL. (2003). Pharmacokinetics, drug interactions, and tolerability of paroxetine and paroxetine CR, *Psychopharmacol Bull*, 37(Suppl 1): 29–41.

Goeringer KE, Raymon L, Christian GD, Logan BK. (2000). Postmortem forensic toxicology of selective serotonin reuptake inhibitors: A review of pharmacology and report of 168 cases, *J Forensic Sci*, 45(3): 633–648.

Lewis RJ, Kemp PM, Johnson RD. (2015). Paroxetine in postmortem fluids and tissues from nine aviation accident victims, *J Anal Toxicol*, 39(8): 637–641.

Velez LI, Shepherd G, Roth BA, Benitez FL. (2004). Serotonin syndrome with elevated paroxetine concentrations, *Ann Pharmacotherapy*, 38(2): 269–272.

Vermeulen T. (1998). Distribution of paroxetine in three postmortem cases, *J Anal Toxicol*, 22(6): 541–544.

Wagstaff AJ, Cheer SM, Matheson AJ, Ormrod D, Goa KL. (2002). Paroxetine: An update of its use in psychiatric disorders in adults, *Drugs*, 62(4): 655–703.

Pentazocine

Brand names: Talwin and Talacen (w/acetaminophen)
Classification: Opioid
λ: 2–3.5 h
V_d: 4–8 L/kg
Usual dosage: 50–100 mg q 3–4 h

Source	Therapeutic/Nontoxic	Toxic	Lethal
Blood	0.05–0.24 mg/L	0.5–2 mg/L	1–9 mg/L
Liver			34–87 mg/kg

Comments

- Tolerance can develop and should be considered when interpreting drug concentrations

Selected Sources

Berkowitz BA, Asling JH, Shnider SM, Way EL. (1969). Relationship of pentazocine plasma levels to pharmacological activity in man, *Clin Pharm Thera*, 10(3): 320–328.

Bexar County Medical Examiner's Office data 1996–2015.

Finkle B. (1974). Pentazocine, *Bull Intl Assoc Forensic Tox*, 10(3): 7.

Poklis A, Mackell MA. (1982). Toxicological findings in deaths due to ingestion of pentazocine: A report of two cases, *Forensic Sci Intl*, 20(1): 89–95.

Stahl SM, Kasser IS. (1983). Pentazocine overdose, *Ann Emer Med*, 12(1): 28–31.

Pentobarbital

Brand name: Nembutal
Classification: Barbiturate
λ: 15–50 h
V_d: 0.5–1 L/kg
Usual dosage: 50–200 mg/dose

Source	Therapeutic/Nontoxic	Toxic	Lethal
Blood	1–5 mg/L	8–24 mg/L	15–241 mg/L
Vitreous			7–27 mg/L
Liver			8–980 mg/kg
Kidney			7–72 mg/kg
Brain			4–48 mg/kg

Selected Sources

Bexar County Medical Examiner's Office data 1996–2015.
Broughton PM, Higgins G, O'Brien JR. (1956). Acute barbiturate poisoning, *Lancet*, 270: 180–184.
Caplan YH, Ottinger WE, Crooks CR. (1983). Therapeutic and toxic drug concentrations in post mortem blood: A six year study in the state of maryland, *J Anal Toxicol*, 7(5): 225–230.
Koyama K, Suzuki R, Yoshida T, Kikuno T. (2007). Usefulness of serum concentration measurement for acute pentobarbital intoxication in patients, *Chudoku Kenkyu*, 20(1): 45–53.
Parker KD, Elliott HW, Wright JA, Nomof H, Hine CH. (1970). Blood and urine concentrations of subjects receiving barbiturates, meprobamate, glutethimide, or diphenylhydantoin, *Clin Toxicol*, 3(1): 131–145.
Robinson AE, McDowall RD. (1979). The distribution of amylobarbitone, butobarbitone, pentobarbitone and quinalbarbitone and the hydroxylated metabolites in man, *J Pharmacy Pharmacol*, 31(6): 357–365.
Romain N, Giroud C, Michaud K, Mangin P. (2003). Suicide by injection of a veterinarian barbiturate euthanasia agent: Report of a case and toxicological analysis, *Forensic Sci Intl*, 131(2–3): 103–107.
Ziminski KR, Wemyss CT, Bidanset JH, Manning TJ, Lukash L. (1984). Comparative study of postmortem barbiturates, methadone, and morphine in vitreous humor, blood, and tissue, *J Forensic Sci*, 29(3): 903–909.

Phencyclidine

Brand name: Not applicable

Street names: PCP, Angel Dust, Peter Pan, Wack, Ozone, Elephant, Super Kools w/ Cocaine: Spaceball, Parachute, Space Base, Tragic Magic, Lovelies, Beam Em Up w/ MJ: Happy Stick, Love Boat, Supergrass, Donk, Killer Joints, Wacky Weed

Classification: Hallucinogen

λ: 7–46 h

V_d: 5–7.5 L/kg

Usual dosage: 3–10 mg/dose

Source	Therapeutic/Nontoxic	Toxic	Lethal
Blood	0.1–1.1 mg/L	0.09–0.5 mg/L	0.3–25 mg/L
Vitreous	0.01–0.5 mg/L		
Liver	0.3–3.4 mg/kg		0.9–170 mg/kg
Brain	0.09–0.9 mg/kg		0.1–32 mg/kg
Lung			0.4–7.6 mg/kg
Kidney			0.1 mg/kg
Spleen			20 mg/kg

Selected Sources

Bexar County Medical Examiner's Office data 1996–2015.

Caplan YH, Orloff KG, Thompson BC, Fisher RS. (1979). Detection of phencyclidine in medical examiner's cases, *J Anal Toxicol*, 3: 47–52.

Cox D, Jufer Phipps RA, Levine B, Jacobs A, Fowler D. (2007). Distribution of phencyclidine into vitreous humor, *J Anal Toxicol*, 31(8): 537–539.

Cravey RH, Reed D, Ragle JL. (1979). Phencyclidine-related deaths: A report of nine fatal cases, *J Anal Toxicol*, 3: 199–201.

deRoux SJ, Sgarlato A, Marker E. (2011). Phencyclidine: A 5-year retrospective review from the New York City Medical Examiner's Office, *J Forensic Sci*, 56(3): 656–659.

Jenkins AJ, Oblock J. (2008). Phencyclidine and cannabinoids in vitreous humor, *Leg Med (Tokyo)*, 10(4): 201–203.

Marshman JA, Ramsay MP, Sellers EM. (1976). Quantitation of phencyclidine in biological fluids and application to human overdose, *Tox Appl Pharm*, 35(1): 129–136.

Noguchi TT, Nakamura GR. (1978). Phencyclidine-related deaths in Los Angeles county, 1976, *J Forensic Sci*, 23(3): 503–507.

Reynolds PC. (1976). Clinical and forensic experiences with phencyclidine, *Clin Tox*, 9(4): 547–552.

Phenelzine

Brand name: Nardil
Classification: Antidepressant (MAOI)
λ: 9–12 h
V_d: Unknown
Usual dosage: 15 mg tid/qd

Source	Therapeutic/Nontoxic	Toxic	Lethal
Blood	0.01–0.2 mg/L	0.5 mg/L	1–2 mg/L

Selected Sources

Caddy BA, Stead AH. (1978). Three cases of poisoning involving the drug phenelzine, *Forensic Sci Soc J*, 18(3–4): 207–208.

Georgotas A, McCue RE, Cooper TB, Nagachandran N, Friedhoff A. (1989). Factors affecting the delay of antidepressant effect in responders to nortriptyline and phenelzine, *Psychiatry Rese*, 28(1): 1–9.

Kallem RR, Jillela B, Ravula AR, Samala R, Andy A, Ramesh M, Rao JS. (2016). Highly sensitive LC-MS/MS-ESI method for determination of phenelzine in human plasma and its application to a human pharmacokinetic study, *J Chromatogr B Analyt Technol Biomed Life Sci*, 1022: 126–132.

Lichtenwalner MR, Tully RG, Cohn RD, Pinder RD. (1995). Two fatalities involving phenelzine, *J Anal Toxicol*, 19: 265–266.

Waring WS, Wallace WAH. (2007). Acute myocarditis after massive phenelzine overdose, *Eur J Clin Pharm*, 63(11): 1007–1009.

Pheniramine

Brand name: Avil; ingredient in many OTC cold medicines
Classification: Antihistamine
λ: 8–19 h
V_d: 1.5–3 L/kg
Usual dosage: 25–50 mg q 8 h

Source	Therapeutic/Nontoxic	Toxic	Lethal
Blood	0.2–0.9 mg/L	No data available	2–30 mg/L
Liver			6.6–115 mg/kg
Kidney			4 mg/kg
Brain			5.3 mg/kg

Selected Sources

Queree EA, Dickson SJ, Missen AW. (1979). Therapeutic and toxic levels of pheniramine in biological specimens, *J Anal Toxicol*, 3: 253–255.

Witte PU, Irmisch R, Hajdú P. (1985). Pharmacokinetics of pheniramine (Avil) and metabolites in healthy subjects after oral and intravenous administration, *Intl J Clin Pharm Ther Tox*, 23(1): 59–62.

Phenobarbital

Brand names: Luminal and Solfoton
Classification: Barbiturate anticonvulsant
λ: 2–6 d
V_d: 0.5–0.7 L/kg
Usual dosage: 30–100 mg qd/bid/tid

Source	Therapeutic/Nontoxic	Toxic	Lethal
Blood	4–40 mg/L	35–253 mg/L	48–348 mg/L
Vitreous			2–22 mg/L
Liver	2.4–5.2 mg/kg		17–275 mg/kg
Kidney	1.7–4.9 mg/kg		12–84 mg/kg
Brain	0.01–3.6 mg/kg		5–75 mg/kg
Skeletal muscle			35–86 mg/kg

Comments

- Metabolized by CYP 2C9 and 2C19

Selected Sources

Amitai Y, Degani Y. (1990). Treatment of phenobarbital poisoning with multiple dose activated charcoal in an infant, *J Emer Med*, 8(4): 449–450.

Bexar County Medical Examiner's Office data 1996–2015.

Bruce AM, Smith H. (1977). The investigation of phenobarbitone, phenytoin and primidone in the death of epileptics, *Med Sci Law*, 17(3): 195–199.

Caplan YH, Ottinger WE, Crooks CR. (1983). Therapeutic and toxic drug concentrations in post mortem blood: A six year study in the state of Maryland, *J Anal Toxicol*, 7(5): 225–230.

Costello JB, Poklis A. (1981). Treatment of massive phenobarbital overdose with dopamine diuresis, *Arch Int Med*, 141(7): 938–940.

Lal R, Faiz S, Garg RK, Baweja KS, Guntupalli J, Finkel KW. (2006). Use of continuous venovenous hemodiafiltration in a case of severe phenobarbital poisoning, *Am J Kidney Dis*, 48(2): e13–e15.

Parker KD, Elliott HW, Wright JA, Nomof H, Hine CH. (1970). Blood and urine concentrations of subjects receiving barbiturates, meprobamate, glutethimide, or diphenylhydantoin, *Clin Tox*, 3(1): 131–145.

Paterson SC. (1985). Drug levels found in cases of fatal self-poisoning, *For Sci Intl*, 27(2): 129–133.

Ziminski KR, Wemyss CT, Bidanset JH, Manning TJ, Lukash L. (1984). Comparative study of postmortem barbiturates, methadone, and morphine in vitreous humor, blood, and tissue, *J Forensic Sci*, 29(3): 903–909.

Phentermine

Brand names: Pro-Fast and Adipex
Classification: Stimulant/anorectic
λ: 19–24 h
V_d: 3–4 L/kg
Usual dosage: 37.5 mg qd

Source	Therapeutic/Nontoxic	Toxic	Lethal
Blood	0.07–0.9 mg/L	0.2–0.9 mg/L	1.5–7.6 mg/L
Liver	4 mg/kg		14–15 mg/kg
Kidney			12–16 mg/kg

Selected Sources

Bexar County Medical Examiner's Office data 1996–2015.

Groenewoud G, Schall R, Hundt HK, Müller FO, van Dyk M. (1993). Steady-state pharmacokinetics of phentermine extended-release capsules, *Intl J Clin Pharm Ther Tox*, 31(8): 368–372.

Levine B, Caplan YH, Dixon AM. (1984). A fatality involving phentermine, *J Forensic Sci*, 29(4): 1242–1245.

Price K. (1974). Phenteramine, *Bull Intl Assoc Forensic Tox*, 10(1): 12.

Phenylephrine

Brand names: Sudafed PE and Neo-Synephrine; ingredient in OTC
  cold medicines
Classification: α-adrenergic agonist
λ: 0.5–3 h
V_d: 3.5–5 L/kg
Usual dosage: 10 mg q 4 h

Source	Therapeutic/Nontoxic	Toxic	Lethal
Blood	0.002–0.04 mg/L	No data available	

Selected Sources

Dubost C, de Saint Maurice G, Vichard A, Berbari H, Lenoir B. (2011). Right to
  the heart: A case of accidental phenylephrine intoxication, *Eur J Anaesthesiol*,
  28(9): 670–672.
Hengstmann JH, Goronzy J. (1982). Pharmacokinetics of 3H-phenylephrine in man,
  Eur J Clin Pharm, 21(4): 335–341.
Ptácek P, J Klíma J, Macek J. (2007). Development and validation of a liquid chroma-
  tography-tandem mass spectrometry method for the determination of phenylephrine in human plasma and its application to a pharmacokinetic study,
  J Chromatography B, 858(1–2): 263–268.

Phenylpropanolamine (PPA)

Brand names: Accutrim and Dexatrim
Classification: α-adrenergic agonist
λ: 3–4.5 h
V_d: 4.5 L/kg
Usual dosage: 25–75 mg q 6–8 h

Source	Therapeutic/Nontoxic	Toxic	Lethal
Blood	0.05–0.3 mg/L	2 mg/L	0.63–48 mg/L

Comments

- Associated with arrhythmias and hemorrhagic cerebrovascular accidents
- No longer available in the United States

Selected Sources

Augenstein WL, Bakerman P, Radetsky M. (1988). PPA overdose resulting in pulmonary edema and death, *Vet Hum Tox*, 30: 365.

Bexar County Medical Examiner's Office data 1996–2015.

Druid H, Holmgren P. (1997). A compilation of fatal and control concentrations of drugs in postmortem femoral blood, *J Forensic Sci*, 42(1): 79–87.

Lake CR, Gallant S, Masson E, Miller P. (1990). Adverse drug effects attributed to phenylpropanolamine: A review of 142 case reports, *Am J Med*, 89(2): 195–208.

Scherzinger SS, Dowse R, Kanfer I. (1990). Steady state pharmacokinetics and dose-proportionality of phenylpropanolamine in healthy subjects, *J Clin Pharm*, 30(4): 372–377.

Phenytoin

Brand name: Dilantin
Classification: Anticonvulsant
λ: 7–60 h
V_d: 0.6–0.7 L/kg
Usual dosage: 100–200 mg tid

Source	Therapeutic/Nontoxic	Toxic	Lethal
Blood	2–25 mg/L	20–101 mg/L	45–242 mg/L
Liver			14–272 mg/kg
Kidney			5.2–112 mg/kg
Brain			15–78 mg/kg

Comments

- Metabolized by CYP 2C9, 2C8, and 2C19

Selected Sources

Bexar County Medical Examiner's Office data 1996–2015.

Brandolese R, Scordo MG, Spina E, Gusella M, Padrini R. (2001). Severe phenytoin intoxication in a subject homozygous for CYP2C9 * 3, *Clin Pharm Therapeutics*, 70(4): 391–394.

Bruce AM, Smith H. (1977). The investigation of phenobarbitone, phenytoin and primidone in the death of epileptics, *Med Sci Law*, 17(3): 195–199.

Coutselinis A, Dimopoulos G, Varsami P. (1975). Fatal intoxication with diphenlhdantoin: Report of two cases, *Forensic Sci*, 6(3): 131–133.

Craig S. (2004). Phenytoin overdose complicated by prolonged intoxication and residual neurological deficits, *Emer Med Australasia*, 16(4): 361–365.

Flanagan RJ. (1998). Guidelines for the interpretation of analytical toxicology results and unit of measurement conversion factors, *Ann Clin Biochem*, 35: 261–267.

Jenkins A. (2006). A case of phenytoin toxicity in a patient with advanced lung cancer, *Palliative Med*, 20(4): 479–480.

Laubscher FA. (1966). Fatal diphenylhydantoin poisoning. A case report, *JAMA*, 198(10): 1120–1121.

Levine M, Jones MW. (1983). Toxic reaction to phenytoin following a viral infection, *Can Med Assoc J*, 128(11): 1270–1271.

Mellick LB, Morgan JA, Mellick GA. (1989). Presentations of acute phenytoin overdose, *Am J Emer Med*, 7(1): 61–67.

Murphy JM, Motiwala R, Devinsky O. (1991). Phenytoin intoxication, *Southern Med J*, 84(10): 1199–1204.

Thimmisetty RK, Gorthi JR, Abu Hazeem M. (2014). Oral phenytoin toxicity causing sinus arrest: A case report, *Case Reports Cardiol*, 2014: 851767.

Pimozide

Brand name: Orap
Classification: Antipsychotic
λ: 55–111 h
V_d: 13–37 L/kg
Usual dosage: 1–5 mg bid

Source	Therapeutic/Nontoxic	Toxic	Lethal
Blood	0.003–0.01 mg/L	0.02 mg/L	0.09[a]–0.5 mg/L

[a] Co-intoxicants present.

Comments

- Prolongs QT interval
- Metabolized by CYP 3A4 as well as 1A2 and 2D6

Selected Sources

Harrison D, Elliot S. (2001). A novel case of fatal pimozide poisoning, *Bull Intl Assoc Forensic Tox*, 31(2): 11–12.

Krähenbühl S, Sauter B, Kupferschmidt H, Krause M, Wyss PA, Meier PJ. (1995). Case report: Reversible QT prolongation with torsades de pointes in a patient with pimozide intoxication, *Am J Med Sci*, 309(6): 315–316.

Sallee FR, Pollock BG, Stiller RL, Stull S, Everett G, Perel JM. (1987). Pharmacokinetics of pimozide in adults and children with tourette's syndrome, *J Clin Pharm*, 27(10): 776–781.

Salness RA, Goetz CM, Gorman RL. (1992). Two cases of pimozide ingestion, *Vet Hum Tox*, 34: 4.

Söderberg C, Wernvik E, Tillmar A, Spigset O, Kronstrand R, Reis M, Jönsson AK, Druid H. (2016). Antipsychotics—Postmortem fatal and non-fatal reference concentrations, *Forensic Sci Int*, 266: 91–101.

Prazepam

Brand names: Centrax, Lysanxia, and Demetrin
Classification: Benzodiazepine
λ: 1–2 h
V_d: 12–14 L/kg
Usual dosage: 30–60 mg qd

Source	Therapeutic/Nontoxic	Toxic	Lethal
Blood	0.008–0.3 mg/L	1–5 mg/L	No data available

Comments

- Active metabolite: Nordiazepam (λ 38–135 h)
- Tolerance can develop and should be considered when interpreting drug concentrations

Selected Sources

Repetto MR, Repetto M. (1997). Habitual, toxic, and lethal concentrations of 103 drugs of abuse in humans, *J Tox Clin Tox*, 35(1): 1–9.
Schulz M, Schmoldt A. (2003). Therapeutic and toxic blood concentrations of more than 800 drugs and other xenobiotics, *Pharmazie*, 58(7): 447–474.
Smith MT, Evans LE, Eadie MJ, Tyrer JH. (1979). Pharmacokinetics of prazepam in man, *Eur J Clin Pharm*, 16(2): 141–147.

Pregabalin

Brand name: Lyrica
Classification: Anticonvulsant
λ: 5–7 h
V_d: 0.5 L/kg
Usual dosage: 150–600 mg divided b/tid

Source	Therapeutic/Nontoxic	Toxic	Lethal
Blood	1.4–14 mg/L	7.7–112 mg/L	36–207 mg/L[a]
Kidney	14 mg/kg		
Liver	3 mg/kg		

[a] All fatalities have either co-intoxicants or significant natural disease present.

Selected Sources

Bexar County Medical Examiner's Office data 1996–2015.
Braga AJ, Chidley K. (2007). Self-poisoning with lamotrigine and pregabalin, *Anaesthesia*, 62(5): 524–527.
Elliot SP, Burke T, Smith C. (2016). Determining the toxicological significant of pregabalin in fatalities, *J Forensic Sci*, 62(1): 169–173.
Häkkinen M, Vuori E, Kalso E, Gergov M, Ojanperä I. (2014). Profiles of pregabalin and gabapentin abuse by postmortem toxicology, *Forensic Sci Int*, 241: 1–6.
Miljevic C, Crnobaric C, Nikolic S, Lecic-Tosevski D. (2012). A case of pregabalin intoxication, *Psychiatriki*, 23(2): 162–165.
Olaizola I, Ellger T, Young P, Bösebeck F, Evers S, Kellinghaus C. (2006). Pregabalin-associated acute psychosis and epileptiform EEG-changes, *Seizure*, 15(3): 208–210.
Priez-Barallon C, Carlier J, Boyer B, Benslima M, Fanton L, Mazoyer C, Gaillard Y. (2014). Quantification of pregabalin using hydrophilic interaction HPLC-high-resolution MS in postmortem human samples: Eighteen case reports, *J Anal Toxicol*, 38(3): 143–148.
Wood DM, Berry DJ, Glover G, Eastwood J, Dargan PI. (2010). Significant pregabalin toxicity managed with supportive care alone, *J Med Toxicol*, 6: 435–437.
Yoo L, Matalon D, Hoffman RS, Goldfarb DS. (2009). Treatment of pregabalin toxicity by hemodialysis in a patient with kidney failure, *Am J Kidney Dis*, 54(6): 1127–1130.

Primidone

Brand names: Mysoline, Myidone, and Sertan
Classification: Anticonvulsant
λ: 5–20 h
V_d: 0.6–1 L/kg
Usual dosage: 100–250 mg tid/qid

Source	Therapeutic/Nontoxic	Toxic	Lethal
Blood	5–19 mg/L	80–209 mg/L	65 mg/L

Comments

- Active metabolite: Phenobarbital

Selected Sources

Bailey DN, Jatlow PI. (1972). Chemical analysis of massive crystalluria following primidone overdose, *Am J Clin Path*, 58(5): 583–589.

Baselt RC, Cravey RH. (1977). A compendium of therapeutic and toxic concentrations of toxicologically significant drugs in human biofluids, *J Anal Toxicol*, 1: 81–103.

Bexar County Medical Examiner's Office data 1996–2015.

Cate JC, Tenser R. (1975). Acute primidone overdosage with massive crystalluria, *Clin Tox*, 8(4): 385–389.

Lehmann DF. (1987). Primidone crystalluria following overdose. A report of a case and an analysis of the literature, *Med Tox*, 2(5): 383–387.

van Heijst AN, de Jong W, Seldenrijk R, van Dijk A. (1983). Coma and crystalluria: A massive primidone intoxication treated with haemoperfusion, *J Tox Clin Tox*, 20(4): 307–318.

Procainamide

Brand names: Pronestyl and Procanbid
Classification: Antidysrhythmic
λ: 2.5–5 h
V_d: 1.5–2.5 L/kg
Usual dosage: 250–1250 mg q 6 h

Source	Therapeutic/Nontoxic	Toxic	Lethal
Blood	4–16 mg/L	8–63 mg/L	30–114 mg/L
Liver			283 mg/kg

Comments

- Concentrations can range from 25–75 mg/L when given during resuscitation
- Active metabolite: *N*-acetylprocainamide (NAPA)
- Prolongs QT interval

Selected Sources

Bexar County Medical Examiner's Office data 1996–2015.
Bizjak ED, Nolan PE, Brody EA, Galloway JM. (1999). Procainamide-induced psychosis: A case report and review of the literature, *Ann Pharmacotherapy*, 33(9): 948–951.
Kopjak L, Jennison TA. (1976). Procainamide—Ingestion or saturation, *Bull Intl Assoc Forensic Tox*, 12(1): 12–13.
Villalba-Pimentel L, Epstein LM, Sellers EM, Foster JR, Bennion LJ, Nadler LM. (1973). Survival after massive procainamide ingestion, *Am J Cardiology*, 32(5): 727–730.
White SR, Dy G, Wilson JM. (2002). The case of the slandered halloween cupcake: Survival after massive pediatric procainamide overdose, *Pediatric Emerg Care*, 18(3): 185–188.

Promazine

Brand names: Sparine and Protactyl
Classification: Antipsychotic
λ: 10–40 h
V_d: 23–43 L/kg
Usual dosage: 50–150 mg im q 4–6 h

Source	Therapeutic/Nontoxic	Toxic	Lethal
Blood	0.003–0.14 mg/L	1–1.8 mg/L	5 mg/L

Selected Sources

Hu OY, Tang HS, Sheeng TY, Chen SC, Lee SK, Chung PH. (1990). Pharmacokinetics
    of promazine: I. Disposition in patients with acute viral hepatitis B, *Biopharm
    Drug Dispos*, 11(7): 557–568.
Larsimont V, Meins J, Fieger-Büschges H, Blume H. (1998). Validated high-performance
    liquid chromatographic assay for the determination of promazine in human
    plasma. Application to pharmacokinetic studies, *J Chromatography—B*,
    719(1–2): 222–226.
Schulz M, Schmoldt A. (2003). Therapeutic and toxic blood concentrations of more
    than 800 drugs and other xenobiotics, *Pharmazie*, 58(7): 447–474.

Promethazine

Brand name: Phenergan
Classification: Antiemetic
λ: 9–16 h
V_d: 9–20 L/kg
Usual dosage: 12.5–50 mg q 4–6 h

Source	Therapeutic/Nontoxic	Toxic	Lethal
Blood	0.004–0.5 mg/L	0.14[a]–2 mg/L	2–64 mg/L
Liver	9–12 mg/kg		23–180 mg/kg
Kidney	7 mg/kg		26–92 mg/kg
Skeletal muscle	0.5 mg/kg		

[a] Concentration obtained 5 h post exposure.

Selected Sources

Allender WJ, Archer AW. (1984). Liquid chromatographic analysis of promethazine and its major metabolites in human postmortem material, *J Forensic Sci*, 29(2): 515–526.

Bexar County Medical Examiner's Office data 1996–2015.

Bonnichsen R, Geertinger P, Maehly AC. (1970). Toxicological data on phenothiazine drugs in autopsy cases, *Zeitschrift für Rechtsmedizin*, 67(3): 158–169.

Druid H, Holmgren P. (1997). A compilation of fatal and control concentrations of drugs in postmortem femoral blood, *J Forensic Sci*, 42(1): 79–87.

Pan CV, Quintela AG, Anuncibay PG, Vic JM. (1989). Topical promethazine intoxication, *DICP: Ann Pharmacother*, 23(1): 89.

Propoxyphene

Brand names: Darvon; Wygesic, Darvocet, and Propacet (w/ acetaminophen)
Classification: Opioid
λ: 6–12 h
V_d: 10–18 L/kg
Usual dosage: 50–100 mg q 4 h

Source	Therapeutic/Nontoxic	Toxic	Lethal
Blood	0.01–1 mg/L	0.8–2 mg/L	1–60 mg/L
Liver	0.05–0.16 mg/kg		2–550 mg/kg
Kidney			3–58 mg/kg
Brain			20 mg/kg
Skeletal muscle	0.2–2 mg/kg		2–20 mg/kg

Comments

- Withdrawn from the U.S. market in 2010
- Active metabolite: Norpropoxyphene
- Tolerance can develop and should be considered when interpreting drug concentrations

Selected Sources

Baselt RC, Wright JA. (1975). Propoxyphene and norpropoxyphene tissue concentrations in fatalities associated with propoxyphene hydrochloride and propoxyphene napsylate, *Arch Tox*, 34(2): 145–152.

Bexar County Medical Examiner's Office data 1996–2015.

Christensen H. (1977). Dextropropoxyphene and norpropoxyphene in blood, muscle, liver and urine in fatal poisoning, *Acta Pharmacologica et Toxicologica*, 40(2): 298–309.

Druid H, Holmgren P. (1997). A compilation of fatal and control concentrations of drugs in postmortem femoral blood, *J Forensic Sci*, 42(1): 79–87.

Garriott JC. (1991). Skeletal muscle as an alternative specimen for alcohol and drug analysis, *J Forensic Sci*, 36(1): 60–69.

Koski A, Vuori E, Ojanperä I. (2005). Relation of postmortem blood alcohol and drug concentrations in fatal poisonings involving amitriptyline, propoxyphene and promazine, *Hum Exp Toxicol*, 24(8): 389–396.

Sturner WQ, Garriott JC. (1973). Deaths involving propoxyphene. A study of 41 cases over a two-year period, *JAMA*, 223(10): 1125–1130.

Wetli CV, Bednarczyk LR. (1980). Deaths related to propoxyphene overdose: A ten-year assessment, *Southern Med J*, 73(9): 1205–1209.

Propranolol

Brand name: Inderal
Classification: β-blocker
λ: 2–6 h
V_d: 3–5 L/kg
Usual dosage: 40–180 mg bid/tid

Source	Therapeutic/Nontoxic	Toxic	Lethal
Blood	0.03–1 mg/L	2–12 mg/L	4–167 mg/L
Liver	0.2 mg/kg		10–170 mg/kg
Kidney	0.025 mg/kg		26–119 mg/kg
Brain			6–67 mg/kg
Skeletal muscle	0.003 mg/kg		

Comments

- Metabolized by CYP 1A2, 2D6, and 2C19

Selected Sources

Bexar County Medical Examiner's Office data 1996–2015.
Fucci N, Offidani C. (2000). An unusual death by propranolol ingestion, *Am J Forensic Med Path*, 21(1): 56–58.
Gault R, Monforte JR, Khasnabis S. (1977). A death involving propranolol (Inderal), *Clin Tox*, 11(3): 295–299.
Hong CY, Yang WC, Chiang BN. (1983). Importance of membrane stabilizing effect in massive overdose of propranolol: Plasma level study in a fatal case, *Hum Tox*, 2(3): 511–517.
Johnson RD, Lewis RJ. (2006). Quantitation of atenolol, metoprolol, and propranolol in postmortem human fluid and tissue specimens via LC/APCI-MS, *Forensic Sci Int*, 156(2–3): 106–117.
Jones JW, Clark MA, Mullen BL. (1982). Suicide by ingestion of propranolol, *J Forensic Sci*, 27(1): 213–216.
Kristinsson J, Jóhannesson T. (1977). A case of fatal propranolol intoxication, *Acta Pharmacologica et Toxicologica*, 41(2): 190–192.
McVey FK, Corke CF. (1991). Extracorporeal circulation in the management of massive propranolol overdose, *Anaesthesia*, 46(9): 744–746.
Paterson SC. (1985). Drug levels found in cases of fatal self-poisoning, *Forensic Sci Intl*, 27(2): 129–133.
Suarez RV, Greenwald MS, Geraghty E. (1988). Intentional overdosage with propranolol. A report of two cases, *Am J Forensic Med Path*, 9(1): 45–47.

Pseudoephedrine

Brand name: Sudafed; component of many OTC cold medicines
Classification: α and β adrenergic agonist
λ: 3–16 h
V_d: 2–3.5 L/kg
Usual dosage: 30–60 mg q 4–6 h

Source	Therapeutic/Nontoxic	Toxic	Lethal
Blood	0.3–1 mg/L	1.4 mg/L	6[a]–33 mg/L
Liver	5 mg/kg		16 mg/kg[a]

[a] Infant.

Selected Sources

Bexar County Medical Examiner's Office data 1996–2015.
Boland DM, Rein J, Lew EO, Hearn WL. (2003). Fatal cold medication intoxication in an infant, *J Anal Toxicol*, 27(7): 523–526.
Hanzlick R. (1995). National association of medical examiners pediatric toxicology (PedTox) registry report 3. Case submission summary and data for acetaminophen, benzene, carboxyhemoglobin, dextromethorphan, ethanol, phenobarbital, and pseudoephedrine, *Am J Forensic Med Path*, 16(4): 270–277.
Sica DA, Comstock TJ. (1989). Pseudoephedrine accumulation inrRenal failure, *Am J Med Sci*, 298(4): 261–263.

Psilocin/Psilocybin

Brand name: Not applicable
Street names: Magic Mushroom and Shrooms
Classification: Hallucinogen
λ: 1.5–4.5 h
V_d: 2.5–5 L/kg
Usual dosage: 5–20 mg/dose

Source	Nontoxic[a]	Toxic[a]	Lethal[a]
Blood	0.005–0.02 mg/L	0.05 mg/L	0.03[b]–4 mg/L

[a] All concentrations are for psilocin.
[b] Heart transplant patient.

Comments

- Psilocybin (λ 0.5–2 h) rapidly metabolized to active metabolite, psilocin
- Component in certain species of *Psilocybe, Conocybe, Copelandia, Panaeolus, Gymnopilus, Pluteus*, and *Stropharia* mushrooms

Selected Sources

Hasler F, Bourquin D, Brenneisen R, Bär T, Vollenweider FX. (1997). Determination of psilocin and 4-Hydroxyindole-3-Acetic acid in plasma by HPLC-ECD and pharmacokinetic profiles of oral and intravenous psilocybin in man, *Pharmaceutica Acta Helvetiae*, 72(3): 175–184.
Lim TH, Wasywich CA, Ruygrok PN. (2012). A fatal case of "magic mushroom" ingestion in a heart transplant recipient. *Intern Med J*, 42(11): 1268–1269.
Sticht G, Käferstein H. (2000). Detection of psilocin in body fluids, *Forensic Sci Intl*, 113(1–3): 403–407.

Quetiapine

Brand name: Seroquel
Classification: Antipsychotic
λ: 5–7 h
V_d: 6–14 L/kg
Usual dosage: 25–300 mg bid/qd

Source	Therapeutic/Nontoxic	Toxic	Lethal
Blood	0.04–1 mg/L	1.8–20 mg/L	4–50 mg/L
Vitreous			0.9–5 mg/L
Liver			1.1–120 mg/kg
Kidney			4.2 mg/kg
Brain	0.01–5.3 mg/kg		1.2–26 mg/kg
Skeletal muscle			5.9 mg/kg
Cardiac muscle			5.3 mg/kg

Comments

- Metabolized by CYP 3A4
- Prolongs QT interval

Selected Sources

Balit CR, Isbister GK, Hackett LP, Whyte IM. (2003). Quetiapine poisoning: A case series, *Ann Emerg Med*, 42(6): 751–758.

Bexar County Medical Examiner's Office data 1996–2015.

Flammia DD, Valouch T, Venuti S. (2006). Tissue distribution of quetiapine in 20 cases in Virginia, *J Anal Toxicol*, 30(4): 287–292.

Hunfeld NGM, Westerman EM, Boswijk DJ, de Haas JAM, van Putten MJAM, Touw DJ. (2006). Quetiapine in overdosage: A clinical and pharmacokinetic analysis of 14 cases, *Ther Drug Monit*, 28(2): 185–189.

Langman LJ, Kaliciak HA, Carlyle S. (2004). Fatal overdoses associated with quetiapine, *J Anal Toxicol*, 28(6): 520–525.

Parker DR, McIntyre IM. (2005). Case studies of postmortem quetiapine: Therapeutic or toxic concentrations?, *J Anal Toxicol*, 29(5): 407–412.

Skov L, Johansen SS, Linnet K. (2015). Postmortem quetiapine reference concentrations in brain and blood, *J Anal Toxicol*, 39(7): 557–561.

Wise S, Jenkins AJ. (2005). Disposition of quetiapine in biological specimens from postmortem cases, *J Forensic Sci*, 50(1): 209–214.

Quinidine

Brand names: Cardioquin, Duraquin, Quinalan, and Quinidex
Classification: Antiarrhythmic/antimalarial
λ: 6–8 h
V_d: 1.5–4 L/kg
Usual dosage: 200–648 mg bid/tid

Source	Therapeutic/Nontoxic	Toxic	Lethal
Blood	2–5 mg/L	8.5–28 mg/L	19–45 mg/L
Liver	8.8 mg/kg		220 mg/kg
Brain	0.29 mg/kg		

Comments

- Metabolized by CYP 3A
- Prolongs QT interval

Selected Sources

Baselt RC, Cravey RH. (1977). A compendium of therapeutic and toxic concentrations of toxicologically significant drugs in human biofluids, *J Anal Toxicol*, 1: 81–103.

Bexar County Medical Examiner's Office data 1996–2015.

Flanagan RJ. (1998). Guidelines for the interpretation of analytical toxicology results and unit of measurement conversion factors, *Ann Clin Biochem*, 35: 261–267.

Geyer R, Snell K. (1983). Detection of mianserin in a digoxin overdose case, *Bull Intl Assoc Forensic Tox* 17(2): 9–11.

Haapanen EJ, Pellinen TJ. (1981). Hemoperfusion in quinidine intoxication, *Acta Medica Scandinavica*, 210(6): 515–516.

Kerr F, Kenoyer G, Bilitch M. (1971). Quinidine overdose. Neurological and cardiovascular toxicity in a normal person, *Br Heart J*, 33(4): 629–631.

Reimold EW, Reynolds WJ, Fixler DE, McElroy L. (1973). Use of hemodialysis in the treatment of quinidine poisoning, *Pediatrics*, 52(1): 95–99.

Shub C, Gau GT, Sidell PM, Brennan LA. (1978). The management of acute quinidine intoxication, *Chest*, 73(2): 173–178.

Woie L, Oyri A. (1974). Quinidine intoxication treated with hemodialysis, *Acta Medica Scandinavica*, 195(3): 237–239.

Quinine

Brand names: Qualaquin, Quinerva, and Quinite
Classification: Antimalarial
λ: 9–18 h
V_d: 1–2 L/kg
Usual dosage: 542–648 mg tid

Source	Therapeutic/Nontoxic	Toxic	Lethal
Blood	3–10 mg/L	6–16 mg/L	11–58 mg/L
Liver			52–350 mg/kg
Kidney			72–370 mg/kg
Brain			63–72 mg/kg

Comments

- Metabolized by CYP 3A4 and 2C19
- Active metabolite: 3-hydroxyquinine
- Prolongs QT interval

Selected Sources

Bodenhamer JE, Smilkstein MJ. (1993). Delayed cardiotoxicity following quinine overdose: A case report, *J Emer Med*, 11(3): 279–285.
Coutselinis A, Boukis D. (1977). Quinine concentrations in blood and viscera in a case of acute fatal intoxication, *Clin Chem*, 23(5): 914.
Dyson EH, Proudfoot AT, Prescott LF, Heyworth R. (1985). Death and blindness due to overdose of quinine, *Br Med J*, 291: 31–33.
Morrison LD, Velez LI, Shepherd G, Bey T, Benitez FL. (2003). Death by quinine, *Vet Hum Tox*, 45(6): 303–306.
Townend BS, Sturm JW, Whyte S. (2004). Quinine associated blindness, *Aust Family Physician*, 33(8): 627–628.
Wenstone R, Bell M, Mostafa SM. (1989). Fatal adult respiratory distress syndrome after quinine overdose, *Lancet*, 1: 1143–1144.
Winek CL, Davis ER, Collom WD, Shanor SP. (1974). Quinine fatality—Case report, *Clin Tox*, 7(2): 129–132.

Reboxetine

Brand names: Edronax and Vestra
Classification: Antidepressant (NRI)
λ: 12–15 h
V_d: 0.5–2 L/kg
Usual dosage: 2–4 mg bid

Source	Therapeutic/Nontoxic	Toxic	Lethal
Blood	0.03–0.7 mg/L	No data available	

Selected Sources

Hendershot PE, Fleishaker JC, Lin KM, Nuccio ID, Poland RE. (2001). Pharmacokinetics of reboxetine in healthy volunteers with different ethnic descents, *Psychopharmacology*, 155(2): 148–153.

Pellizzoni C, Poggesi I, Jørgensen NP, Edwards DM, Paus E, Benedetti MS. (1996). Pharmacokinetics of reboxetine in healthy volunteers. single against repeated oral doses and lack of enzymatic alterations, *Biopharm Drug Dispos*, 17(7): 623–633.

Poggesi I, Pellizzoni C, Fleishaker JC. (2000). Pharmacokinetics of reboxetine in elderly patients with depressive disorders, *Int J Clin Pharmacol Ther*, 38(5): 254–259.

Ricin

Brand name: Not applicable
Classification: Plant lectin
λ: Unknown
V_d: Unknown
Usual dosage: Not applicable

Source	Nontoxic[a]	Toxic[a]	Lethal[a]
Blood	0.25–10 ng/mL	0.3–1.5 ng/mL ricin 46 ng/mL ricinine [b]	2.3–33 ng/mL ricinine [b]
Urine	None detected ricin 0.2–4.2 ricinine [b]	0.06–0.3 ng/mL ricin 20–8540 ng/mL ricinine [b]	0.3 ng/mL ricin 0.08–58 ng/mL ricinine [b]

[a] Note units are in ng/mL.
[b] Ricinine is a marker for ricin exposure.

Comments

- From *Ricinus communis* (castor bean)
- Inhibits protein synthesis
- Death usually occurs 48–72 h post exposure

Selected Sources

Audi J, Belson M, Patel M, Schier J, Osterloh J. (2005). Ricin poisoning: A comprehensive review, *JAMA*, 294(18): 2342–2351.

Fodstad O, Kvalheim G, Godal A, Lotsberg J, Aamdal S, Høst H. (1984). Phase I study of the plant protein ricin, *Cancer Res*, 44(2): 862–865.

Godal A, Olsnes S, Pihl A. (1981). Radioimmunoassays of abrin and ricin in blood, *J Tox Environ Health*, 8(3): 409–417.

Johnson RC, Lemire SW, Woolfitt AR, Ospina M, Preston KP, Olson CT. (2005). Quantification of ricinine in rat and human urine: A biomarker for ricin exposure, *J Anal Toxicol*, 29(3): 149–155.

Kopferschmitt J, Flesch F, Lugnier A, Sauder P, Jaeger A, Mantz JM. (1983). Acute voluntary intoxication by ricin, *Hum Tox*, 2(2): 239–242.

Pittman CT, Guido JM, Hamelin EI, Blake TA, Johnson RC. (2013). Analysis of a ricin biomarker, ricinine, in 989 individual human urine samples, *J Anal Toxicol*, 37(4): 237–240.

Røen BT, Opstad AM, Haavind A, Tønsager J. (2013). Serial ricinine levels in serum and urine after ricin intoxication, *J Anal Toxicol*, 37(5): 313–317.

Risperidone

Brand name: Risperdal
Classification: Antipsychotic
λ: 2.5–20 h
V_d: 1–2 L/kg
Usual dosage: 0.5–8 mg bid/qd

Source	Therapeutic/Nontoxic	Toxic	Lethal
Blood	0.009–0.1 mg/L	0.3–1.1 mg/L	0.5–1.8 mg/L

Comments

- Active metabolite: 9-hydroxyrisperdone (paliperidone)
- Metabolized by CYP 2D6
- Prolongs QT interval

Selected Sources

Brown K, Levy H, Brenner C, Leffler S, Hamburg EL. (1993). Overdose of risperidone, *Ann Emer Med*, 22(12): 1908–1910.
Hitosugi M, Tsukada C, Yamauchi S, Nagai T. (2014). A case of fatal risperidone poisoning alerts physicians, *J Clin Psychopharmacol*, 34(2): 268–269.
Lee HS, Tan CH, Au LS, Khoo YM. (1997). Serum and urine risperidone concentrations in an acute overdose, *J Clin Psychopharm*, 17(4): 325–326.
Linnet K, Johansen SS. (2014). Postmortem femoral blood concentrations of risperidone, *J Anal Toxicol*, 38(1): 57–60.
Springfield AC, Bodiford E. (1996). An overdose of risperidone, *J Anal Toxicol*, 20(3): 202–203.

Scopolamine

Brand names: Scopace, Scopoderm, and Hyoscine (ophthalmologic gtts)
Classification: Anticholinergic/antiemetic
λ: 2–9.5 h
V_d: 1.5–5 L/kg
Usual dosage: 0.4–0.8 mg q 8 h; 1 mg q 3 d (transdermal)

Source	Therapeutic/Nontoxic	Toxic	Lethal
Blood	0.0002–0.02 mg/L	0.0005–0.01 mg/L	0.005–0.3 mg/L[a]

[a] Co-intoxicant: Citalopram, 0.5–0.7 mg/L.

Comments

- Metabolized by CYP 3A

Selected Sources

Balíková M. (2002). Collective poisoning with hallucinogenous herbal tea, 128(1–2): 50–52.

Lusthof KJ, Bosman IJ, Kubat B, Vincenten-van Maanen MJ. (2017). Toxicological results in a fatal and two non-fatal cases of scopolamine-facilitated robberies, *Forensic Sci Intl*, 274: 79–82.

Putcha L, Cintrón NM, Tsui J, Vanderploeg JM, Kramer WG. (1989). Pharmacokinetics and oral bioavailability of scopolamine in normal subjects, *Pharmaceutical Res*, 6(6): 481–485.

Renner UD, Oertel R, Kirch W. (2005). Pharmacokinetics and pharmacodynamics in clinical use of scopolamine, *Ther Drug Monit*, 27(5): 655–665.

Vallersnes OM, Lund C, Duns AK, Netland H, Rasmussen I. (2009). Epidemic of poisoning caused by scopolamine disguised as Rohypnol tablets, *Clin Toxicol (Phila)*, 47(9): 889–893.

Secobarbital

Brand name: Seconal
Classification: Barbiturate
λ: 15–40 h
V_d: 1.5–2 L/kg
Usual dosage: 100–300 mg qd

Source	Therapeutic/Nontoxic	Toxic	Lethal
Blood	0.48–2.2 mg/L	3.2–22 mg/L	4–40 mg/L
Vitreous			2–10 mg/L
Liver	3.1–3.2 mg/kg		3–213 mg/kg
Kidney	1.8–2.8 mg/kg		3–30 mg/kg
Brain	0.6–1.8 mg/kg		1–25 mg/kg

Comments

- Tolerance can develop and should be considered when interpreting drug concentrations

Selected Sources

Bexar County Medical Examiner's Office data 1996–2015.
Caplan YH, Ottinger WE, Crooks CR. (1983). Therapeutic and toxic drug concentrations in post mortem blood: A six year study in the state of Maryland, *J Anal Toxicol*, 7(5): 225–230.
Finkle BS. (1971). Ubiquitous reds: A local perspective on secobarbital abuse, *Clin Tox*, 4(2): 253–264.
Sunshine I, Hackett E. (1957). Chemical findings in cases of fatal barbiturate intoxications, *J Forensic Sci*, 2(2): 149–158.

Selegiline

Brand names: Eldepryl, Zelapar, Emsam, Deprenyl, and Anipryl
Classification: Anti-Parkinson's (MAOI)
λ: 1–3 h
V_d: 4–25 L/kg
Usual dosage: 5 mg bid

Source	Therapeutic/Nontoxic	Toxic	Lethal
Blood	0.002–0.005 mg/L selegiline 0.04–0.08 mg/L l-meth 0.02–0.05 mg/L l-amphet	No data available	0.2–0.3 mg/L l-meth 0.07–0.08 mg/L l-amphet
Liver			0.7 mg/kg l-meth 0.4 mg/kg l-amphet

Comments

- Active metabolites: l-methamphetamine, l-amphetamine, and l-desmethylselegiline

Selected Sources

Kupiec TC, Chaturvedi AK. (1999). Stereochemical determination of selegiline metabolites in postmortem biological specimens, *J Forensic Sci*, 44(1): 222–226.
Meeker JE, Reynolds PC. (1990). Postmortem tissue methamphetamine concentrations following selegiline administration, *J Anal Toxicol*, 4(5): 330–331.

Sertraline

Brand name: Zoloft
Classification: Antidepressant (SSRI)
λ: 13–45 h
V_d: 20–76 L/kg
Usual dosage: 50–200 mg qd

Source	Therapeutic/Nontoxic	Toxic	Lethal
Blood	0.03–0.9 mg/L	1–2.9 mg/L	5.6–26 mg/L
Vitreous	0.001–0.03 mg/L		
Liver	0.2–36 mg/kg		
Kidney	0.1–8.7 mg/kg		
Skeletal muscle	0.07–2.4 mg/kg		8.3 mg/kg
Lung	0.8–13 mg/kg		
Spleen	0.1–21 mg/kg		
Brain	0.08–5.2 mg/kg		
Cardiac muscle	0.02–2.2 mg/kg		

Comments

- Active metabolite: Desmethylsertraline
- Prolongs QT interval
- Metabolized by CYP 2B6, 2C9, and 2C19

Selected Sources

Bexar County Medical Examiner's Office data 1996–2015.
Brendel DH, Bodkin JA, Yang JM. (2000). Massive sertraline overdose, *Ann Emer Med*, 36(5): 524–526.
Goeringer KE, Raymon L, Christian GD, Logan BK. (2000). Postmortem forensic toxicology of selective serotonin reuptake inhibitors: A review of pharmacology and report of 168 cases, *J Forensic Sci*, 45(3): 633–648.
Levine B, Jenkins AJ, Smialek JE. (1994). Distribution of sertraline in postmortem cases, *J Anal Toxicol*, 18(5): 272–274.
Lewis RJ, Angier MK, Williamson KS, Johnson RD. (2013). Analysis of sertraline in postmortem fluids and tissues in 11 aviation accident victims, *J Anal Toxicol*, 37(4): 208–216.
McIntyre IM, Mallett P. (2012). Sertraline concentrations and postmortem redistribution, *Forensic Sci Int*, 223(1–3): 349–352.
Rohrig TP, Goodson LJ. (2004). A sertraline-intoxicated driver, *J Anal Toxicol*, 28(8): 689–691.

Sildenafil

Brand names: Revatio and Viagra
Classification: Phosphodiesterase inhibitor
λ: 3–5 h
V_d: 1.5–3.5 L/kg
Usual dosage: 25–100 mg qd

Source	Therapeutic/Nontoxic	Toxic	Lethal[a]
Blood	0.04–0.9 mg/L	3.9–22 mg/L	6.3 mg/L[b]
Vitreous	0.09 mg/L		
Liver	0.2–5.5 mg/kg		
Kidney	0.02–4.3 mg/kg		
Brain	0.01–6.4 mg/kg		
Skeletal muscle	0.002–0.04 mg/kg		
Cardiac muscle	0.03–6.1 mg/kg		
Lung	0.3–5.4 mg/kg		
Spleen	0.09–1.4 mg/kg		

[a] Multiple fatalities reported without concentrations due to heart disease.
[b] Concomitant heart disease.

Comments

- Metabolized by CYP 3A4 and 2C9
- Active metabolite: *N*-desmethylsildenafil

Selected Sources

Lewis RJ, Johnson RD, Blank CL. (2006). Quantitative determination of silde-nafil (Viagra) and its metabolite (UK-103,320) in fluid and tissue specimens obtained from six aviation fatalities, *J Anal Toxicol*, 30(1): 14–20.
Matheeussen V, Maudens KE, Anseeuw K, Neels H. (2015). A non-fatal self-poisoning attempt with sildenafil, *J Anal Toxicol*, 39(7): 572–576.
Pagani S, Mirtella D, Mencarelli R, Rodriguez D, Cingolani M. (2005). Postmortem distribution of sildenafil in histological material, *J Anal Toxicol*, 29(4): 254–257.
Tracqui A, Miras A, Tabib A, Raul JS, Ludes B, Malicier D. (2002). Fatal overdosage with sildenafil citrate (Viagra): First report and review of the literature, *Hum Exp Tox*, 21(11): 623–629.

Strychnine

Brand names: Component of pesticides
Classification: Alkaloid
λ: 10–11 h
V_d: 13 L/kg
Usual dosage: Not applicable

Source	Nontoxic	Toxic	Lethal
Blood	Negative	0.1–4.7 mg/L	0.2–61 mg/L
Vitreous			0.4 mg/L
Liver			0.3–175 mg/kg
Kidney			0.5–70 mg/kg
Brain			0.9–2.4 mg/kg
Skeletal muscle			2.3 mg/kg
Cardiac muscle			16 mg/kg

Comments

- From *Strychnos nux vomica*
- Causes muscular convulsions

Selected Sources

Bexar County Medical Examiner's Office data 1996–2015.

Duverneuil C, de la Grandmaison GL, de Mazancourt P, Alvarez J-C. (2004). Liquid chromatography/photodiode array detection for determination of strychnine in blood: A fatal case report, *Forensic Sci Intl*, 141(1): 17–21.

Heiser JM, Daya MR, Magnussen AR, Norton RL, Spyker DA, Allen DW. (1992). Massive strychnine intoxication: Serial blood levels in a fatal case, *J Tox Clin Tox*, 30(2): 269–283.

Lindsey T, O'Hara J, Irvine R, Kerrigan S. (2004). Strychnine overdose following ingestion of gopher bait, *J Anal Toxicol*, 28(2): 135–137.

Marques EP, Gil F, Proenca P, Monsanto P, Oliveira MF, Castanheira A. (2000). Analytical method for the determination of strychnine in tissues by gas chromatography/mass spectrometry: Two case reports, *Forensic Sci Intl*, 110(2): 145–152.

Palatnick W, Meatherall R, Sitar D, Tenenbein M. (1997). Toxicokinetics of acute strychnine poisoning, *J Tox Clin Tox*, 35(6): 617–620.

Rosano TG, Hubbard JD, Meola JM, Swift TA. (2000). Fatal strychnine poisoning: Application of gas chromatography and tandem mass spectrometry, *J Anal Toxicol*, 24(7): 642–647.

Wood D, Webster E, Martinez D, Dargan P, Jones A. (2002). Case report: Survival after deliberate strychnine self-poisoning, with toxicokinetic data, *Critical Care*, 6(5): 456–459.

Suvorexant

Brand name: Belsomra
Classification: Hypnotic
λ: 8–15 h
V_d: 0.7 L/kg
Usual dosage: 5–20 mg qHS

Source	Nontoxic	Toxic	Lethal
Blood	0.1–1.5 mg/L	No data available	

Comments

• Metabolized by CYP 3A

Selected Sources

Belsomra Prescribing Information (package insert) Merck & Co, Inc. 2014.
Sun H, Yee KL, Gill S et al. (2015). Psychomotor effects, pharmacokinetics and safety of the orexin receptor antagonist suvorexant administered in combination with alcohol in healthy subjects, *J Psychopharmacol*, 29(11): 1159–1169.
Sutton EL. (2015). Profile of suvorexant in the management of insomnia, *Drug Des Devel Ther*, 9: 6035–6042.
Uemura N, McCrea J, Sun H et al. (2015). Effects of the orexin receptor antagonist suvorexant on respiration during sleep in healthy subjects, *J Clin Pharmacol*, 55(10): 1093–1100.

Tadalafil

Brand name: Cialis
Classification: Phosphodiesterase inhibitor
λ: 16–22 h
V_d: 0.5–1 L/kg
Usual dosage: 5–20 mg qd

Source	Therapeutic/Nontoxic	Toxic	Lethal
Blood	0.02–0.4 mg/L	No data available	

Selected Sources

Forgue ST, Phillips DL, Bedding AW, Payne CD, Jewell H, Patterson BE. (2007). Effects of gender, age, diabetes mellitus and renal and hepatic impairment on tadalafil pharmacokinetics, *Br J Clin Pharm*, 63(1): 24–35.

Mehrotra N, Gupta M, Kovar A, Meibohm B. (2007). The role of pharmacokinetics and pharmacodynamics in phosphodiesterase-5 inhibitor therapy, *Intl J Impotence Res*, 19(3): 253–264.

Proença P, Mustra C, Marcos M, Franco JM, Corte-Real F, Vieira DN. (2013). Validated UPLC-MS/MS assay for the determination of synthetic phosphodiesterase type-5 inhibitors in postmortem blood samples. *J Forensic Leg Med*, 20(6): 655–658.

Trocóniz IF, Tillmann C, Staab A, Rapado J, Forgue ST. (2007). Tadalafil population pharmacokinetics in patients with erectile dysfunction, *Eur J Clin Pharm*, 63(6): 583–590.

Tapentadol

Brand name: Nucynta
Classification: Opioid
λ: 4–5 h
V_d: 6–9 L/kg
Usual dosage: 50–100 mg q 4–6 h

Source	Therapeutic/Nontoxic	Toxic	Lethal
Blood	0.02–0.4 mg/L	No data available	0.8[a]–6.6 mg/L
Vitreous			0.9 mg/L[a]
Liver	0.5 mg/kg		1.7–9.9 mg/kg[a]
Brain	0.4 mg/kg		1.6 mg/kg[a]

[a] Co-intoxicants: Blood tapentadol, 0.8–1.1 mg/L.

Comments

- Metabolized by CYP2C9 and CYP2C19
- Can contribute to serotonin system if combined with other seroto-nergic drugs

Selected Sources

Anderson D, deQintana S, Valencia KH. (2010). New drug: Tapentadol (Nucynta), *Toxtalk*, 34(3): 22–23.

Bexar County Medical Examiner's Office data 1996–2015.

Cantrell FL, Mallett P, Aldridge L, Verilhac K, McIntyre IM. (2016). A tapentadol related fatality: Case report with postmortem concentrations, *Forensic Sci Int*, 266: e1–e3.

Franco DM, Ali Z, Levine B, Middleberg RA, Fowler DR. (2014). Case report of a fatal intoxication by nucynta, *Am J Forensic Med Pathol*, 35(4): 234–236.

Kemp W, Schlueter S, Smalley E. (2013). Death due to apparent intravenous injection of tapentadol, *J Forensic Sci*, 58(1): 288–291.

Larson SJ, Pestaner J, Prashar SK, Bayard C, Zarwell LW, Pierre-Louis M. (2012). Postmortem distribution of Tapentadol and N-desmethyltapentadol, *J Anal Toxicol* 36: 440–443.

Temazepam

Brand names: Restoril and Normison
Classification: Benzodiazepine
λ: 7–18 h (biphasic)
V_d: 1–1.5 L/kg
Usual dosage: 7.5–30 mg qHS

Source	Therapeutic/Nontoxic	Toxic	Lethal
Blood	0.1–1 mg/L	1 mg/L	2.9–10 mg/L
Liver			39–107 mg/kg
Brain	0.003–0.2 mg/kg		
Skeletal muscle	0.5–0.6 mg/kg		3–8.8 mg/kg

Comments

- Active metabolite: Oxazepam
- Metabolite of diazepam
- Tolerance can develop and should be considered when interpreting drug concentrations

Selected Sources

Bexar County Medical Examiner's Office data 1996–2015.
Forrest AR, Marsh I, Bradshaw C, Braich SK. (1986). Fatal temazepam overdoses, *Lancet*, 2: 226.
Langford AM, Taylor KK, Pounder DJ. (1998). Drug concentration in selected skeletal muscles, *J Forensic Sci*, 43(1): 22–27.
Martin CD, Chan SC. (1986). Distribution of temazepam in body fluids and tissues in lethal overdose, *J Anal Toxicol*, 10(2): 77–78.
Skov L, Dollerup HKM, Johansen SS, Linnet K. (2016). Postmortem brain and blood reference concentrations of alprazolam, bromazepam, chlordiazepoxide, diazepam, and their metabolites and a review of the literature, *J Anal Tox*, 40(7): 529–536.
Williams KR, Pounder DJ. (1997). Site-to-site variability of drug concentrations in skeletal muscle, *Am J Forensic Med Path*, 18(3): 246–250.

Terbutaline

Brand names: Brethine and Bricanyl
Classification: β-agonist
λ: 2.5–4.5 h
V_d: 1–2 L/kg
Usual dosage: 2.5–5 mg q 6 h

Source	Therapeutic/Nontoxic	Toxic	Lethal
Blood	0.002–0.01 mg/L	0.04–0.2 mg/L	0.04 mg/L[a]
Liver	0.009–0.05 mg/kg		
Kidney	0.05 mg/kg		
Skeletal muscle	0.06 mg/kg		
Cardiac muscle	0.004–0.04 mg/kg		

[a] Concomitant natural disease.

Selected Sources

Couper FJ, Drummer OH. (1996). Gas chromatographic-mass spectrometric determination of beta 2-agonists in postmortem blood: Application in forensic medicine, *J Chromatogr B Biomed Appl*, 685(2): 265–272.

Heath A, Hultén BA. (1987). Terbutaline concentrations in self-poisoning: A case report, *Hum Tox*, 6(6): 525–526.

Jarvie DR, Thompson AM, Dyson EH. (1987). Laboratory and clinical features of self-poisoning with salbutamol and terbutaline, *Clin Chem Acta* 168(3): 313–322.

Leferink JG, Wagemaker-Engels I, Maes RA, Van der Straeten M. (1979). Determination of terbutaline in post mortem human tissues by gas chromatography-mass spectrometry, *Vet Hum Tox*, 21 (Suppl): 164–167.

Tetrahydrocannabinol

Brand names: Marinol, Cesamet, and Sativex (dronabinol, nabilone)
Alternate name: delta-9-tetrahydrocannabinol (Δ^9THC, THC)
Street names: Pot, Weed, Grass, Mary Jane, Dope, Doobie, Hashish, and Hash
Classification: Cannabinoid/psychoactive
λ: 2–57 h
V_d: 1–10 L/kg
Usual dosage: 10–30 mg/dose

Source	Therapeutic/Nontoxic		Toxic	
	THC	11-OH-THC	THC	Lethal
Blood	0.001–0.20 mg/L	0.02–0.1 mg/L	0.2 mg/L	See below[a]
Serum/plasma	0.005–0.04 mg/L	0.006–0.04 mg/L		
Liver	0.02–0.05 mg/kg	0.001–0.07 mg/kg		
Lung	0.002–0.15 mg/kg	0.001–0.01 mg/kg		
Kidney	0.001–0.45 mg/kg	0.002–0.02 mg/kg		
Spleen	0.001–0.02 mg/kg	0.01–0.02 mg/kg		
Muscle	0.001–0.4 mg/kg	0.01 mg/kg		
Brain	0.001–0.04 mg/kg	0.001–0.04 mg/kg		
Heart	0.002–0.5 mg/kg	0.002–0.2 mg/kg		

[a] May be associated with sudden cardiac death in the presence of severe coronary artery diease.

Comments

- Active ingredient in *Cannabis*
- Metabolized to 11-OH-THC (λ 12–36 h) (active) and THC-COOH (λ 1–6 d)
- Metabolized by CYP 2C9, CYP 3A4
- PM concentrations should be interpreted with caution as cannabinoids exhibit moderate PMR and have been detected 30 days after sustained abstinence in live chronic users
- Distribution of cannabinoids between plasma and whole blood is not equal
- Second hand smoke
  - In high-intensity environment (whole blood)—THC 0.0–0.006 mg/L; COOH-THC 0.0–0.005 mg/L
  - In coffee shop (serum)—THC 0.0–0.0007 mg/L; COOH-THC 0.0–0.002 mg/L

Selected Sources

André C, Jaber-Filho JA, Bento RMQ, Damasceno LMP, Aquino-Neto FR. (2006). Delirium following ingestion of marijuana present in chocolate cookies, *CNS Spectrums*, 11(4): 262–264.

Bergamaschi MM, Karschner EL, Goodwin RS, Scheidweiler KB, Hirvonen J, Queiroz RHC, Huestis MA. (2013). Impact of prolonged cannabinoid excretion in chronic daily cannabis smokers' blood on per se drugged driving laws, *Clin Chem*, 59(3): 519–523.

Cone EJ, Bigelow GE, Herrmann ES, Mitchell JM, LoDico C, Flegel R, Vandrey R. (2015). Nonsmoker exposure to secondhand cannabis smoke. III. Oral fluid and blood drug concentrations and corresponding subjective effects, *J Anal Toxicol*, 39: 497–509.

Cone EJ, Mitchell JM, Bigelow GE, Herrmann ES, LoDico C, Flegel R, Vandrey R et al. (2015). Passive exposure to secondhand cannabis smoke. Disposition in Urine, Oral Fluid and Blood. *Presented at Society for Forensic Toxicologists Annual Meeting.* Atlanta, GA.

Garrett CP, Braithwaite RA, Teale JD. (1977). Unusual case of tetrahydrocannabinol intoxication confirmed by radioimmunoassay, *Br Med J*, 2: 166.

Gaziano JM. (2008). Marijuana use among those at risk for cardiovascular events, *Am Heart J*, 155: 395–396.

Giroud C, Menetrey A, Augsburger M, Buclin T, Sanchez-Mazas P, Mangin P. (2001). Delta(9)-THC, 11-OH-Delta(9)-THC and Delta(9)-THCCOOH plasma or serum to whole blood concentrations distribution ratios in blood samples taken from living and dead people, *Forensic Sci Int*, 123(2–3): 159–164.

Holland MG, Schwope DM, Stoppacher R, Gillen SB, Huestis MA. (2011). Postmortem redistribution of delta-9-tetrahydrocannabinol (THC), 11-hydroxy-THC (11-OH-THC), and 11-nor-9-carboxy-THC (THCCOOH) *Forensic Sci Int*, 212(1–3): 247–251.

Hunt CA, Jones RT. (1980). Tolerance and disposition of tetrahydrocannabinol in man, *J Pharm Exp Therapeutics*, 215(1): 35–44.

Law B. (1981). Cases of cannabis abuse detected by analysis of body fluids, *Forensic Sci Soc J*, 21(1): 31–39.

Rohrich J, Schimmel I, Zörntlein S, Becker J, Drobnik S, Kaufmann T, Kuntz V, Urban R. (2010). Concentrations of delta9-tetrahydrocannabinol and 11-nor-9-carboxytetrahydrocannabinol in blood and urine after passive exposure to cannabis smoke in a coffee shop, *J Anal Toxicol*, 34: 196–203.

Saenz SR, Lewis RJ, Angies MK, Wagner JR. (2017). Postmortem fluid and tissues concentrations of THC, 11-OH-THC and THC-COOH, *J Anal Toxicol*, 41: 508–516.

Schwilke EW, Karschner EL, Lowe RH, Gordon AM, Cadet JL, Herning RI, Huestis MA. (2009). Intra- and intersubject whole blood/plasma cannabinoid ratios determined by 2-dimensional, electron impact GC/MS with cryofocusing, *Clin Chem*, 55(6): 1188–1195.

Tewari SN, Sharma JD. (1980). Detection of delta-9-tetrahydrocannabinol in the organs of a suspected case of cannabis poisoning, *Tox Lett*, 5(3–4): 279–281.

Theophylline

Brand names: Quibron-T, Slo-phyllin, Senophylline, Theo-24, Theodur, and Slo-bid
Classification: Bronchodilator
λ: 3–8 h
V_d: 0.3–0.7 L/kg
Usual dosage: 5–20 mg/kg/d divided q 4–6 h

Source	Therapeutic/Nontoxic	Toxic	Lethal
Blood	1–20 mg/L	31–170 mg/L	63–290 mg/L
Liver			108–275 mg/kg
Kidney			212 mg/kg
Brain			120–231 mg/kg

Comments

• Metabolized by CYP 1A2 and 2E1

Selected Sources

Anderson JR, Poklis A, Slavin RG. (1983). A fatal case of theophylline intoxication, *Arch Int Med*, 143(3): 559–560.

Bexar County Medical Examiner's Office data 1996–2015.

Druid H, Holmgren P. (1997). A compilation of fatal and control concentrations of drugs in postmortem femoral blood, *J Forensic Sci*, 42(1): 79–87.

Ehlers SM, Zaske DE, Sawchuk RJ. (1978). Massive theophylline overdose. Rapid elimination by charcoal hemoperfusion, *JAMA*, 240(5): 474–475.

Korsheed S, Selby NM, Fluck RJ. (2007). Treatment of severe theophylline poisoning with the molecular adsorbent recirculating system (MARS), *Nephrol Dial Transplant*, 22(3): 969–970.

Loveland MR. (1974). Fatal theophylline poisoning, *Bull Intl Assoc Forensic Tox*, 10(1): 16.

Rutten J, van den Berg B, van Gelder T, van Saase J. (2005). Severe theophylline intoxication: A delay in charcoal haemoperfusion solved by oral activated charcoal, *Nephrol Dial Transplant*, 20(12): 2868–2869.

Tsokos M, Sperhake JP. (2002). Coma blisters in a case of fatal theophylline intoxication, *Am J Forensic Med Path*, 23(3): 292–294.

Winek CL, Bricker JD, Collom WD, Fochtman FW. (1980). Theophylline fatalities, *Forensic Sci Intl*, 15(3): 233–236.

Thiopental

Brand name: Pentothal
Classification: Barbiturate
λ: 3–28 h
V_d: 0.4–4 L/kg
Usual dosage: 25–250 mg/dose

Source	Therapeutic/Nontoxic	Toxic	Lethal
Blood	3–50 mg/L[a]	8–10 mg/L	11–279 mg/L
Liver			32–114 mg/kg
Kidney			16–41 mg/kg
Brain			3.3–22 mg/kg
Skeletal muscle			5.4–55 mg/kg
Cardiac muscle			5–64 mg/kg

[a] Therapeutic concentrations during surgical anesthesia.

Comments

- Active metabolite: Pentobarbital
- Therapeutic concentrations can be fatal if drug not administered in a monitored, medical setting

Selected Sources

Backer RC. (1975). Thiopental suicide—Case report, *J Tox Clin Tox*, 8(3): 283–287.

Bruce AM, Oliver JS, Smith H. (1977). A suicide by thiopentone injection, *Forensic Sci*, 9(3): 205–207.

Campbell JE. (1960). Deaths associated with anesthesia, *J Forensic Sci*, 5: 501–549.

Druid H, Holmgren P. (1997). A compilation of fatal and control concentrations of drugs in postmortem femoral blood, *J Forensic Sci*, 42(1): 79–87.

Fernando GC. (1990). A suicide by thiopentone infusion, *Am J Forensic Med Path*, 11(4): 309–311.

Sanganalmath PU, Nagaraju PM, Mohan BM. (2013). HPTLC method for the assay of thiopental in post-mortem blood in a fatal case of suicide, *J Pharm Biomed Anal*, 80: 89–93.

Winek CL, Collom WD, Davis ER. (1969). Death from rectal thiopental, *J Tox Clin Tox*, 2: 75–79.

Thioridazine

Brand name: Mellaril
Classification: Antipsychotic
λ: 7–36 h
V_d: 18 L/kg
Usual dosage: 20–200 mg bid/tid/qid

Source	Therapeutic/Nontoxic	Toxic	Lethal
Blood	0.1–0.7 mg/L	2.4–12 mg/L	1.8–28 mg/L
Liver	3–7 mg/kg		25–513 mg/kg
Kidney			18–135 mg/kg
Brain			6.4 mg/kg
Skeletal muscle	0.3–1.4 mg/kg		

Comments

- Active metabolite: Mesoridazine
- Metabolized by CYP 2D6
- Prolongs QT interval
- Causes agranulocytosis and hepatitis

Selected Sources

Baselt RC, Wright JA, Gross EM. (1978). Human tissue distribution of thioridazine during therapy and after poisoning, *J Anal Toxicol*, 2: 41–43.

Bexar County Medical Examiner's Office data 1996–2015.

Bonnichsen R, Geertinger P, Maehly AC. (1970). Toxicological data on phenothiazine drugs in autopsy cases, *Zeitschrift für Rechtsmedizin*, 67(3): 158–169.

Caplan YH, Ottinger WE, Crooks CR. (1983). Therapeutic and toxic drug concentrations in post mortem blood: A six year study in the State of Maryland, *J Anal Toxicol*, 7(5): 225–230.

Donlon PT, Tupin JP. (1977). Successful suicides with thioridazine and mesoridazine: A result of probable cardiotoxicity, *Arch Gen Psychiatry*, 34(8): 955–957.

Druid H, Holmgren P. (1997). A compilation of fatal and control concentrations of drugs in postmortem femoral blood, *J Forensic Sci*, 42(1): 79–87.

Langford AM, Taylor KK, Pounder DJ. (1998). Drug concentration in selected skeletal muscles, *J Forensic Sci*, 43(1): 22–27.

Murray LM, Hackett LP, Hett KF. (2001). Delayed absorption and peak cardiotoxicity following massive thioridazine overdose, *Clin Tox*, 39(5): 493–494.

Poklis A, Wells CE, Juenge EC. (1982). Thioridazine and its metabolites in post mortem blood, including two stereoisomeric ring sulfoxides, *J Anal Toxicol*, 6(5): 250–252.

Tiagabine

Brand name: Gabitril
Classification: Anticonvulsant
λ: 4–9 h
V_d: 0.5–2 L/kg
Usual dosage: 2–16 mg bid

Source	Therapeutic/Nontoxic	Toxic	Lethal
Blood	0.04–0.5 mg/L	0.4–4.6 mg/L	7–9 mg/L

Comments

- Metabolized by CYP 3A

Selected Sources

Forbes RA, Kalra H, Hackett LP, Daly FFS. (2007). Deliberate self-poisoning with tiagabine: An unusual toxidrome, *Emer Med Australasia*, 19(6): 556–558.

Fulton JA, Hoffman RS, Nelson LS. (2005). Tiagabine overdose: A case of status epilepticus in a non-epileptic patient, *Clin Tox*, 43(7): 869–871.

Gustavson LE, Mengel HB. (1995). Pharmacokinetics of tiagabine, a γ-aminobutyric acid-uptake inhibitor, in healthy subjects after single and multiple doses, *Epilepsia*, 36(6): 605–611.

Kazzi ZN, Jones CC, Morgan BW. (2006). Seizures in a pediatric patient with a tiagabine overdose, *J Med Toxicol*, 2(4): 160–162.

Leach JP, Stolarek I, Brodie MJ. (1995). Deliberate overdose with the novel anticonvulsant tiagabine, *Seizure*, 4(2): 155–157.

Ostrovskiy D, Spanaki MV, Morris GL. (2002). Tiagabine overdose can induce convulsive status epilepticus, *Epilepsia*, 43(7): 773–774.

Viner, K, Clifton JC, Hryhorczuk DO. (1999). Status epilepticus following acute tiagabine overdose, *Clin Tox*, 37(5): 638.

Topiramate

Brand name: Topamax
Classification: Anticonvulsant
λ: 19–25 h
V_d: 0.6–0.8 L/kg
Usual dosage: 50–400 mg bid

Source	Therapeutic/Nontoxic	Toxic	Lethal
Blood	1.7–20 mg/L	4.2[a]–10 mg/L	36–170 mg/L
Vitreous			65–118 mg/L
Liver	12–14 mg/kg		140–234 mg/kg
Kidney	9–10 mg/kg		55 mg/kg
Brain			157 mg/kg

[a] Pediatric patient.

Selected Sources

Beer B, Libiseller K, Oberacher H, Pavlic M. (2010). A fatal intoxication case involving topiramate, *Forensic Sci Int*, 202(1–3): e9–e11.

Easterling DE, Zakzewski T, Moyer MD. (1988). Plasma pharmacokinetics of topiramate, a new anticonvulsant in humans, *Epilepsia*, 29: 662.

Kiely ER, Uptegrove RL, Marinetti LJ. (2004). A case report of fatal topiramate toxicity, *ToxTalk*, 28(2): 9.

Langman LJ, Kaliciak HA, Boone SA. (2003). Fatal acute topiramate toxicity, *J Anal Toxicol*, 27(5): 323–324.

Levine B, Phipps RJ, Naso C, Fahie K, Fowler D. (2010). Tissue distribution of newer anticonvulsant drugs in postmortem cases, *J Anal Toxicol*, 34(8): 506–509.

Lin G, Lawrence R. (2006). Pediatric case report of topiramate toxicity, *J Tox Clin Tox*, 44(1): 67–69.

Perucca E. (1996). Pharmacokinetic profile of topiramate in comparison with other new antiepileptic drugs, *Epilepsia*, 37 (Suppl 2): S8–S13.

Traub SJ, Howland MA, Hoffman RS, Nelson LS. (2003). Acute topiramate toxicity, *J Tox Clin Tox*, 41(7): 987–990.

Tramadol

Brand names: Ultram and Ultracet (w/acetaminophen)
Classification: Opioid
λ: 5–7 h
V_d: 3–5 L/kg
Usual dosage: 50–100 mg q 4–6 h

Source	Therapeutic/Nontoxic	Toxic	Lethal
Blood	0.1–3.0 mg/L	1–24 mg/L	1.3–89 mg/L
Liver	0.3 mg/kg		6.2–69 mg/kg
Kidney	0.4 mg/kg		3–37 mg/kg
Skeletal muscle			1.1 mg/kg
Brain			44 mg/kg
Lung			106 mg/kg

Comments

- Metabolized by CYP 2D6 and CYP 3A4
- Active metabolite: O-desmethyltramadol, 200x more active than parent drug
- Tolerance may develop and should be considered when interpreting drug concentrations
- Can contribute to serotonin system if combined with other serotonergic drugs

Selected Sources

Barbera N, Fisichella M, Bosco A, Indorato F, Spadaro G, Romano G. (2013). A suicidal poisoning due to tramadol. A metabolic approach to death investigation, *J Forensic Leg Med*, 20(5): 555–558.

Bexar County Medical Examiner's Office data 1996–2015.

De Backer B, Renardy F, Denooz R, Charlier C. (2010). Quantification in postmortem blood and identification in urine of tramadol and its two main metabolites in two cases of lethal tramadol intoxication, *J Anal Toxicol*, 34(9): 599–604.

Levine B, Ramcharitar V, Smialek JE. (1997). Tramadol distribution in four postmortem cases, *Forensic Sci Intl*, 86(1–2): 43–48.

Moore KA, Cina SJ, Jones R, Selby DM, Levine B, Smith ML. (1999). Tissue distribution of tramadol and metabolites in an overdose fatality, *Am J Forensic Med Path*, 20(1): 98–100.

Oertel R, Pietsch J, Arenz N, Zeitz SG, Goltz L, Kirch W. (2011). Distribution of metoprolol, tramadol, and midazolam in human autopsy material, *J Chromatogr A*, 1218(30): 4988–4994.

Randall C, Crane J. (2014). Tramadol deaths in Northern Ireland: A review of cases from 1996 to 2012, *J Forensic Leg Med*, 23: 32–36.

Trazodone

Brand name: Desyrel
Classification: Antidepressant
λ: 3–9 h
V_d: 0.9–1.5 L/kg
Usual dosage: 50–400 mg bid

Source	Therapeutic/Nontoxic	Toxic	Lethal
Blood	0.5–2.0 mg/L	1.5–26 mg/L	5–25 mg/L
Liver	0.6–2.2 mg/kg		26–82 mg/kg
Kidney			40 mg/kg
Brain			21 mg/kg
Skeletal muscle			6.6–9 mg/kg

Comments

- Active metabolite: m-chlorophenylpiperzine
- Metabolized by CYP 3A4
- May prolong QT interval

Selected Sources

Bexar County Medical Examiner's Office data 1996–2015.
de Meester A, Carbutti G, Gabriel L, Jacques JM. (2001). Fatal overdose with trazodone: Case report and literature review, *Acta Clinica Belgica*, 56(4): 258–261.
Flanagan RJ. (1998). Guidelines for the interpretation of analytical toxicology results and unit of measurement conversion factors, *Ann Clin Biochem*, 35: 261–267.
Henry JA, Ali CJ, Caldwell R, Flanagan RJ. (1984). Acute trazodone poisoning: Clinical signs and plasma concentrations, *Psychopathology*, 17(Suppl 2): 77–81.
Lesar T, Kingston R, Dahms R, Saxena K. (1983). Trazodone overdose, *Ann Emer Med*, 12(4): 221–223.
Martin A, Pounder DJ. (1992). Post-mortem toxico-kinetics of trazodone, *Forensic Sci Intl*, 56(2): 201–207.
Martínez MA, Ballesteros S, de la Torre CS, Almarza E. (2005). Investigation of a fatality due to trazodone poisoning: Case report and literature review, *J Anal Toxicol*, 29(4): 262–268.
McIntyre IM, Mallett P, Stabley R. (2015). Postmortem distribution of trazodone concentrations, *Forensic Sci Intl*, 251: 195–201.
Root I, Ohlson GB. (1984). Trazodone overdose: Report of two cases, *J Anal Toxicol*, 8(2): 91–94.

Triazolam

Brand name: Halcion
Classification: Benzodiazepine
λ: 1–5 h
V_d: 1–3 L/kg
Usual dosage: 0.125–0.5 mg qHS

Source	Therapeutic/Nontoxic	Toxic	Lethal
Blood	0.002–0.02 mg/L	0.004–0.04 mg/L	0.01–0.4 mg/L
Liver			0.09–0.5 mg/kg
Kidney			0.07–0.3 mg/kg
Brain			0.1 mg/kg
Skeletal muscle			0.1 mg/kg

Comments

- Metabolized by CYP 3A4
- Tolerance can develop and should be considered when interpreting drug concentrations

Selected Sources

Bexar County Medical Examiner's Office data 1996–2015.

Joynt BP. (1993). Triazolam blood concentrations in forensic cases in Canada, *J Anal Toxicol*, 17(3): 171–177.

Levine B, Grieshaber A, Pestaner J, Moore KA, Smialek JE. (2002). Distribution of triazolam and alpha-hydroxytriazolam in a fatal intoxication case, *J Anal Toxicol*, 26(1): 52–54.

Moriya F, Hashimoto Y. (2003). A case of fatal triazolam overdose, *Legal Med*, 5(Suppl 1): S91–S95.

Olson KR, Yin L, Osterloh J, Tani A. (1985). Coma caused by trivial triazolam overdose, *Am J Emer Med*, 3(3): 210–211.

Steentoft A, Worm K. (1993). Cases of fatal triazolam poisoning, *Forensic Sci Soc J*, 33(1): 45–48.

Sunter JP, Bal TS, Cowan WK. (1988). Three cases of fatal triazolam poisoning, *Br Med J*, 297: 719.

Takayasu T, Kondo T, Sato Y, Ohshima T. (2000). Determination of triazolam by GC-MS in two autopsy cases: Distribution in body fluids and organs, *Leg Med*, 2(4): 206–211.

Trihexylphenidyl

Brand names: Artane, Trihexane, and Benzhexal
Classification: Anti-Parkinson's agent
λ: 3–10 h
V_d: Unknown
Usual dosage: 1–20 mg qd

Source	Therapeutic/Nontoxic	Toxic	Lethal
Blood	0.005–0.06 mg/L	No data available	0.1–1.8 mg/L[a]
Liver			0.5 mg/kg[a]

[a] All fatalities have either co-intoxicants or significant natural disease present.

Comments

- Toxicities associated with torsade de pointes

Selected Sources

Bexar County Medical Examiner's Office data 2003–2015.

Gall JA, Drummer OH, Landgrem AJ. (1995). Death due to benzhexol toxicity, *Forensic Sci Int*, 71: 9–14.

Hadidi KA. (2004). Development of a screening method for the most commonly abused anticholinergic drugs in Jordan; trihexyphenidyl, procyclidine and biperiden, *Leg Med (Tokyo)*, 6(4): 233–241.

Liao WB, Bullard MJ, Kuo CT, Hsiao CT, Chu PH, Chiang CW. (1996). Anticholinergic overdose induced torsade de pointes successfully treated with verapamil, *Jpn Heart J*, 37(6): 925–931.

Petković S, Durendić-Brenesel M, Dolai M, Samojlik I. (2011). Fatal intoxication because of trihexyphenidyl, *J Forensic Sci*, 56(5): 1383–1386.

Trimipramine

Brand name: Surmontil
Classification: Antidepressant (TCA)
λ: 16–39 h
V_d: 17–48 L/kg
Usual dosage: 50–100 mg qHS

Source	Therapeutic/Nontoxic	Toxic	Lethal
Blood	0.01–0.4 mg/L	0.4–2 mg/L	1.8–12 mg/L
Liver			51–544 mg/kg

Comments

- Active metabolite: Desmethyl-trimipramine
- May prolong QT interval

Selected Sources

Bexar County Medical Examiner's Office data 1996–2015.
Druid H, Holmgren P. (1991). Fatal seizures associated with trimipramine poisoning, *Forensic Sci Intl*, 49(1): 75–79.
Fraser AD, Isner AF, Perry RA. (1987). Distribution of trimipramine and its major metabolites in a fatal overdose case, *J Anal Toxicol*, 11(4): 168–170.
Gutscher K, Rauber-Lüthy C, Haller M, Braun M, Kupferschmidt H, Kullak-Ublick GA, Ceschi A. (2013). Patterns of toxicity and factors influencing severity in acute adult trimipramine poisoning, *Br J Clin Pharmacol*, 75(1): 227–235.
Hucker RS. (1983). A fatal clomipramine and trimipramine poisoning, *Bull Intl Assoc Forensic Tox*, 17(2): 20–22.

Valproic Acid

Brand names: Depakene, Depacon, and Depakote
Alternate names: Valproate, divalproex, and dipropylacetic acid
Classification: Anticonvulsant
λ: 5–20 h
V_d: 0.1–0.4 L/kg
Usual dosage: 250–500 mg tid

Source	Therapeutic/Nontoxic	Toxic	Lethal
Blood	17–100 mg/L	200–1440 mg/L	556–2204 mg/L
Vitreous			516–821 mg/L
Liver			104–985 mg/kg
Kidney			69–1580 mg/kg
Brain			510–545 mg/kg
Skeletal muscle	30–124 mg/kg		482 mg/kg
Cardiac muscle			670 mg/kg

Comments

- Metabolized by CYP 2C9 and 2C19

Selected Sources

Andersen GO, Ritland S. (1995). Life threatening intoxication with sodium valproate, *J Tox Clin Tox*, 33(3): 279–284.

Bexar County Medical Examiner's Office data 1996–2015.

Christianson GS, Mowry JB, Furbee RB. (2001). Death associated with massive valproic acid ingestion, *J Tox Clin Tox*, 39: 498.

Garnier R, Boudignat O, Fournier PE. (1982). Valproate poisoning, *Lancet*, 2: 97.

Graudins A, Aaron CK. (1996). Delayed peak serum valproic acid in massive divalproex overdose—treatment with charcoal hemoperfusion, *J Tox Clin Tox*, 34(3): 335–341.

Lee WL, Yang CC, Deng JF, Chen YF, Lin HD, Wang PH. (1998). A case of severe hyperammonemia and unconsciousness following sodium valproate intoxication, *Vet Hum Tox*, 40(6): 346–348.

Lokan RJ, Dinan AC. (1988). An apparent fatal valproic acid poisoning, *J Anal Toxicol*, 12(1): 35–37.

Poklis A, Poklis JL, Trautman D, Treece C, Backer R, Harvey CM. (1998). Disposition of valproic acid in a case of fatal intoxication, *J Anal Toxicol*, 22(6): 537–540.

Proença P, Franco JM, Mustra C, Marcos M, Pereira AR, Corte-Real F, Vieira DN. (2011). An UPLC-MS/MS method for the determination of valproic acid in blood of a fatal intoxication case, *J Forensic Leg Med*, 18(7): 320–324.

Vardenafil

Brand name: Levitra
Classification: Phosphodiesterase inhibitor
λ: 4–5 h
V_d: 2–3 L/kg
Usual dosage: 5–20 mg qd

Source	Therapeutic/Nontoxic	Toxic	Lethal
Blood	0.003–0.3 mg/L	No data available	
Liver	0.09 mg/kg		
Kidney	0.02 mg/kg		
Skeletal muscle	0.008 mg/kg		
Cardiac muscle	0.03 mg/kg		
Lung	0.2 mg/kg		

Comments

- May prolong QT interval
- Metabolized by CYP3A4; also CYP3A5 and CYP2C

Selected Sources

Johnson RD, Lewis RJ, Angier MK. (2007). The postmortem distribution of vardenafil (Levitra) in an aviation accident victim with an unusually high blood concentration, *J Anal Toxicol*, 31(6): 328–333.

Ku HY, Shon JH, Liu KH, Shin JG, Bae SK. (2009). Liquid chromatography/tandem mass spectrometry method for the simultaneous determination of vardenafil and its major metabolite, N-desethylvardenafil, in human plasma: Application to a pharmacokinetic study, *J Chromatogr B Analyt Technol Biomed Life Sci*, 877(1–2): 95–100.

Lake ST, Altman PM, Vaisman J, Addison RS. (2010). Validated LC-MS/MS assay for the quantitative determination of vardenafil in human plasma and its application to a pharmacokinetic study, *Biomed Chromatogr*, 24(8): 846–851.

Venlafaxine

Brand name: Effexor
Classification: Antidepressant (SNRI)
λ: 2.5–8 h
V_d: 4–12 L/kg
Usual dosage: 37.5–225 mg qd

Source	Therapeutic/Nontoxic	Toxic	Lethal
Blood	0.05–2.1 mg/L	1.8–15 mg/L	6.5–130 mg/L
Vitreous			6.7–58 mg/L
Liver			81–425 mg/kg
Kidney			420 mg/kg
Brain			543 mg/kg
Skeletal muscle	0.5–1.9 mg/kg		

Comments

- Active metabolite: O-desmethylvenlafaxine (Pristiq)
- Metabolized by CYP 2D6
- Prolongs QT interval

Selected Sources

Bexar County Medical Examiner's Office data 1996–2015.

Jaffe PD, Batziris HP, van der Hoeven P, DeSilva D, McIntyre IM. (1999). A study involving venlafaxine overdoses: Comparison of fatal and therapeutic concentrations in postmortem specimens, *J Forensic Sci*, 44(1): 193–196.

Koken L, Dart RC. (1996). Life-threatening hypotension from venlafaxine overdose, *J Tox Clin Tox*, 34: 559.

Levine B, Jenkins AJ, Queen M, Jufer R, Smialek JE. (1996). Distribution of venlafaxine in three postmortem cases, *J Anal Toxicol*, 20(6): 502–505.

Long C, Crifasi J, Maginn D, Graham M, Teas S. (1997). Comparison of analytical methods in the determination of two venlafaxine fatalities, *J Anal Toxicol*, 21(2): 166–169.

Mazur JE, Doty JD, Krygiel AS. (2003). Fatality related to a 30 g venlafaxine overdose, *Pharmacotherapy*, 23(12): 1668–1672.

Parsons AT, Anthony RM, Meeker JE. (1996). Two fatal cases of venlafaxine poisoning, *J Anal Toxicol*, 20(4): 266–268.

Verapamil

Brand name: Calan
Classification: Calcium channel blocker
λ: 4–14 h
V_d: 2.5–6.5 L/kg
Usual dosage: 40–120 mg tid/qid

Source	Therapeutic/Nontoxic	Toxic	Lethal
Blood	0.03–1 mg/L	1.5–4 mg/L	1.5–85 mg/L
Liver			2.4–258 mg/kg
Kidney			1.5–33 mg/kg
Skeletal muscle	0.2–0.5 mg/kg		

Comments

- Active metabolite: Norverapamil
- Metabolized by CYP 1A2 and 3A

Selected Sources

Batalis NI, Harley RA, Schandl CA. (2007). Verapamil toxicity: An unusual case report and review of the literature, *Am J For Med Path*, 28(2): 137–140.

Bexar County Medical Examiner's Office data 1996–2015.

Chan LF, Chhuy LH, Crowley RJ. (1987). Verapamil tissue concentrations in fatal cases, *J Anal Toxicol*, 11(4): 171–174.

Crouch DJ, Crompton C, Rollins DE, Peat MA, Francom P. (1986). Toxicological findings in a fatal overdose of verapamil, *J Forensic Sci*, 31(4): 1505–1508.

Gelbke HP, Schlicht HJ, Schmidt G. (1977). Fatal poisoning with verapamil, *Arch Tox*, 37(2): 89–94.

Kivistö KT, Neuvonen PJ, Tarssanen L. (1997). Pharmacokinetics of verapamil in overdose, *Hum Exp Tox*, 16(1): 35–37.

Koepke JF, McBay AJ. (1987). Fatal verapamil poisoning, *J Forensic Sci*, 32(5): 1431–1434.

Oe H, Taniura T, Ohgitani N. (1998). A case of severe verapamil overdose, *Jap Circ J*, 62(1): 72–76.

Szekely LA, Thompson BT, Woolf A. (1999). Use of partial liquid ventilation to manage pulmonary complications of acute verapamil-sustained release poisoning, *J Tox Clin Tox*, 37(4): 475–479.

Thomson BM, Pannell LK. (1981). The analysis of verapamil in postmortem specimens by HPLC and GC, *J Anal Toxicol*, 5(3): 105–109.

Wilimowska J, Piekoszewski W, Krzyanowska-Kierepka E, Florek E. (2006). Monitoring of verapamil enantiomers concentration in overdose, *Clin Tox*, 44(2): 169–171.

Vigabatrin

Brand names: Sabril and Sabrilex
Classification: Anticonvulsant
λ: 5–8 h
V_d: 0.8 L/kg
Usual dosage: 500–3000 mg/d divided bid

Source	Therapeutic/Nontoxic	Toxic	Lethal
Blood	1–43 mg/L	No data available	40–49 mg/L[a]

[a] Fatality was due to hepatotoxicity in a child.

Selected Sources

Deeb S, McKeown DA, Torrance HJ, Wylie FM, Logan BK, Scott KS. (2014). Simultaneous analysis of 22 antiepileptic drugs in postmortem blood, serum and plasma using LC-MS-MS with a focus on their role in forensic cases, *J Anal Toxicol*, 38(8): 485–494.

Kellermann K, Soditt V, Rambeck B, Klinge O. (1996). Fatal hepatotoxicity in a child treated with vigabatrin, *Acta Neurol Scand*, 93(5): 380–381.

Rey E, Pons G, Olive G. (1992). Vigabatrin: Clinical pharmacokinetics, *Clin Pharmacokinetics*, 23(4): 267–278.

Vilazodone

Brand name: Viibryd
Classification: Antidepressant (SSRI)
λ: 25–37 h
V_d: 13–17 L/kg
Usual dosage: 20–40 mg/qd

Source	Therapeutic/Nontoxic	Toxic	Lethal
Blood	0.01–0.2 mg/L	No data available	

Comments

• Metabolized by CYP 3A4 as well as 2C19 and 2D6

Selected Sources

Boinpally R, Alcorn H, Adams MH, Longstreth J, Edwards J. (2013). Pharma-cokinetics of vilazodone in patients with mild or moderate renal impairment, *Clin Drug Investig*, 33(3): 199–206.

Carstairs SD, Griffith EA, Alayin T, Ejike JC, Cantrell FL. (2012). Recurrent seizure activity in a child after acute vilazodone ingestion, *Ann Emerg Med*, 60(6): 819–820.

Cruz MP. (2012). Vilazodone HCl (Viibryd): A serotonin partial agonist and reuptake inhibitor for the treatment of major depressive disorder, *Pharm Therapeutics*, 37(1): 28–31.

Warfarin

Brand name: Coumadin
Classification: Anticoagulant
λ: 20–60 h
V_d: 0.1–0.2 L/kg
Usual dosage: 1–10 mg qd

Source	Therapeutic/Nontoxic	Toxic[a]	Lethal[a]
Blood	0.7–9 mg/L		>10 mg/L

[a] Toxicity/lethality results from bleeding diatheses.

Comments

- Metabolized by CYP 2C9, 2C19, 2C8, 2C18, 1A2, and 3A4
- Toxicity can be diagnosed by prothrombin time

Selected Sources

Midha KK, McGilveray IJ, Cooper JK. (1974). GLC determination of plasma levels of warfarin, *J Pharmaceutical Sci*, 63(11): 1725–1729.
Orme M, Breckenridge A, Brooks RV. (1972). Interactions of benzodiazepines with warfarin, *Br Med J*, 3(5827): 611–614.
Sutcliffe FA, MacNicoll AD, Gibson GG. (1987). Aspects of anticoagulant action: A review of the pharmacology, metabolism and toxicology of warfarin and congeners, *Rev Drug Metab Drug Interact*, 5(4): 225–272.

Yohimbine

Brand names: Aphrodyne, Yocon, Viritab, and Yohimex
Classification: α-adrenergic blocker
λ: 0.5–1 h
V_d: 0.3–2 L/kg
Usual dosage: 5–15 mg per dose

Source	Therapeutic/Nontoxic	Toxic	Lethal
Blood	0.04–0.4 mg/L	5–5.2 mg/L	5.4–7.4 mg/L

Comments

- Active metabolite: 11-OH-yohimbine

Selected Sources

Anderson C, Anderson D, Harre N, Wade N. (2013). Case study: Two fatal case reports of acute yohimbine intoxication, *J Anal Toxicol*, 37(8): 611–614.

Giampreti A, Lonati D, Locatelli C, Rocchi L, Campailla MT. (2009). Acute neurotoxicity after yohimbine ingestion by a body builder, *Clin Toxicol* (*Phila*), 47(8): 827–829.

Varkey S. (1992). Overdose of yohimbine, *Br Med J*, 304(6826): 548.

Zaleplon

Brand name: Sonata
Classification: Sedative/hypnotic
λ: 1–1.5 h
V_d: 1–1.5 L/kg
Usual dosage: 5–20 mg qHS

Source	Therapeutic/Nontoxic	Toxic	Lethal
Blood	0.01–0.4 mg/L	No data available	2.2 mg/L[a]

[a] Co-intoxicants: Promethazine and butalbital.

Comments

- Metabolized by CYP 3A

Selected Sources

Drover D, Lemmens H, Naidu S, Cevallos W, Darwish M, Stanski D. (2000). Pharmacokinetics, pharmacodynamics, and relative pharmacokinetic/pharmacodynamic profiles of zaleplon and zolpidem, *Clin Therapeutics*, 22(12): 1443–1461.

Jönsson AK, Söderberg C, Espnes KA, Ahlner J, Eriksson A, Reis M, Druid H. (2014). Sedative and hypnotic drugs—Fatal and non-fatal reference blood concentrations, *Forensic Sci Int*, 236: 138–145.

Moore KA, Zemrus TL, Ramcharitar V, Levine B, Fowler DR. (2003). Mixed drug intoxication involving zaleplon ("Sonata"), *Forensic Sci Intl*, 134(2–3): 120–122.

Ziprasidone

Brand name: Geodon
Classification: Antipsychotic
λ: 3–7 h
V_d: 1–1.5 L/kg
Usual dosage: 20–80 mg bid

Source	Therapeutic/Nontoxic	Toxic	Lethal
Blood	0.02–0.1 mg/L	0.3–2.0 mg/L[a]	5.7 mg/L[b]

[a] Toddler.
[b] Co-intoxicants: Ethanol, 0.16 g/dL; venlafaxine, 120 mg/L; and zolpidem, 0.08 mg/L.

Comments

- Prolongs QT interval; may develop Torsades de Pointes in overdose
- Metabolized by CYP 3A4

Selected Sources

Gresham C, Ruha AM. (2010). Respiratory failure following isolated ziprasidone ingestion in a toddler, *J Med Toxicol*, 6: 41–43.

Manini AF, Raspberry D, Hoffman RS, Nelson LS. (2007). QT prolongation and torsades de pointes following overdose of ziprasidone and amantadine, *J Med Toxicol*, 3(4): 178–181.

Roman M, Kronstrand R, Lindstedt D, Josefsson M. (2008). Quantitation of seven low-dosage antipsychotic drugs in human postmortem blood using LC-MS-MS, *J Anal Toxicol*, 32(2): 147–155.

Zolpidem

Brand name: Ambien
Classification: Sedative/hypnotic
λ: 1.5–5 h
V_d: 0.5–1 L/kg
Usual dosage: 5–10 mg qHS

Source	Therapeutic/Nontoxic	Toxic	Lethal
Blood	0.05–2.2 mg/L	0.1–1.4 mg/L	0.6–7.9 mg/L
Vitreous			0.5–1.6 mg/L
Liver	0.4–1.3 mg/kg		12–23 mg/kg
Skeletal muscle	0.2–0.5 mg/kg		

Comments

- Metabolized by CYP 3A4

Selected Sources

Bexar County Medical Examiner's Office data 1996–2015.
Druid H, Holmgren P. (1997). A compilation of fatal and control concentrations of drugs in postmortem femoral blood, *J Forensic Sci*, 42(1): 79–87.
Gock SB, Wong SH, Nuwayhid N, Venuti SE, Kelley PD, Teggatz JR. (1999). Acute zolpidem overdose—Report of two cases, *J Anal Toxicol*, 23(6): 559–562.
Jones AW, Holmgren A. (2012). Concentrations of zolpidem and zopiclone in venous blood samples from impaired drivers compared with femoral blood from forensic autopsies, *Forensic Sci Int*, 222(1–3): 118–123.
Jönsson AK, Söderberg C, Espnes KA, Ahlner J, Eriksson A, Reis M, Druid H. (2014). Sedative and hypnotic drugs—Fatal and non-fatal reference blood concentrations, *Forensic Sci Int*, 236: 138–145.
Keller T, Schneider A, Tutsch-Bauer E. (1999). GC/MS determination of zolpidem in postmortem specimens ina voluntary intoxication, *Forensic Sci Intl*, 106(2): 103–108.
Lheureux P, Debailleul G, De Witte O, Askenasi R. (1990). Zolpidem intoxication mimicking narcotic overdose: Response to flumazenil, *Hum Exp Tox*, 9(2): 105–107.
Winek CL, Wahba WW, Janssen JK, Rozin L, Rafizadeh V. (1996). Acute overdose of zolpidem, *Forensic Sci Intl*, 78(3): 165–168.

Zonisamide

Brand name: Zonegran
Classification: Anticonvulsant
λ: 27–105 h (~63 h)
V_d: 1–2 L/kg
Usual dosage: 25–200 mg bid/qd

Source	Therapeutic/Nontoxic	Toxic	Lethal
Blood	2.3–40 mg/L	40–202 mg/L	44 mg/L[a]

[a] Other confounding variables present; not definitive zonisamide intoxication.

Comments

- Metabolized by CYP 3A4

Selected Sources

Frampton JE, Scott LJ. (2005). Zonisamide: A review of its use in the management of partial seizures in epilepsy, *CNS Drugs*, 19(4): 347–367.

Hofer KE, Trachsel C, Rauber-Lüthy C, Kupferschmidt H, Kullak-Ublick GA, Ceschi A. (2011). Moderate toxic effects following acute zonisamide overdose, *Epilepsy Behav*, 21(1): 91–93.

Naito H, Itoh N, Matsui N, Eguchi T. (1988). Monitoring plasma concentrations of zonisamide and clonazepam in an epileptic attempting suicide by an overdose of the drugs, *Curr Ther Res*, 43: 463–467.

Sztajnkrycer MD, Huang EE, Bond GR. (2003). Acute zonisamide overdose: A death revisited, *Vet Hum Tox*, 45(3): 154–156.

Wilfong AA, Willmore LJ. (2006). Zonisamide—A review of experience and use in partial seizures, *Neuropsychiatr Dis Treat*, 2(3): 269–280.

Zopiclone

Brand names: Imovane, Zimovane; Lunesta (eszopiclone)
Classification: Sedative/hypnotic
λ: 3–8 h
V_d: 1–2 L/kg
Usual dosage: 3.75–7.5 mg qHS

Source	Therapeutic/Nontoxic	Toxic	Lethal
Blood	0.02–1.3 mg/L	0.25–1.6 mg/L	0.4–4.1 mg/L
Vitreous			94 mg/L
Liver			4.9–8.7 mg/kg
Kidney			1.7 mg/kg
Spleen			5.8 mg/kg
Brain			2.8 mg/kg
Skeletal muscle			1.9–3.3 mg/kg
Cardiac muscle			1.6 mg/kg

Comments

- Eszopiclone is the s-enantiomer of zopiclone and *laboratories usually do not differentiate between zopiclone and eszopiclone*

Selected Sources

Bexar County Medical Examiner's Office data 1996–2015.

Cienki JJ, Burkhart KK, Donovan JW. (2005). Zopiclone overdose responsive to flumazenil, *Clin Tox*, 43(5): 385–386.

Gebauer MG, Alderman CP. (2002). Validation of a high-performance liquid chromatographic method for the enantiospecific quantitation of zopiclone in plasma, *Biomed Chromatogr*, 16(4): 241–246.

Jones AW, Holmgren A. (2012). Concentrations of zolpidem and zopiclone in venous blood samples from impaired drivers compared with femoral blood from forensic autopsies, *Forensic Sci Int*, 222(1–3): 118–123.

Jönsson AK, Söderberg C, Espnes KA, Ahlner J, Eriksson A, Reis M, Druid H. (2014). Sedative and hypnotic drugs—Fatal and non-fatal reference blood concentrations, *Forensic Sci Int*, 236: 138–145.

Meatherall RC. (1997). Zopiclone fatality in a hospitalized patient, *J Forensic Sci*, 42(2): 340–343.

Pounder DJ, Davies JI. (1994). Zopiclone poisoning: Tissue distribution and potential for postmortem diffusion, *Forensic Sci Intl*, 65(3): 177–183.

Zuclopenthixol

Brand names: Clopixol, Cisordinol, and Ciatyl-Z
Classification: Antipsychotic
λ: 12–30 h
V_d: 15–20 L/kg
Usual dosage: 10–20 mg po bid; 50–150 mg im qod

Source	Therapeutic/Nontoxic	Toxic	Lethal
Blood	0.005–0.1 mg/L	0.15–0.3 mg/L	0.3–0.9 mg/L
Liver			0.75 mg/kg
Lung			5.2 mg/kg
Kidney			1.4 mg/kg
Brain			0.1 mg/kg

Comments

- Metabolized by CYP 2D6

Selected Sources

Kollroser M, Henning G, Gatternig R, Schober C. (2001). HPLC-ESI-MS/MS determination of zuclopenthixol in a fatal intoxication during psychiatric therapy, *Forensic Sci Intl*, 123(2–3): 243–247.

Kratzsch C, Peters FT, Kraemer T, Weber AA, Maurer HH. (2003). Screening, library-assisted identification and validated quantification of fifteen neuroleptics and three of their metabolites in plasma by liquid chromatography/ mass spectrometry with atmospheric pressure chemical ionization, *J Mass Spectrum*, 38(3): 283–295.

Roman M, Kronstrand R, Lindstedt D, Josefsson M. (2008). Quantitation of seven low-dosage antipsychotic drugs in human postmortem blood using LC-MS-MS, *J Anal Toxicol*, 32(2): 147–155.

Rop PP. (2001). Concentrations of cis(Z)-clopenthixol and trans(E)-clopenthixol in a lethal case involving zuclopenthixol, diazepam, and cyamemazine, *J Anal Toxicol*, 25(5): 348–352.

Tracqui A, Kintz P, Cirimele V, Berthault F, Mangin P, Ludes B. (1997). HPLC-DAD and HPLC-MS findings in fatality involving (Z)-Cis-clopenthixol (Zuclopenthixol), *J Anal Toxicol*, 21(4): 314–318.

Appendix A

Specimen Types and Collection

- **Blood**
  - Most common and preferable sample.
  - Peripheral blood is more desirable than central blood because it is less affected by postmortem redistribution.
    - Femoral blood, followed by subclavian, heart, and cavity blood are recommended.
  - Used for screening and confirmatory testing.
  - Should be collected into glass tubes because drugs can bind to polymers of plastic tubes.
    - Collect at least 20 mL into glass tube with appropriate preservative for testing, such as sodium fluoride/potassium oxalate or EDTA.
    - For volatile testing, collect a full Teflon-lined screw top tube.
    - Additional tubes can be used for serology and/or genetic testing.
- **Urine**
  - Relatively easy to obtain and store.
  - Good screening sample.
  - Drug concentrations in urine do not accurately reflect the corresponding blood concentrations or indicate acute toxicity.
  - May reflect a drug that was ingested many hours, and sometimes days, prior to testing.
  - Can be used as a confirmatory sample.
  - Collect 5–10 mL into glass red top tube (no preservative).
- **Vitreous**
  - Excellent specimen with good stability.
  - Only available in a limited quantity.
  - Most often used for electrolyte testing.
  - Good for detection of short-lived metabolites like 6-MAM.
  - Collected into glass, red top tubes (no preservative); usually 2–4 mL.

- **Bile**
  - Not recommended to detect drug toxicity deaths.
  - Certain drugs are concentrated in the bile making interpretation of elevated levels difficult.
  - Collect into glass, red top tubes (no preservative); usually 2–10 mL.
- **Synovial Fluid**
  - Available in limited quantities.
  - Can be used to confirm drug presence.
- **Tissue**
  - Usually readily available in large quantities.
  - Interpretation of drug concentration can be difficult as concentrations may be elevated in chronically administered drugs.
  - Collect at least 50 g into clean, unused specimen containers.
  - Collect at least 50 g into clean, unused specimen containers.
    - Muscle speciments should be collected from quadriceps.
    - Liver from the deep right lobe.
    - Lung from the apex.
  - Specific issues to be considered:
    - Liver may concentrate drugs.
    - Kidney is good for heavy metal testing.
    - Brain is good for lipophilic drugs, including volatiles.
    - Lung is good for inhaled toxins, such as volatile compounds.
    - Spleen can be used as an alternative sample for carbon monoxide testing.
    - Adipose tissue can be used for pesticide and volatile analysis.
- **Stomach/Gastric Contents**
  - The presence of a drug in gastric contents, even at elevated concentrations may not indicate drug toxicity.
  - May be useful in directing blood testing.
- **Hair**
  - Not routinely used in the postmortem setting.
  - Yields information about drug intake over a period of months to years, depending on the length of hair sampled.
  - Often used as screening source for arsenic poisoning.
  - To collect, shave 100–200 mg, usually of scalp hair, tie the root end to mark direction, and place into a new, unused, dry specimen container.

- **Labeling and Storage**
  - Samples should be labeled with the following: the type of specimen, case number, date of collection, name of deceased, and the names of medical examiner and person securing the sample (if they are different).
  - Blood samples should be labeled with the exact site of collection rather than simply "peripheral" or "central."
  - Samples should be immediately refrigerated or frozen until ready for transport to the toxicology laboratory.

Appendix B

Common Methodologies

Screening Tests

- **Immunoassay**
  - *Theory*: An antibody reacts against a particular drug or drug class.
  - *Types*: Radioimmunoassay (RIA), enzyme multiplied immunoassay technique (EMIT), fluorescent polarization immunoassays (FPIA), kinetic interaction of microparticles in solution (KIMS), and enzyme linked immunosorbent assay (ELISA).
  - *Advantages*: Relatively easy to use and to perform, good sensitivity, and requires small amount of sample.
  - *Disadvantages*: Limited specificity; interfering substances may result is false positive or false negative results.
- **Spectrophotometry**
  - *Theory*: Measures the changes in the wavelength of light passing through a substance.
  - *Types*: Ultraviolet (UV), visible spectra, and infrared (IR).
  - *Advantages*: Ease of use.
  - *Disadvantages*: Lack of sensitivity and specificity.
- **Chromatography**
  - *Theory*: Drugs are identified based upon the time it takes to transverse the stationary phase.
  - *Types:* Can be gas (GC) or liquid (LC).
  - *Advantages*: Sensitive; specific when paired with a mass spectrometer.
  - *Disadvantages*: Time consuming; requires significant sample preparation; expensive.

Confirmatory Tests

- Usually more specific than screening tests.
- Performed by a different methodology than the screening test and on a different sample, if possible.
- Preferred methods are GC or LC paired with mass spectrometry.
- Confirmation of an immunoassay by another immunoassay is not acceptable.

Appendix C

Normal Laboratory Values

Blood

Cell Counts

WBC	$4.1–10.9 \times 10^3/\mu L$
Hb	13.2–17.2 g/dL Male
	12.0–15.2 g/dL Female
Hct	40%–52% Male
	37%–48% Female
Plt	$140–450 \times 10^3/\mu L$
PT/PTT	12–14/18–28 s

Electrolytes

Ca	8.5–10.5 mg/dL
Cl	98–108 mEq/L
K	3.5–5 mEq/L
Na	135–145 mEq/L

Liver Function

NH_4	12–55 μmol/L
Bilirubin (total)	0.2–1.3 mg/dL
AST/ALT	5–35/7–56 U/L
GGT	8–78 U/L

Renal Function

BUN	7–21 mg/dL
Cr	0.6–1.5 mg/dL
Glucose	65–110 mg/dL

Blood Gases

pH	7.35–7.45
pCO_2	35–45 mmHg
pO_2	75–100 mmHg

Cardiac

CPK (total)	38–120 ng/mL
Troponin	<0.4 ng/mL

Enzymes

Amylase	30–110 U/L
Lipase	7–60 U/L
Alk phos	38–126 U/L

Vitreous

K	3.5–10 mEq/L (levels > 15 mEq/L indicate decomposition)[a]
Na	130–155 mEq/L[a]
Cl	105–135 mEq/L[a]
Ca	6–8.4 mg/dL
Urea nitrogen	7–30 mg/dL
Cr	<1.5 mg/dL
Glucose	<60 mg/dL (or ½ serum level)

[a] After death, potassium increases while sodium and chloride decrease.

Average Blood Volume

Neonates	85–95 mL/kg
Infants	80 mL/kg
Adults	75 mL/kg Male
	65 mL/kg Female

Appendix D

Conversion Charts

Metric Units

$k = kilo = 10^3$
$d = deci = 10^{-1}$
$c = centi = 10^{-2}$
$m = milli = 10^{-3}$
$\mu = micro = 10^{-6}$
$n = nano = 10^{-9}$
$p = pico = 10^{-12}$

Volume

1 L = 1000 mL = 1000 cc
30 mL ~ 1 fluid ounce

Weight

65 mg = 1 grain
437.5 grain = 1 oz
28.35 g = 1 oz
1 kg = 2.2 lbs
1 g = 0.035 oz

Length

1 cm = 0.4 inch
2.54 cm = 1 inch
1 meter = 39.37 inches

Temperature

$^{\circ}C = (^{\circ}F - 32) \times 0.555$
$^{\circ}F = (^{\circ}C \times 1.8) + 32$

Concentration

$\mu g/mL = mg/L$
$\mu g/g = mg/kg$
$\mu g/L = ng/mL$
$\mu g/\mu L = mg/mL$
mmol/L * molecular weight (g/mol) = mg/L

Density

blood = 1.055 g/mL
1 mL blood = 1.055 g

Index